Welcome to Peru

Peru is as complex as its most intricate and exquisite weavings. Festivals mark ancient rites, the urban vanguard fuels innovation and nature bestows splendid diversity.

Peru is a place of ancient beliefs where age-old pageants unfold to the tune of booming brass bands. Its rich cultural heritage is never more real and visceral than when you are immersed streetside in the swirling madness of a festival. Deities of old are reincarnated as Christian saints, pilgrims climb mountains in the dead of night and icons are paraded through crowded plazas as once were the mummies of Inca rulers.

Visitors flock to the glorious Inca citadel of Machu Picchu, yet this feted site is just a flash in a 5000-year history of Peruvian settlement. Explore the dusty remnants of Chan Chan, the largest pre-Columbian ruins in all the Americas. Fly over the puzzling geoglyphs etched into the arid earth at Nazca. Or peruse Lima's great museums that reveal in full detail the sophistication, skill and passion of these lost civilizations.

Save time for adventure too. Giant sand dunes, chiseled peaks and Pacific breaks are a few heartbeats away from rush-hour traffic: this vast country translates to paradise for the active traveler. Take it in small bites and don't rush. Festivals can swallow you whole for days. And that's when you realize that in Peru the adventure usually lies in getting there.

Peru is a place where age-old pageants unfold to the tune of booming brass bands

Machu Picchu (p200)

NORTH
PACIFIC
OCEAN

✪ QUITO

ECUADOR

PERU

Napo

Santiago

Golfo de Guayaquil

Tumbes ◉

Tumbes

Talara ◉

Piura ◉

Jaén ◉ ◉ Bagua Grande

Moyobamba ◉

Marañón

Huallaga

Lagunas ◉

Reserva
Nacional
Pacaya-Samíria

◉ Yurimaguas

◉ Tarapoto

Chiclayo ◉

Cajamarca ◉

Juanjuí ◉

Ucayali

Pacasmayo ◉

TRUJILLO p221 ◉

Reserva
Nacional
Calipuy

Parque
Nacional
Río Abiseo

Parque
Nacional
Cordillera Azul

◉ Pucallpa

Chimbote ◉

Casma ◉

Huaraz ◉

THE CORDILLERAS
p235

Parque
Nacional
Huascarán

◉ Huánuco

Parque Nacional
Yanachaga
Chemillen

Santuario Histórico
Chacamarca

Río Tambo

Chancay ◉

LIMA p35 ✪

Río Cañete

◉ Tarma

Huancayo ◉

Pa
Nac
O

SOUTH
PACIFIC
OCEAN

Reserva Nor
Yauyos-Cochas

Huancavelica ◉

Ayacucho ◉

Pisco ◉

Andahuaylas

PARACAS & THE ISLAS BALLESTAS p69

◉ Ica

Reserva
Nacional
Paracas

NAZCA p79

Ca

⊙N   0 |————————| 400 km
      0 |————————| 200 miles

A

![Lonely Planet]

PERU

TOP SIGHTS, AUTHENTIC EXPERIENCES

Brendan Sainsbury, Alex Egerton, Carolyn McCarthy,
Phillip Tang, Luke Waterson

Contents

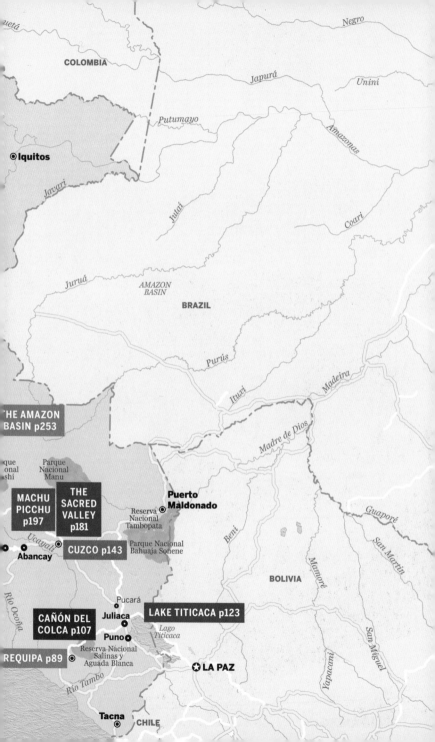

COLOMBIA

Iquitos

BRAZIL

AMAZON BASIN

Parque Nacional Manu

Puerto Maldonado

Reserva Nacional Tambopata

Abancay

Parque Nacional Bahuaja Sonene

BOLIVIA

Pucará

Juliaca

Puno

Lago Titicaca

Reserva Nacional Salinas y Aguada Blanca

LA PAZ

Tacna

CHILE

Woman in traditional dress holding a baby llama, Cuzco (143)
MEDIAPRODUCTION/GETTY IMAGES ©

Plan Your Trip
Peru's Top 12

ANTOM_IVANOV/SHUTTERSTOCK ©

Machu Picchu

One of the most famous ruins on the planet

A fantastic Inca citadel lost to the world until its rediscovery in the early 20th century, Machu Picchu stands as a marvel among ruins. With its emerald terraces backed by steep peaks, the sight simply surpasses imagination. This wondrous feat of engineering has withstood six centuries of earthquakes, foreign invasion and howling weather. Discover it for yourself: wander through the stone temples and scale the dizzying heights.

WILDZERO/SHUTTERSTOCK ©

1

Lake Titicaca

Floating reed islands and traditional living

Less a lake than a highland ocean, Titicaca is home to fantastical sights – none more surreal than the floating islands crafted entirely of tightly woven *totora* reeds. Requiring near constant renovation, the reeds are also used to build thatched homes and elegant boats. There are plenty of islands to choose from, such as Isla Taquile, where rural Andean life from centuries long gone lives on, and the quinoa soup recipe has been perfected.

GALYNA ANDRUSHKO//SHUTTERSTOCK ©

The Cordilleras

The starting point for outdoor adventure in Peru

The dramatic peaks of the Cordilleras make up one of the pre-eminent hiking, trekking and backpacking spots in South America. Every which way you throw your gaze, razor-sharp white peaks tower over expansive mantles of green valleys. The Cordillera Blanca is one of the highest mountain ranges in the world and boasts the enigmatic 3000-year-old ruins of Chavín de Huántar.

3

Arequipa

Cuisine and architecture in an ethereal cityscape

Crowned by dazzling baroque architecture hewn out of the local white *sillar* rock, Arequipa is primarily a Spanish colonial city that hasn't strayed far from its conception. Its beautiful natural setting amid volcanoes and high pampa is complemented by a 400-year-old monastery, a huge cathedral and innovative fusion cuisine.

Cuzco

The ancient Inca capital

With ancient cobblestone streets, grandiose baroque churches and the remnants of masterful Inca temples, no city looms larger in Andean history than Cuzco, which has been inhabited continuously since precolonial times. Cuzco also serves as the gateway to Machu Picchu. Mystic, commercial and chaotic, this unique city is still a stunner. Where else would you find ornately dressed women walking llamas on leashes, a museum for magical plants, and the wildest nightlife in the high Andes?

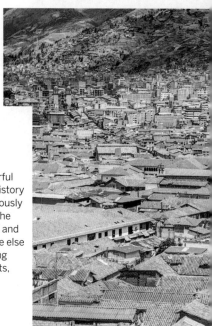

Cañón del Colca

Scenic hiking, biking, rafting and zip lining

First colonized by pre-Inca civilizations, the cultural history of the Colca Canyon is as alluring as the endless trekking possibilities. Stretching 100km from end to end and plunging over 3400m at its deepest, the canyon has been embellished with terraced agricultural fields, pastoral villages, colonial churches, and ruins that date back to pre-Inca times.

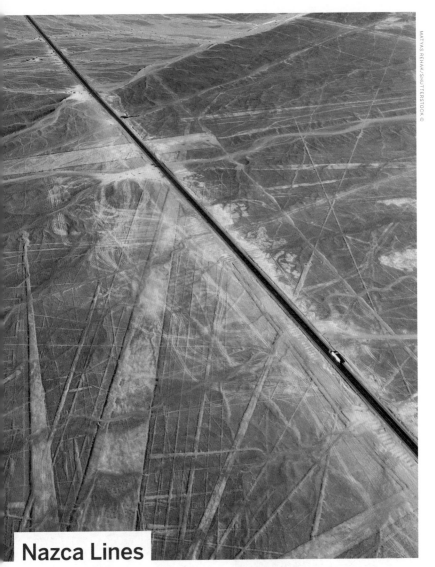

MATYAS REHAK/SHUTTERSTOCK ©

Nazca Lines

Mysterious giant geoglyphs

Made by aliens? Laid out by prehistoric balloonists? Conceived as a giant astronomical chart? No two evaluations of Peru's giant geoglyphs – known as the Nazca Lines – are the same. The mysteries have attracted outsiders since the 1940s, but no one has been able to fully crack the code. The lines remain unfathomed, enigmatic and loaded with historic intrigue.

7

The Amazon Basin

The world's most biodiverse forest

The Amazon Basin is as close to visiting an alien planet as you can get on Earth. The abundance of plants and animal life can make it seem like new creatures are created here. The forest's diversity is matched only by the uniqueness of its people, with tribes that have never interacted with external civilization. Set aside ample time to visit the national parks, which grow more intriguing the deeper you get.

TERRI BUTLER PHOTOGRAPHY/SHUTTERSTOCK ©

9

Sacred Valley

Village markets and ancient ruins

Andean villages, crumbling Inca military outposts and agricultural terraces used since time immemorial are linked by the Río Urubamba as it curves through the Sacred Valley. Located between Cuzco and Machu Picchu, this picturesque destination is an ideal base for exploring the area's famed markets, historic structures and remote agricultural villages.

TR3GIN/SHUTTERSTOCK ©

Lima

World-class food and museums

Want to understand Peru's ancient civilizations? Begin your trip
here. The city's museums hold the treasures of millennia. Want
to understand modern living in Peru? It's all about the diversity
reflected in Lima's cuisine. The coastal capital is replete with
options ranging from street food to haute cuisine.

10

CHRISTIAN DECLERCQ/SHUTTERSTOCK ©

Trujillo

Colonial architecture and modern culture

Old Trujillo boasts a dazzling display of preserved splendor. The city's historic center is chock full of elegant churches, mansions and otherwise unspoiled colonial constructions, which are steeped today in a modern motif that lends the city a lovely, livable feel. Add the close proximity of impressive Chimú ruins such as Chan Chan, and the Moche pyramids at Huacas del Sol y de la Luna, and Trujillo easily trumps its northern rivals in style and grace.

CHRISTIAN VINCES/SHUTTERSTOCK ©

Islas Ballestas

The Pacific Ocean's most astonishing fauna

A barren collection of guano-covered rocks, the Islas Ballestas support an extraordinary ecosystem of birds, sea mammals and fish. They also represent one of Peru's most successful conservation projects. Boat trips around the island's cliffs and arches allow close encounters with barking sea lions, huddled Humboldt penguins and tens of thousands of birds.

Plan Your Trip
Need to Know

When to Go

Trujillo•
GO year-round

Huaraz
• **GO** May–Sep

Lima•
GO year-round

Cuzco
•**GO** Jun–Sep

Puno
• **GO** Jun–Sep

Alpine desert (including snow)
Warm to hot summers, mild winters
Semi-tropical climate, wet & dry seasons
Tropical climate, rain year-round

High Season (Jun–Aug)

○ Dry season in Andean highlands and eastern rainforest.

○ Best time for festivals and highland sports, including treks.

○ Busiest time due to North American and European holidays.

Shoulder (Sep–Nov & Mar–May)

○ Spring and fall weather in the highlands.

○ Ideal for less-crowded visits.

○ September to November good for rainforest trekking.

Low Season (Dec–Feb)

○ Rainy season in the highlands and Amazon basin.

○ The Inca Trail closes during February for cleanup.

○ High season for the coast and beach activities.

Currency
Nuevo sol (S)

Languages
Spanish, Quechua, Aymara

Visas
Visas are generally not required for travelers entering Peru.

Money
ATMs widely available in larger towns and cities. Credit cards accepted in most establishments.

Cell Phones
Local SIM cards (and top-up credits) are cheap and widely available, and can be used on unlocked triband GSM 1900 world phones.

Time
Eastern Standard Time (EST), five hours behind Greenwich Mean Time (GMT); same as New York City, without Daylight Savings Time.

Daily Costs

Budget: **Less than S190**

o Inexpensive hotel room or dorm bed: S28–165

o Set lunches: less than S15; supermarkets have takeout

o Entry fee to historic sights: average S10

Midrange: **S190–650**

o Double room in midrange hotel: S85–435

o Main dish at midrange restaurant: S40

o Group tours: from S120

Top End: **More than S650**

o Double room in top-end hotel: from S250–435

o Private city tour: from S200 per person

o Fine restaurant dinner: from S60

Useful Websites

Lonely Planet (www.lonelyplanet.com/peru) Destination information, hotel bookings, traveler forum and more.

Latin America Network Information Center (www.lanic.utexas.edu/la/peru) Diverse, informative links including academic research.

Living in Peru (www.livinginperu.com) An English-language guide with articles and restaurant reviews.

Peru Reports (www.perureports.com) Alternative English-language news.

Peruvian Times (www.peruviantimes.com) The latest news, in English.

Expat Peru (www.expatperu.com) Useful for government offices and customs regulations.

Opening Hours

Opening hours vary throughout the year. We've provided high-season opening hours; hours will generally decrease in the shoulder and low seasons.

Banks 9am to 6pm Monday to Friday, some 9am to 6pm Saturday

Government offices and businesses 9am to 5pm Monday to Friday

Museums Often close on Monday

Restaurants 10am to 10pm, many close 3pm to 6pm

Shops 9am to 6pm Monday to Friday, some open Saturday

Arriving in Peru

Aeropuerto Internacional Jorge Chávez (☏01-517-3500, schedules 01-511-6055; www.lima-airport.com; Callao) Many flights arrive in the wee hours, so be sure to have a hotel booked ahead.

Taxis from the airport take forty-five minutes to one hour (rush hour) to Miraflores, Barranco or San Isidro, faster for downtown Lima; should cost S60.

Getting Around

Public transport in Peru is cheap, with options plentiful and frequent.

Light Rail Lima's Metropolitano offers efficient, fast service to downtown.

Train Expensive and geared towards tourists.

Car Useful for traveling at your own pace, though cities can be difficult to navigate and secure parking is a must.

Bus Cheapest option with reclining seats on better long-distance buses.

Taxi A good option for sightseeing, shared taxis are common in the provinces.

For more on **getting around**, see p308

Plan Your Trip
Hot Spots For...

Peruvian Cuisine

Peru's food scene is going through a delicious renaissance, bringing modern appreciation to the classics from the coast to the Andes.

AOSTOJSKA/SHUTTERSTOCK ©

Lima
The capital caters to fancy fusion tastes with modern Asian and European influences and Andean classics.

Gastronomic Tours
Discover culinary gems with Lima Tasty Tours. (p56)

Iquitos
Great restaurants show off local Amazon flavors such as river fish ceviche and tasty *chupín de pollo* soup.

Real Amazonian Food
Food of the jungle at manic Belén Mercado. (p265)

Cuzco
An unbelievable range of Andean crops from highland potatoes and quinoa to avocados.

Iconic Drink
Andean-style cocoa at the Museo de la Coca. (p163)

Ancient Ruins

Machu Picchu is just the start with plenty of ruins, temples and secrets from the Incas and other cultures to discover.

MATYAS REHAK/SHUTTERSTOCK ©

Sacred Valley
The Andean countryside is dotted with villages, high-altitude hamlets and isolated ruins.

Machu Picchu
This Inca citadel will live up to the hype. (p200)

Cuzco
The cosmic realm of the ancient Incas, fused with the colonial and religious splendors of Spanish conquest.

Inti Raymi
Celebrate the solstice at Sacsaywamán. (p152)

Chan Chan
Wander the ruins of the largest pre-Columbian city in the Americas (pictured above), north of Trujillo.

Bird's-Eye View
The museum's exhibits reveal the city's sprawl. (p224)

Trekking in the Andes

The Andes are the interlocking vertebrae of Peru, running the entire length of the country from gaping canyons to glacier-frosted peaks.

BYELIKOVA OKSANA/SHUTTERSTOCK ©

Cordillera Blanca
The vast Cordilleras are Peru's trekking highlight in both size and grandeur.

Santa Cruz Trek
Quieter than the Inca Trail; can be done solo. (p238).

Cañón del Colca
A spectacular canyon of many flavors (and trails) that's guarded by iconic Andean condors.

'El Clásico' Trek
Romp through ancient terraces and villages. (p114)

Inca Trail
South America's most famous trek deposits hikers at the entrance to its most spectacular ruins.

Guided Treks
A guided-only trek that books up fast. (p210)

Wildlife Adventures

Natural wonders are outdoors and free in Peru. Catch sight of wildlife soaring over canyons and swimming in jungle waters.

MARKTUCAN/SHUTTERSTOCK ©

Islas Ballestas
Incredible ecosystem of birds, sea mammals and fish, nicknamed the 'poor man's Galápagos.'

Boat Tours
You can't get onto the island but tours go close. (p72)

Reserva Nacional Salinas y Aguada Blanca
Canyons that are as deep as the mountains are high, full of untamed beauty stretching to the horizon.

Pampa de Toccra
Watch vicuñas dart across the high plains. (p116)

Amazon Basin
This vast and impenetrable area has protected the diverse wildlife from the outside world.

Parque Nacional Manu
One of the best places to see tropical critters. (p256)

Plan Your Trip
Essential Peru

OLEKSANDRA KOROBOVA/GETTY IMAGES ©

Activities

You can scale the highest tropical mountain peaks in the world, stay in the capital, hang glide over the ocean and still have time for a coastal walk. Peru is big, with huge opportunities in the jungle, snow, desert and ocean to raft, zip and ride. Or get your heart racing without breaking a sweat: spot a pink dolphin in the Amazon, watch the sun dissolve over ruins, see a condor ride canyon air currents, whip up your own pisco (Peruvian grape brandy) or set foot on an island made of reeds.

Shopping

Peru has a bonanza of arts and crafts. Popular souvenirs include alpaca wool sweaters and scarves, woven textiles, ceramics, masks, gold and silver jewelry and, the backpacker favorite, Inca Kola T-shirts. While Lima offers a wealth of crafts, highly specialized regional items may be difficult to find. Bargaining is the norm at street stalls and markets, where it's cash only.

Eating

There are dining and snacking options galore in Peru. Traveler hot spots, where you can dine on Peruvian classics with modern twists, are having a foodie boom. Traditional meals can be tried in local restaurants with a *menú* (set meal). Eating with a family at a homestay can be a rewarding experience, for both your palate and the family, especially if you pay directly. Staples such as beans and quinoa soup are easy options for vegetarians. Even in small towns, simple *chifas* (Chinese restaurants) are a common fallback. Peru caters to heat lovers with *ají* (chili) but it is easily avoided for the spice phobic.

Street snacks aren't meant to be complete meals, but tasty whims, and include charcoal corn, *anticuchos* (beef skewers) or quail eggs.

Every region has its specialty. Standouts are coastal seafood, tropical *chonta* (palm hearts) and river snails in the Amazon, and soups and *cuy* (guinea pig) in the highlands. In the land where potatoes originated, the humble spud is elevated to a starring role.

STUDIOLASKA/SHUTTERSTOCK ©

Drinking & Nightlife

Peruvians are passionate about their drinks: pisco is a source of pride and competition (it originated in Peru, not Chile, you'll be told); if you love the fluorescent soft-drink brand Inca Kola, you have truly become a local; and lunch without a jug of *chicha* (fermented corn beer) isn't a Peruvian lunch. In the mountains, coca-leaf tea might get you through altitude sickness but is also a homely drink. Coffee bars with high-quality Peruvian beans and espresso drinks are proliferating.

Lima is the capital of Peruvian nightlife, with a huge selection of bars and clubs for all budgets and ages. The coast does nightlife better than the Andes, with the exception of Cuzco, which has a buzzing club scene. In rural areas nightlife is nonexistent.

Entertainment

Peru's larger towns and cities have plenty to keep your weekends full. The club scene begins well after midnight and keeps up the energy until dawn. Electronic beats, live bands and a range of Latin and jazz styles are all on offer, sometimes in restaurants.

Peruvian folk music and dance is performed at weekends at *peñas* (bars or clubs featuring live music). The *folklórica* style here is typical of the Andean highlands, while *criollo* is a coastal music pulsing with African-influenced beats. Dinner is often included.

★ Best Restaurants

Central, Lima (p42)

Chicha, Arequipa (p103)

Inti-Mar, Paracas (El Chaco; p76)

Cicciolina, Cuzco (p171)

Maido, Lima (p43

From left: Woven textiles; Cocktail bar, Lima

Plan Your Trip
Month by Month

January

January through March is the busiest (and most expensive) season on the coast. In the mountains and canyons, it's rainy season and best avoided by trekkers and mountaineers.

✺ Año Nuevo

New Year's Day is particularly big in Huancayo, where the fiesta continues until Epiphany (January 6).

☆ Fiesta de la Marinera

(last week of January) Trujillo's national dance festival.

February

The Inca Trail is closed all month. Many Peruvian festivals echo the Catholic calendar and are celebrated with great pageantry, especially in highland villages.

✺ La Virgen de la Candelaria

(February 2) This highland fiesta, also known as Candlemas, is particularly colorful around Puno, where folkloric music and dance celebrations last for two weeks.

March

Beach-resort prices go down and crowds disperse, though the coast remains sunny. Orchids bloom on the Inca Trail.

April

Crowds and high-season prices mark Holy Week, a boon of national tourism in March/April. Hotel prices spike and availability is low, so reserve ahead.

✺ Semana Santa

(week before Easter Sunday) Semana Santa is celebrated with spectacular religious processions almost daily.

Above: Q'oyoriti (p149)

May

The heaviest rains have passed, leaving the highlands lush and green. With the return of drier weather, trekking season starts to take off in Huaraz and around Cuzco.

☆ Noche en Blanco

(early May) Inspired by Europe's White Nights, the streets of Miraflores in Lima are closed to cars to allow arts, music and dance to take over.

☆ Q'oyoriti

(May or June) A fascinating indigenous pilgrimage to the holy mountain of Ausangate, outside of Cuzco. (p149)

☆ Festival of the Crosses

(May 3) This religious festival is held in Lima, Apurímac, Ayacucho, Junín, Ica and Cuzco.

June

High season for international tourism runs June through August, with Machu Picchu requiring advance reservations for train

★ Best Festivals

Q'oyoriti May/June
Semana Santa March/April
Inti Raymi June
Mistura September
Puno Week November

tickets and entry. It's also the busiest time for festivals in and around Cuzco.

☆ Corpus Christi

(ninth Thursday after Easter) Processions of this Catholic celebration in Cuzco are especially dramatic. (p148)

☆ Inti Raymi

(June 24) The Festival of the Sun (also the Feast of St John the Baptist and Peasant's Day) is the greatest of Inca festivals, celebrating the winter solstice. (p149)

Above: La Virgen de la Candelaria

♣ San Juan

(June 24) The feast of San Juan is all debauchery in Iquitos, where dancing, feasting and cockfights go until the wee hours on the evening before and the actual day.

♣ San Pedro y San Pablo

(June 29) The feasts of Saints Peter and Paul provide more fiestas in June, especially around Lima and in the highlands.

July

The continuation of high-season tourism. In Lima the weather is marked by *garúa,* a thick sea mist that lingers over the city for the next few months.

♣ La Virgen del Carmen

(July 16) This holiday is mainly celebrated in the southern sierra – Paucartambo and Pisac near Cuzco and Pucará near Lake Titicaca are especially important centers. (p138)

♣ Fiestas Patrias

(July 28 and 29) The National Independence Days are celebrated nationwide; festivities in the southern sierra begin with the Feast of St James on July 25.

August

The last month of high tourist visitation throughout Peru is also the most crowded at Machu Picchu. Book well ahead.

♣ Feast of Santa Rosa de Lima

(August 30) Commemorating the country's first saint, major processions are held in Lima, Arequipa and Junín to honor the patron saint of Lima and of the Americas.

September

Low season everywhere, September and October can still offer good weather to highland trekkers without the crowds.

✗ Mistura

For one week in September, this massive food festival with international acclaim draws up to half a million visitors.

♣ El Festival Internacional de la Primavera

(last week of September) The International Spring Festival in Trujillo features supreme displays of horsemanship, as well as dancing and cultural celebrations. Not to be missed.

October

The best time to hit the Amazon runs from September to November when drier weather results in better wildlife-watching.

✦ Great Amazon River Raft Race

(September/early October) The longest raft race in the world flows between Nauta and Iquitos.

♣ La Virgen del Rosario

(October 4) This saint is celebrated in Lima, Apurímac, Arequipa and Cuzco. Its biggest event is held in Ancash, with a symbolic confrontation between Moors and Christians.

November

A good month for festivals, with plenty of events to choose from. Waves return, calling all surfers to the coast.

♣ Día de los Muertos

(November 2) All Souls' Day is celebrated by taking gifts of food, drink and flowers to family graves.

♣ Puno Week

(starting November 5) This festival involves several days of spectacular costumes and street dancing to celebrate the legendary emergence of the first Inca, Manco Capac.

December

Beach season returns with warmer Pacific temperatures. Skip the Amazon, where heavy rains start falling from the end of the month through early April.

♣ Fiesta de la Purísima Concepción

(December 8) The Feast of the Immaculate Conception is a national holiday celebrated with religious processions in honor of the Virgin Mary.

Plan Your Trip
Get Inspired

Read

The Last Days of the Inca (Kim MacQuarrie; 2007) A clash between civilizations.

Aunt Julia and the Scriptwriter (Mario Vargas Llosa; 1977) A classic unconventional love story.

Cradle of Gold (Christopher Heaney; 2010) Story of Hiram Bingham, the 'real' Indiana Jones.

At Play in the Fields of the Lord (Peter Matthiessen; 1965) Inspired by Amazon conflicts.

Eight Feet in the Andes (Devla Murphy; 1983) A travel writer and her daughter venture through the Andes.

The Conquest of the Incas (John Hemming; 1970) Two cultures colliding.

Watch

La Teta Asustada (The Milk of Sorrow; 2009) Claudia Llosa's feature film examines the life of a girl suffering from a trauma-related affliction.

Undertow (2009) A married fisherman coming to terms with his dead boyfriend's ghost.

Días de Santiago (Days of Santiago; 2004) A military veteran struggles with his return to civilian life in the slums of Lima.

Aguirre, the Wrath of God (1972) Werner Herzog's historical masterpiece about a fruitless search for El Dorado, the city of gold.

Listen

Lo mejor de Uchpa (Uchpa; 2005) Quechua band lacing Peruvian punk rock with blues.

Ch'usay (Novalima; 2018) Internationally popular Afro–Peruvian electronica.

Ves lo que quieres ver (Bareto; 2012) Alt rock and Peruvian rhythms.

Contigo Peru (Arturo 'Zambo' Cavero) Legendary crooner singing a national classic.

Yuyu (Pauchi Sasaki; 2007) Peruvian–Japanese violinist incorporating diverse, modern influences.

Cafe Inkaterra (Miki Gonzalez; 2004) Peruvian pioneer mixing rock with Afro–Peruvian and Andean music.

Above: Inca ruins at Sacsaywamán (p152)

Plan Your Trip
Five-Day Itineraries

South Coast Sortie

A couple of Peru's flagship sights lie on the southern Pacific coast, within punting distance of Lima, and provide an interesting mix of wildlife-spotting and mysterious pre-Columbian, Pre-Inca history amid stark desert landscapes.

Lima (p35) Get over your jet lag in Lima's sedate Miraflores neighborhood, a great place to sample progressive *cocina novoandina* (New Andean cuisine). 🚌 3½ hrs to Paracas

Islas Ballestas (p72) Enjoy day two with a boat trip to these wildlife-rich, guano-covered islands. 🚲 or 🚗 into the Península de Paracas

Reserva Nacional de Paracas (p74) Spend day three traversing this arid reserve, exploring its beaches and coastal geology. 🚌 2 hrs to Nazca

Nazca (p79) Make an overflight of the Nazca Lines and reserve an extra day for South America's biggest sand dune.

Southern Highland Jaunt

This brisk itinerary allows two days to see the capital's sights, then heads south to the charming highland city of Arequipa, known for its rich history and spicy cuisine, and throws in the fabulous Cañón del Colca for good measure.

Lima (p35) Spend a couple of days in Lima, exploring colonial churches and the Museo Larco. ✈ 1½ hrs to Arequipa

①

Cañón del Colca (p107) On the last day, get an early start for a day trip to see one of Peru's most famous natural sights.

③
②

Arequipa (p89) Allocate the next two days to handsome Arequipa. 🚌 4 hrs to Cañón del Colca

③

②

Plan Your Trip
10-Day Itinerary

A Tour of Inca Country

Ten days allows you ample time to soak up the wonders of the ancient Inca capital and the Sacred Valley. Starting with a couple of days in Lima ensures that you won't head to the highlands without a few exquisite meals in your belly.

Ollantaytambo (p194)
This charismatic indigenous village retains its inherently Inca form.
🚌 2 hrs to Aguas Calientes

Lima (p35) Two days in Lima is a great start to any adventure.
✈ 1¼ hrs to Cuzco

Aguas Calientes (p216)
Arrange to spend two to three nights at Aguas Calientes exploring local hikes. 🚌 25 mins to Machu Picchu

Machu Picchu (p197)
Explore these spectacular Inca ruins.

Cuzco (p143) Spend a couple of days here and include visits to Sacsaywamán fortress and the Qorikancha temple. 🚐 40 mins to Ollantaytambo

Plan Your Trip
Two-Week Itinerary

Highland/ Jungle Combo

On this two-week trip through the Andes and down into the Amazon, you'll see a little bit of everything that Peru has to offer: Inca ruins, pastoral highland settings, steamy lowland jungle, and more wildlife than you've ever dreamed of.

Machu Picchu (p197) Base yourself at Aguas Calientes. Stick around for at least two days. 🚆 3 hrs to Cuzco, then 🚌 4½ hrs to Parque Nacional Manu

Lima (p35) Ease into the journey with a relaxed day in Lima. ✈ 2 hrs, then 🚗 1 hr to Puno

JESS KRAFT/SHUTTERSTOCK ©

Parque Nacional Manu (p256) Factor in at least three nights in this Amazon jungle park.

6

Cuzco (p143) Admire the ancient capital of the Inca empire, starting with Qorikancha and Sacsaywamán.
4 🚌 3 hrs to Aguas Calientes

5

Puno (p132) High above sea level, spend one day acclimatizing in town while visiting museums. 🚤 to Lake Titicaca

2 **3** Lake Titicaca (p123) Spend a day exploring the floating reed islands.
🚤 to Puno, then ✈ 1 hr to Cuzco

5

6

Plan Your Trip
Family Travel

Traveling to Peru with children can bring some distinct advantages. It is a family-oriented society, and children are treasured. For parents, it makes an easy conversation starter with locals and helps break down cultural barriers. In turn, Peru can be a great place for kids, with plenty of opportunities to explore and interact.

Inspiration

Routine travel, such as train rides or jungle canoe trips, can amount to adventure for kids. In rural areas, community tourism is a great option. Many of the activities aimed at adults can be scaled down for children. Activities such as guided horseback rides and canyoning often have age limits (usually eight and up), but are invariably OK for teenagers. Some rivers may be suitable for children to float or raft; make sure outfitters have life vests and wet suits in appropriate sizes.

Good ideas for families include rafting near Cuzco, horseback riding in the Andean foothills, splashing about in the hot pools in Cañón del Colca's La Calera, canopy zip lining in the Sacred Valley, cycling the coastal paths of Lima and spying wildlife in the Amazon.

Need to Know

Flights Children under the age of 12 may receive discounts on airline travel, while infants under two pay only 10% of the fare, provided they sit on their parent's lap.

Accommodations Most midrange and top-end hotels will have reduced rates for children under 12 years of age, provided the child shares a room with parents. Cots are not normally available, except at the most exclusive hotels. Cabins or apartments, more common in beach destinations, usually make a good choice, with options for self-catering.

Expecting and New Mothers Expecting mothers enjoy a boon of special parking spaces and grocery store lines. Breastfeeding in public is not uncommon, but most women will discreetly cover themselves.

JOERG STEBER/SHUTTERSTOCK ©

Dining While restaurants don't offer special kids' meals, most offer a variety of dishes suitable for children or may accommodate a special request. You can also always order meals *sin picante* (without spice). High chairs are available in some larger restaurants.

Infant supplies Stock up on diapers (nappies) in Lima or other major cities before heading to rural areas. Bring your own infant medicines and a thermometer. Formula and baby food are easily found.

Babysitting Babysitting services or children's activity clubs tend to be limited to upmarket hotels and resorts.

Driving Car seats are not widely available with rental cars, so it is best to bring one with you.

Public Toilets In general, public toilets are poorly maintained. Always carry toilet paper with you. While a woman may take a young boy into the ladies' room, it would be socially unacceptable for a man to take a girl into the men's room.

★ **Best Destinations for Kids**

Lima (p35)

Cuzco (p143)

Islas Ballestas (p72)

Machu Picchu (p197)

Public Transportation In Peru, kids are a common sight on public transportation. Often someone will give up a seat for a parent and child or offer to put your child on their lap. On buses, children aren't normally charged if they sit on their parent's lap.

From left: Beach near Arequipa; Parque Nacional Manu (p256)

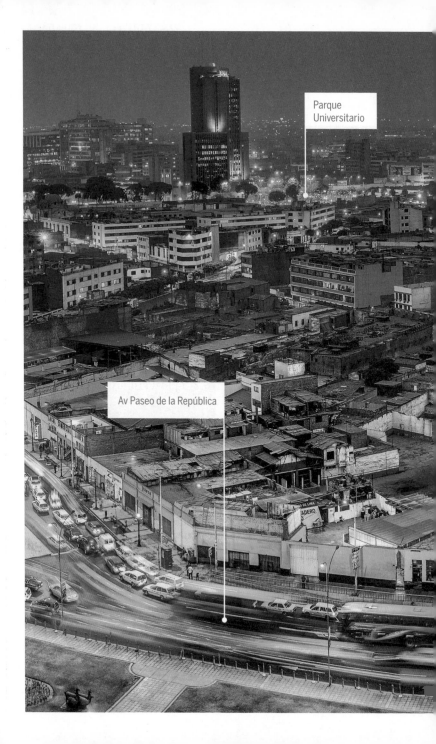

Parque
Universitario

Av Paseo de la República

LIMA

Lima at a Glance...

Fresh sophistication has come to a civilization that dates back millennia. Galleries debut edgy art, stately museums give new angles to sacrifice vessels, solemn religious processions recall the 18th century, and crowded nightclubs dispense tropical beats. No visitor can miss the capital's culinary genius, part of a gastronomic revolution more than 400 years in the making. This is Lima. Shrouded in history, gloriously messy and full of aesthetic delights. Don't even think of missing it.

Lima in Two Days

Start the day with a **walking tour** (p48) of the city's colonial heart and end the day with a most important pilgrimage: a pisco sour, either at **Dada** (p61) or **Museo del Pisco** (p61). On the second day, go pre-Columbian and view breathtaking Moche pottery at **Museo Larco** (p38) and explore **Huaca Pucllana** (p53), a centuries-old adobe temple in the middle of Miraflores. The temple also boasts a sophisticated **restaurant** (p53).

Lima in Three Days

Make the day trip to **Pachacamac** (p44) to explore sandy ruins with several civilizations' worth of temples. Spend the afternoon haggling for crafts at the **Mercado Indio** (p57) in Miraflores before side-stepping to Barranco where you can hit **Isolina** (p61) for dinner and **Red Cervecera** (p61) for craft beer.

Estación
mparados

Lima Centro
The city's colonial heart, filled with bustling narrow streets and ornate baroque churches (p50)

MUSEO DE ARTE DE LIMA

ASTRID Y GASTÓN CASA MOREYRA

FUNDACIÓN USEO AMANO

ÁMAZ

PACHACAMAC

(8km)

EO PEDRO OSMA

CENTRAL

Lima Centro Map (p52)
Miraflores & San Isidro Map (p54)
Barranco Map (p60)

Palacio de Justicia

Paseo de los
Héroes Navales

N
0 ———————————— 2 km
0 ———————————— 1 mile

✈ Jorge Chávez
(3km)

Des.

**MUSEO ANDRÉS
DEL CASTILLO**

MUSEO LARCO ●

San Isidro
Swanky area with
sumptuous hotels,
frothy cocktails and
fusion haute cuisine
(p51)

●

Miraflores
Lima's modern hub,
full of restaurants, shops
and nightspots (p52)

●

MAID

*PACIFIC
OCEAN*

Barranco
Lima's nightlife
epicenter, packed with
thumping clubs and
bars (p53)

MUS
D

Buskers, Plaza de Armas (p50)

Arriving in Lima

Aeropuerto Internacional Jorge Chávez Lies 12km west of downtown, or 20km northwest of Miraflores. Take the 45- to 60-minute trip in an official airport taxi, Taxi Green, for about S60.

Bus There is no central terminal; each company operates independent arrival points. Cruz del Sur has most luxury arrivals at La Victoria, a 15-minute taxi ride south to Miraflores.

Where to Stay

From diminutive family *pensións* to hotel towers armed with spas, Lima has every type of accommodations imaginable. It is also one of the most expensive destinations in the country (other than the tourist mecca of Cuzco).

The favored traveler neighborhood is Miraflores, which offers a bounty of hostels, inns and upscale hotel chains plus vigilant neighborhood security. Nearby Barranco is certainly one of the most walkable areas, with lots of gardens and colonial architecture. More upscale – and generally more tranquil – is the financial hub of San Isidro.

Museo Andrés del Castillo

RICHARD CUMMINS/GETTY IMAGES ©

Top Museums

Lima is a masterpiece of cultures, artifacts and architecture. A glut of art of the pre-Inca, colonial and contemporary kind is matched with eye-openers such as erotic pots, Mario Testino snaps and Inquisition torture devices.

Great For...

☑ Don't Miss

Museo Larco's gold ceremonial suit, and the erotic ceramics of indigenous cultures.

Museo Larco

In an 18th-century viceroy's mansion, **Museo Larco** (☎01-461-1312; www.museolarco.org; Bolívar 1515, Pueblo Libre; adult/child under 15 S30/15; ☺9am-10pm) offers one of the largest, best-presented displays of ceramics in Lima. Founded by pre-Columbian collector Rafael Larco Hoyle in 1926, the collection includes more than 50,000 pots, with ceramic works from the Cupisnique, Chimú, Chancay, Nazca and Inca cultures. Highlights include the sublime Moche portrait vessels, presented in simple, dramatically lit cases, and a Wari weaving in one of the rear galleries that contains 398 threads to the linear inch – a record.

Museo de Arte de Lima

Known locally as MALI, the **Museo de Arte de Lima** (☎01-204-0000; www.

Sculpture, Museo Larco

SAIKO3P/SHUTTERSTOCK ©

textiles produced by the coastal Chancay culture. There's an optional 1 ½ hour guided tour in English, Portuguese or Spanish.

Museo Andrés del Castillo

Housed in a pristine 19th-century mansion with Spanish tile floors, the **Museo Andrés del Castillo** (Map p122; 📞01-433-2831; www.madc.com.pe; Jirón de la Unión 1030; admission S10; ⊗9am-6pm, Mon-Sat, from 10am Sun) showcases a vast collection of minerals, as well as Nazca textiles and Chancay pottery, including some remarkable representations of Peruvian hairless dogs.

Museo Pedro de Osma

In a lovely beaux-arts mansion surrounded by gardens, the **Museo Pedro de Osma** (Map p127; 📞01-467-0141; www.museopedrodeosma.org; Av Pedro de Osma 423; admission S30; ⊗10am-6pm Tue-Sun) is an undervisited museum that has an exquisite collection of colonial furniture, silverwork and art, some of which dates back to the 1500s. Among the many fine pieces, standouts include a 2m-wide canvas that depicts a Corpus Christi procession in turn-of-the-17th-century Cuzco.

mali.pe; Paseo Colón 125; adult/child S30/15; ⊗10am-7pm Tue,Thu & Fri, to 5pm Sat & Sun) is the capital's principal fine-art museum and is housed in a striking beaux-arts building that was renovated in 2015. Subjects range from pre-Columbian to contemporary art, and there are also guided visits to special exhibits. On Sunday entry is just S1. A satellite museum is under construction in Barranco.

Fundación Museo Amano

The well-designed **Fundación Museo Amano** (Map p124; 📞01-441-2909; www.museoamano.org; Retiro 160; ⊗10am-5pm) **FREE** features a fine private collection of ceramics, with a strong representation of wares from the Chimú and Nazca cultures. It also has a remarkable assortment of lace and other

Ceviche (raw seafood marinated in lime juice)

Eating in Lima

The gastronomic capital of the continent, you will find sublime culinary creations in Lima: from simple cevicherías (restaurants serving ceviche) and corner anticucho (beef skewer) stands to outstanding molecular cuisine, ají de gallina (spicy chicken and walnut stew) from Arequipa and cocktails infused with Amazon berries.

Great For...

❶ Need to Know

A *menú* (set meal) is a delicious way to taste-test local flavors.

★ **Top Tip**

In Miraflores, casual places with cheap *menús* abound on the tiny streets east of Av José Larco, just off the Parque Kennedy.

Outstanding Eateries

Lima's prime position on the coast gives it access to a wide variety of fresh seafood, while showcasing regional specialties. The city has such a vast assortment of cuisine, in fact, that it's possible to spend weeks here without tasting it all. Pack your appetite, you'll need it.

Central   Peruvian $$$

(Map p127; ☎01-242-8515; www.centralrestau-rante.com.pe; Av Pedro de Osma 301; mains S52-95; ⏰seating 12:45-1:15pm & 7:45-8:30pm Mon-Sat) ✐ Part restaurant, part laboratory, Central reinvents Andean cuisine and rescues age-old Peruvian ingredients not used elsewhere. Dining is an experience, evidenced by tender native potatoes served in edible clay. Chef Virgilio Martinez wants you to taste the Andes. He paid his dues in Europe and Asia's top kitchens, but it's his work here that dazzles.

Seafood – such as the charred octopus starter – is a star, but classics like suckling pig served with pickled vegetables and spiced squash deliver. A menu supplied by sustainable fishing and organic gardens enhance the ultra-fresh appeal.

ámaZ   Amazonian $$

(Map p124; ☎01-221-9393; www.amaz.com.pe; Av La Paz 1079; mains S20-65; ⏰12:30-11:30pm Mon-Sat, 12:30-4:30pm Sun; ✐) Chef Pedro Miguel's wonder is wholly dedicated to the abundance of the Amazon. Start with tart jungle-fruit cocktails and oversized *tostones* (plantain chips). Banana-leaf wraps, aka *juanes,* hold treasures such as fragrant Peking duck with rice. There's excellent *encurtido* (pickled vegetables) and the

Andean cuisine, Central

generous vegetarian set menu for two is a delicious way to sample the diversity.

ÁmaZ has a popular circular bar and coveted thatched-roof tables.

Maido   Japanese $$$

(Map p124; ☑01-446-2512; www.maido.pe; San Martín 399; mains S26-110; ☺12:30-4pm & 7:30-11pm Mon-Sat, 12:30-4pm Sun) ✿ True artistry and exquisite flavors make Maido an excellent stop for top-notch *nikkei* (Japanese-Peruvian) fare that has put it on World's Best lists. The menu of chef Mitsuharu 'Micha' Tsumura ranges from sushi to tender 50-hour ribs, *okonomiyaki* (Japanese pancake) and ramen, with a Peruvian

☑ Don't Miss

The experience of tucking into ceviche (raw seafood marinated in lime juice) with a view of the moody ocean.

NICHOLAS GILL/ALAMY STOCK PHOTO ©

accent. Desserts – such as the yucca *mochi* or a white-chocolate egg with sorbet yolk – delight. It supports sustainable fishing.

Astrid y Gastón
Casa Moreyra   Fusion $$$

(Map p124; ☑01-442-2775; www.astridygaston. com; Av Paz Soldan 290; mains S53-89; ☺1-3pm & 7-11pm Mon-Sat) The standard-bearer of *novoandina* (Peruvian nouvelle cuisine) cooking in Lima, Gastón Acurio's flagship French-influenced restaurant, run by Lima native Diego Muñoz, remains a culinary tour de force. The seasonal menu features traditional Peruvian fare, but it's the exquisite fusion specialties that make this a sublime fine-dining experience. The 28-course tasting menu showcases the depth and breadth of possibility here – just do it.

Seafood at La Punta

A quiet residential neighborhood with great views of the water, La Punta is perfect for a leisurely lunch. The gregarious owner of **Caleta la Punta** (☑01-453-1380; Malecón Pardo 180, Callao; mains S40-65; ☺10am-5:30pm; ☑) will lure you in with a complimentary cup of cold *chicha* (blue corn juice). Its mango ceviche won a prize at the prestigious Mistura food festival – seafood die-hards line up for fresh ceviche and whole fried garlic fish.

Dine in style at the waterfront **La Rana Verde** (☑973-752-959; Parque Gálvez s/n, Chorrillos; mains S42-59; ☺noon-6pm), ideal for Sunday dinner, with views of Isla San Lorenzo. Dishes are all deftly prepared and the *pulpo al olivo* (octopus in olive oil) is one of the best in Lima. It's located on the pier inside the Club Universitario de Regatas.

While you're here, check out the galleries and street art around nearby Monumental Callao (p53).

✕ Take a Break

For eating on the go, grab a tasty Peruvian *sanguche* – 'sandwich' by name, panini by flavor.

Pachacamac

Situated about 31km southeast of the city center, the archaeological complex of Pachacamac is a pre-Columbian citadel made up of adobe and stone palaces and temple pyramids.

Great For...

Chosica

⭐ Lima

☸ **Pachacamac**

ℹ Need to Know

☏01-321-5606; http://pachacamac.cultura. pe; Antigua Carr Panamericana Sur Km 31.5, Lurín; adult/child S15/5; ⊙9am-5pm Tue-Sat, to 4pm Sun

★ **Top Tip**

In summer, take water and a hat – there is no shade to speak of once you hit the trail.

History

If you've been to Machu Picchu, Pacha-camac may not look like much, but this was an important Inca site and a major city when the Spanish arrived. It began as a ceremonial center for the Lima culture beginning at about AD 100, and was later expanded by the Waris before being taken over by the Ichsma. The Inca added numerous other structures upon their arrival to the area in 1450. The name Pachacamac, which can be variously translated as 'He who Animated the World' or 'He who Created Land and Time,' comes from the Wari god, whose wooden, two-faced image can be seen at the on-site museum.

The Site

Most of the buildings are now little more than piles of rubble that dot the desert landscape, but some of the main temples have been excavated to reveal their ramps and stepped sides. You can climb the switchback trail to the top of the **Templo del Sol** (Temple of the Sun), which on clear days offers excellent views of the coast. The most remarkable structure on-site, however, is the **Palacio de las Mamacuna** (House of the Chosen Women), commonly referred to as the **Acllahuasi**, which boasts a series of Inca-style trapezoidal doorways. Unfortunately, a major earthquake in 2007 has left the structure highly unstable. As a result, visitors can only admire it from a distance. Without funding to repair the

extensive damage, it has been listed as one of the planet's most endangered sites.

New Discoveries in Pachacamac

The widespread looting of Peru's archaeological treasures has left many ruins with more puzzling questions than answers. So the discovery in 2012 of an untouched 80-person burial chamber in Pachacamac is considered nothing less than a coup. Archaeologists from the Free University of Brussels discovered an 18m (60ft) oval chamber in front of the Temple of Pachacamac, hidden under newer burials.

The perimeter was laced with infants and newborns encircling over 70 skeletons in the center of the tomb. The mummies were wrapped in textiles and buried with valuables, offerings, and even dogs and guinea pigs. According to *National Geographic,* investigators think the tomb may contain pilgrims who were drawn to the site to seek cures for serious illnesses.

Visiting Pachacamac

Various agencies in Lima offer guided tours that include transport and a guide (S120). Mountain-bike tours can be an excellent option.

A simple map can be obtained from the ticket office, and a track leads from here into the complex. Those on foot should allow at least two hours to explore. Those with a vehicle can drive from site to site.

Alternatively, catch a minibus signed 'Pachacamac' from Av 28 de Julio or the sunken roadway at the corner of Andahuaylas and Grau in Central Lima (S3, 45 minutes); minibuses leave every 15 minutes during daylight hours. From Miraflores, take a bus on Av Benavides headed east to the Panamericana and Puente Primavera, change here for the bus marked 'Pachacamac/Lurín' (S4, 30 minutes). For both services, tell the driver to let you off near the *ruinas* (ruins) or you'll end up at Pachacamac village, about 1km beyond the entrance. To get back to Lima, flag down any bus outside the gate, but expect to stand for the duration of the ride. You can also hire a taxi per hour (from S45) from Lima.

> ☑ **Don't Miss**
>
> The Templo del Sol for vistas of the Pacific Ocean and the Andes foothills.

MARKTUCAN/SHUTTERSTOCK ©

> ✕ **Take a Break**
>
> There is a visitor center and cafe at the site entrance, which is on the road to Lurín.

Downtown Lima Walking Tour

In the historical center of Lima, every turn is a blast from the city's colonial past. This is the best of its architecture in churches, palaces, plazas and catacombs.

Start Plaza San Martín
End El Barrio Chino
Length 3km; two hours

Classic Photo Colonial buildings in the Plaza de Armas

4 Explore **Plaza de Armas** (p50), including the **Catedral de Lima** (p50) and the **Palacio Arzobispal**, home to some of the city's best-preserved ornate Moorish balconies.

2 Walk the pedestrian street of **Jirón de la Unión**; once the heart of aristocratic city life, it's now lined with cinemas and bargain shoe stores.

Plaza de Armas
(Plaza Mayor) **4**

Callao

Camaná

Ica

Ucayali

Carabaya

Emancipación

Estacion Jiron de la Union

Miró Quesada

Lampa

1 Begin in **Plaza San Martín** to imbibe the faded grandeur of **Gran Hotel Bolívar** (☎01-619-7171; www.granhotelbolivar.com.pe), the city's first fine hotel.

Nicolás de Piérola (Colmena)

Camaná

START

Plaza San Martín

3 Iglesia de la Merced (☎01-427-8199; ☾10am-noon & 5-7pm) was originally built in 1541. It held the first Mass in Lima. Peek inside at the impressive mahogany altars.

5 To the northeast, the grandiose baroque **Palacio de Gobierno** (☏01-311-3908; www.presidencia.gob.pe; ☉tours 9am & 9:45am Sat & Sun) serves as Peru's presidential palace; pass at noon for the ceremonious changing of the guard.

7 Follow Río Rimac to **Parque de la Muralla**, a spacious city park installed alongside remains of the original city wall.

0 ———— 200 m
0 ———— 0.1 miles

Río Rimac

Estación Desamparados

Parque de la Muralla

Amazonas

5

6

7

8

Lampa

Ancash

Jirón Junín

Av Abancay

Huallaga

Azángaro

Plaza Bolívar

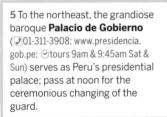

8 Return to Lampa and **Monasterio de San Francisco** (p51) to check out the monastery's catacombs that hold skulls and bones laid out in geometric designs.

6 Across the street, the **Museo del Pisco** (p61) merits a stop, though you might want to save it to end your walk with a handcrafted pisco cocktail instead.

9 The **Mercado Central** (☏958-849-731; ☉7am-9pm Mon-Sat, to 6pm Sun) overflows with goods, from soccer jerseys to piles of tropical and Andean fruit.

Ucayali

9

10 Finish your tour in **El Barrio Chino** (Chinatown) for tea or lunch at a Cantonese eatery.

Av Abancay

Ayacucho

Capón

Huallaga

Cuzco

10

FINISH

Huanta

Take a Break...
Wa Lok (p57) is the quintessential Peruvian *chifa* (Chinese restaurant).

Miró Quesada

3. JAVARMAN/SHUTTERSTOCK © 4. SAIKO3P/GETTY IMAGES © 8. DOUGLASDEFFIS/SHUTTERSTOCK ©

◎ SIGHTS

The majority of museums are located in the busy downtown area of Central Lima. If you have a few days here, try visiting them on a weekend morning when traffic is calmer. The neighborhoods of Miraflores and Barranco can be walked in their entirety, and there are pleasant parks and seaside walks to retreat to when you've had your fill of urban attractions.

◎ Lima Centro

The city's historic heart, Lima Centro (Central Lima) is a grid of crowded streets laid out in the 16th-century days of Francisco Pizarro, and home to most of the city's surviving colonial architecture.

Plaza de Armas   Plaza
(Map p122) Lima's 140-sq-meter Plaza de Armas, also called the Plaza Mayor, was not only the heart of the 16th-century settlement established by Francisco Pizarro, it was a center of the Spaniards' continent-wide empire. Though not one original building remains, at the center of the plaza is an impressive bronze fountain erected in 1650.

La Catedral de Lima   Church
(Map p122; ☏01-427-9647; Plaza Mayor s/n; museum admission S10; ◷9am-5pm Mon-Fri, 10am-1pm Sat) Next to the Palacio Arzobispal, the cathedral resides on the plot of land that Pizarro designated for the city's first church in 1535. Though it retains a baroque facade, the building has been built and rebuilt numerous times: in 1551, in 1622 and after the earthquakes of 1687 and 1746. The last major restoration was in 1940.

Iglesia de Santo Domingo   Church
(Map p122; ☏01-427-6793; cnr Camaná & Conde de Superunda; church free, convent S7; ◷9am-1pm & 5-7:30pm Mon-Sat) One of Lima's most historic religious sites, the Iglesia de Santo Domingo and its expansive **convent** are built on land granted to the Dominican friar Vicente de Valverde, who accompanied Pizarro throughout the conquest and was instrumental in persuading him to execute the captured Inca Atahualpa. Originally completed in the 16th century, this

La Catedral de Lima

impressive pink church has been rebuilt
and remodeled at various points since.

Monasterio de
San Francisco
Monastery

(Map p122; ✆ext 300 01-426-7377; www.
museocatacumbas.com; cnr Lampa & Ancash;
adult/child under 15 S15/3; ⏱9am-8pm) This
bright-yellow Franciscan monastery and
church is most famous for its bone-lined
catacombs (containing an estimated
70,000 remains) and its remarkable **library**
housing 25,000 antique texts, some of
which pre-date the conquest. Admission
includes a 30-minute guided tour in English
or Spanish. Tours leave as groups gather.

El Circuito Mágico
del Agua
Fountain

(Parque de la Reserva, Av Petit Thouars, cuadra
5; admission S4; ⏱3-10:30pm Wed-Sun) This
indulgent series of illuminated fountains is
so over the top it can't help but induce stu-
pefaction among even the most hardened
travel cynic. A dozen different fountains are
capped, at the end, by a laser light show
at the 120m-long Fuente de la Fantasía
(Fantasy Fountain). The whole display is set
to a medley of tunes comprising everything
from Peruvian waltzes to ABBA. It has to be
seen to be believed.

Iglesia de las Nazarenas
Church

(Map p122; ✆01-423-5718; cnr Tacna &
Huancavelica; ⏱7am-1pm & 4-8:30pm) One of
Lima's most storied churches was part of a
17th-century shantytown inhabited by former slaves. One of them painted an image
of the Crucifixion on a wall here. It survived
the devastating earthquake of 1655 and
a church was built around it (the painting
serves as the centerpiece of the main altar)
in the 1700s. The church has been rebuilt
many times since but the wall endures.

◉ San Isidro & Around

Well-to-do San Isidro is Lima's banking
center and one of its most affluent areas.
Its residential neighborhoods offer some
important sights.

Getting Oriented
in Lima

Lima has more than 30 municipalities,
with Lima Centro (Central Lima) its
historic heart. Av Arequipa, one of the
city's principal thoroughfares, plunges
southeast toward wealthy San Isidro,
the contemporary seaside neighborhood of Miraflores, and Barranco to the
south.

Streets in Lima can have several
names; for instance, Av Arequipa is also
known as Garcilaso de la Vega or Wilson.
Some names reappear in different
districts, so be sure to indicate the right
neighborhood to taxi drivers. Streets
also may change names – for practicali-
ty we use the most common names.

Even finding street names in this area
can be maddening, and to top it off,
you'll see tiles indicating colonial street
names that are no longer in use. Your
best bet is to look for the green street
signs and use well-known landmarks for
orientation.

Lima street sign
HARRY PAPAS/ALAMY STOCK PHOTO ©

Espacio Fundacion
Telefonica
Arts Center

(✆01-210-1327; http://espacio.fundaciontelefon-
ica.com.pe; Av Arequipa 1155; ⏱10am-8pm Tue-
Sat, noon-7pm Sun) **FREE** This cultural center
focuses on the arts, particularly technology
and digital formats. Though it's part of the
largest Spanish multinational and housed on
the ground level of the corporate building,
Espacio is a non-profit that brings some of
the most forward-thinking artists (national
and international) to the forefront. Entry to

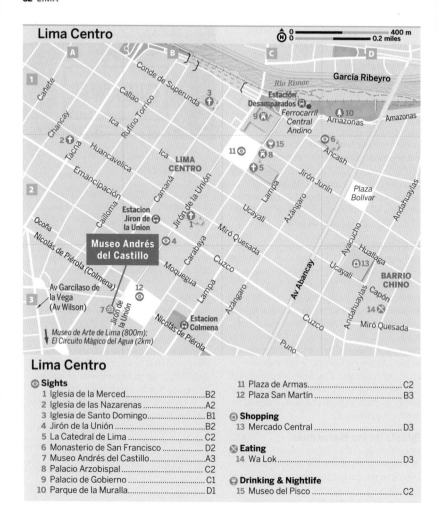

Lima Centro

Sights
1 Iglesia de la Merced.....................................B2
2 Iglesia de las Nazarenas A2
3 Iglesia de Santo Domingo.........................B1
4 Jirón de la Unión B2
5 La Catedral de Lima C2
6 Monasterio de San Francisco D2
7 Museo Andrés del Castillo........................A3
8 Palacio Arzobispal..C2
9 Palacio de Gobierno C1
10 Parque de la Muralla...................................D1

11 Plaza de Armas..C2
12 Plaza San Martín B3

Shopping
13 Mercado Central D3

Eating
14 Wa Lok..D3

Drinking & Nightlife
15 Museo del Pisco C2

exhibits, screenings, lectures and audio performances is free; frequent classes, ranging from animation to how to organize cultural events, have varying costs – see the website for what's coming up.

◎ Miraflores

The seaside neighborhood of Miraflores, which serves as Lima's contemporary core, bustles with commerce, restaurants and nightlife. A long greenbelt overlooks the Pacific from a set of ragged cliffs.

Impakto   Gallery
(Map p124; ☏01-368-7060; www.galeria-impakto.
com; Av Santa Cruz 857, Miraflores; ◎noon-8pm
Mon-Fri, 9am-5pm Sat) Located on the 1st floor of a towering and dark office building, this contemporary art museum has a glass facade that reveals just enough of the stark white interior to pique your interest. Both national and international artists are continually exhibited here to provide diverse yet always fresh perspectives.

Huaca Pucllana　　　　Ruins

(Map p124; 📞01-617-7138; cnr Borgoño & Tara-pacá; adult/child S12/6; ☺9am-4:30pm; 🐾) Located near the Óvalo Gutiérrez, this *huaca* is a restored adobe ceremonial center from the Lima culture that dates back to AD 400. In 2010, an important discovery of four Wari mummies, untouched by looting, was made. Though vigorous excavations continue, the site is accessible by regular guided tours in Spanish (for a tip). In addition to a tiny on-site **museum**, there's a celebrated **restaurant** (Map p124; 📞01-445-4042; www.resthuacapucllana.com; Gral Borgoño cuadra 8; mains S24-72; ☺12:30pm-4:30pm, 7pm-midnight Mon-Sat, to 4pm Sun) that offers incredible views of the illuminated ruins at night.

⊚ Barranco

A tiny resort back at the turn of the 20th century, Barranco is lined with grand old *casonas* (large houses), many of which have been turned into galleries and boutique hotels. With some rough edges, this hip bohemian center has hopping bars and nice areas to stroll.

**Museo de Arte
Contemporaneo**　　　　Museum

(MAC; 📞01-514-6800; www.maclima.pe; Av Grau 1511; adult/child S10/6; ☺10am-6pm Tue-Sun; 🅿🚹) The permanent collection at MAC is a quick study but visiting exhibits, such as a David LaChapelle retrospective, are major draws. There's also a good on-site **cafe** and a **sculpture park** (free access) with shady lawns that provide a good city respite for families. Guided tours available in English.

Museo Mario Testino　　　Museum

(MATE; Map p127; 📞01-200-5400; www.mate.pe; Av Pedro de Osma 409; admission S25; ☺11am-7pm Tue-Sun) Though quite small, this is a wonderful museum dedicated to the work of world-renowned photographer Mario Testino, a native of Peru and a *barranquino*. The permanent exhibition includes iconic portraits of Princess Diana, Kate Moss and notable actors. There are also beautiful portraits of Andean highlanders in traditional dress.

⊚ West Lima & Callao

To the west of downtown, cluttered lower-middle-class and poor neighborhoods eventually give way to the port city of Callao, where the Spanish once shipped gold. Travelers should approach Callao with caution, since some areas are dangerous, even during the day.

Monumental Callao　　Cultural Center

(www.monumentalcallao.com; Jirón Constitución 250; ☺11am-6pm) Superstar graffiti artists are helping to revive the rough neighborhood surrounding Casa Ronald, a 1920 architectural masterpiece. Now a center for creatives, Monumental Callao incorporates restaurants and artists' studios, as well as galleries, with tenants intermittently donating their time to the surrounding community. Every weekend you can find rooftop parties with DJs or live salsa concerts, and even fashion shows using the colorful Spanish-style tiling as the catwalk.

🎯 ACTIVITIES

Surfing has long been Lima's go-to sport, but with the city becoming more active options are expanding. Cycling and running along coastal paths have become widely popular. The adventurous can paraglide right from coastal Miraflores. Off the coast of Callao, you can dive in waters in which sea lions cavort.

Peru Fly　　　　Paragliding

(Map p124; 📞959-524-940, 01-444-5004; www.perufly.com; Parque del Amor, Miraflores; ☺10am-6pm) A paragliding school that also offers tandem flights in Miraflores.

Wayo Whilar　　　　Surfing

(📞01-254-1344; www.wayowhilar.com.pe; Alameda Garzas Reales Mz-FA 7, Chorrillos; ☺9am-7pm Mon-Thu, to 4pm Fri & Sat) The shop of a longtime Peruvian surfer who sells his own line of coveted hand-shaped surfboards.

Perú Divers　　　　Diving

(📞997-205-500, 01-251-6231; www.perudivers.com; Av Defensores del Morro 175, Chorrillos;

Miraflores & San Isidro

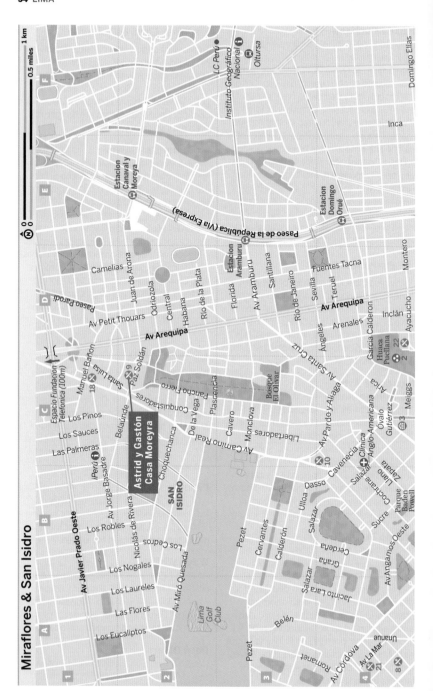

Astrid y Gastón
Casa Moreyra

SAN
ISIDRO

Lima
Golf
Club

Bosque
El Olivar

Paseo de la República (Vía Expresa)

Av Arequipa

Av Javier Prado Oeste

Espacio Fundación
Telefónica (100m)

iPerú

Estacion
Canaval y
Moreyra

Estacion
Aramburu

Estacion
Domingo
Orué

Instituto Geográfico
Naciona

LC Perú

Oltursa

Paseo Parodi

Camelias

Juan de Arona

Av Petit Thouars

Odriozola

Central

Habana

Río de la Plata

Florida

Av Aramburu

Santillana

Río de Janeiro

Sevilla

Fuentes Tacna

Teruel

Av Arequipa

Ángeles

Arenales

Inclán

García Calderón

Huaca
Pucllana

Ayacucho

Av Santa Cruz

Arica

Meiggs

Óvalo
Gutiérrez

Clínica
Anglo-Americana

Av Pardo y Aliaga

Libertadores

Monclova

Cavero

De la Vega

Plascencia

Pancho Fierro

Conquistadores

Belaúnde

Choquechanca

Av Camino Real

Paz Soldán

Santa Luisa

Manuel Bañón

Los Pinos

Los Sauces

Las Palmeras

Los Robles

Av Jorge Basadre

Nicolás de Rivera

Los Cedros

Los Nogales

Los Laureles

Las Flores

Los Eucaliptos

Av Miró Quesada

Pezet

Pezet

Cervantes

Calderón

Graña

Cerdeña

Salazar

Jacinto Lara

Belén

Romanet

Av Córdova

Av La Mar

Unanue

Av Angamos Oeste

Sucre

Parque
Baden
Powell

Zapata

Llano
Zapata

Cochrane

Salazar

Cavenecia

Dasso

Ulloa

Salazar

Montero

Inca

Domingo Elías

9

18

22

2

3

10

21

8

0.5 miles

1 km

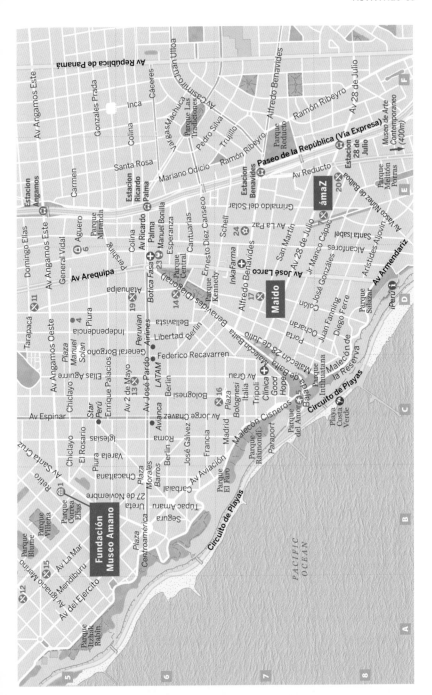

Miraflores & San Isidro

⊙9am-5pm Mon-Sat) Deep-sea diving off Peru's southern coast is reasonably priced. Luis Rodríguez, a PADI-certified instructor, owns this excellent dive shop with equipment for sale, and offers certification and diving trips. Regular excursions visit a year-round sea-lion colony at Islas Palomino, off the coast of Callao.

⊙ TOURS

Andean Photo Expeditions Tours
(☑960-724-103; www.andeanphotoexpeditions. com) Excellent photography tours of Lima led by French and Peruvian photographers, with tailor-made options. There's no office, meet ups are in Parque Kennedy or Central Lima.

Lima Tasty Tours Food & Drink
(☑958-313-939, 01-249-4594; www.limatasty-tours.com; Av Grau 1113, Barranco; ⊙by appointment) Gastronomic tours that reveal Lima as the locals know it, with plenty of sampling at markets. It offers a friendly rapport with clients, tailored options and insider access to lesser-known culinary treasures; tours are available in English.

Lima Vision Tours
(Map p124; ☑01-447-7710; www.limavision. com; Chiclayo 444, Miraflores) Lima Vision has

various four-hour city tours (S116), as well as day trips to the ruins at Pachacamac (p44).

⊙ SHOPPING

Clothing, jewelry and handicrafts from all over Peru can be found in Lima. Shop prices tend to be high, but bargain hunters can haggle their hearts out at craft markets. Credit cards and traveler's checks can be used at some spots, but you'll need photo ID.

Quality pisco can be bought duty-free at the airport prior to departure.

El Cacaotal Chocolate
(Map p127; ☑937-595-812; www.elcacaotal. com; Colina 108, 2nd fl; ⊙11am-8pm Mon-Thu & Sat, to 7pm Fri, to 6pm Sun) ✦ A sustainable chocolate shop with delicious bars and connoisseur expertise. It's the perfect opportunity to appease friends and family back home, and it offers fair-trade compensation for small-scale farmers around Peru. Products are organized by region and portraits of the farmers themselves grace the walls. It also does tastings and excellent workshops in English with an adjacent chocolate lab.

Las Pallas Arts & Crafts
(Map p127; ☑01-477-4629; Cajamarca 212, Barranco; ⊙10am-7pm Mon-Sat) For special gifts, check out this handicrafts shop featuring

a selection of the highest-quality products from all over Peru; it's even on the radar of Sotheby's. Ring the bell if the gate is closed during opening hours.

La Zapateria
Shoes

(Map p127; ☑01-249-9609; www.lazapateria-handmade.pe; Av Pedro de Osma 135, Barranco; ⊗10am-8pm Mon-Sat, noon-6pm Sun) Though it appears quite small, there's a lot going on inside La Zapateria, one part showroom, one part workshop. Handmade leather shoes can be made to order, and there are plenty of stylish models ready-made on the shelves for both men and women.

Mercado Indio
Market

(Map p124; Av Petit Thouars 5245, Miraflores; ⊗9:30am-8pm) This sprawling market is the best place to find everything from pre-Columbian-style clay pottery to alpaca rugs to knock-offs of Cuzco School canvases. Prices vary; shop around.

EATING

For the highlights of Lima's dining scene, see p42.

Lima Centro

Lima's downtown spots offer cheap deals and history, from functional *comedores* (cheap restaurants) packed with office workers to atmospheric eateries that count Peruvian presidents among their clientele.

Agallas
Ceviche $$

(☑01-390-4012; www.facebook.com/agallas-cantina; Av Manco Cápac 1100; mains S22-28; ⊗12:30-5:30pm Tue-Sun) A country mile from the tourist traps, this hip cantina and *cevichería* in La Victoria serves six heavenly versions of marinated fish with metal cups of beer. It's worth sharing an order of the northern-style seafood rice served in aluminum casserole dishes.

The portraits of working *limeños* lining the walls pay homage to the real heart of the city.

Wa Lok
Chinese $$

(Map p122; ☑01-447-1314; Paruro 878; mains S15-80; ⊗9am-11pm Mon-Sat, to 10pm Sun; ☑) Serving seafood, fried rice as light and fresh as it gets, and sizzling meats that come on steaming platters, Wa Lok is among the best *chifas* (Chinese restaurants) in Chinatown. The 16-page Cantonese menu includes dumplings, noodles, stir-fries and a good selection of vegetarian options (try the braised tofu casserole). Portions are enormous; don't over-order.

San Isidro

Chic dining rooms, frothy cocktails and fusion haute cuisine: San Isidro is a bastion of fine dining – and not much else.

Coffee Road
Cafe $

(☑01-637-2028; Av Prescott 365; mains S6-12; ⊗7am-10pm Mon-Fri, from 9am Sat, from 2pm Sun) Calling all coffee connoisseurs: this cafe of long bars and leather stools will brew you delicious espresso, Chemex, French press, Aeropress and more, using quality Peruvian beans. It's some of the best in town. Also serves quiches and desserts.

Barra Chalaca
Ceviche $$

(Map p124; ☑01-422-1465; Av Camino Real 1239; mains S14-39; ⊗11am-5pm) This casual ceviche and seafood bar combines masterful cooking and playful rapport for the win. Watching the prep cooks from your bar stool, order *curatodo* (cures everything) – a fishbowl of tropical juices and fresh herbs. There's mouthwatering *tiradito chichuito* (sashimi with capers, avocado and garlic); crisp, lightly battered *pejerrey* (silverside fish), and seafood fried rice that you can't put down.

Matsuei
Japanese $$

(Map p124; ☑981-310-180; www.matsueiperu.com.pe; Atahualpa 195; mains S16-70; ⊗12:30-3:30pm & 7:30-11pm Mon-Sat) Venerated Japanese super-chef Nobu Matsuhisa once co-owned this sushi bar. Its new location is posh and atmospheric. Diners come to try some of the most spectacular sashimi

From left: Museo del Pisco (p61); *Acevichado* (shrimp and avocado sushi roll); La Mar (p61)

and *maki* (sushi rolls) in Lima. A must-have: the *acevichado*, a roll stuffed with shrimp and avocado, then doused in a house-made mayo infused with ceviche broth. Your brain will tingle.

Cafe A Bistro
American $$

(☎01-264-5856; www.facebook.com/cafeabistro; Av Del Ejercito 2193; mains S25-35; ☺8am-11pm Fri-Wed, to 4pm Thu) Sandwiched between a gas station and a Chinese restaurant, this restaurant is unexpected, and then some. Serving up classic American breakfasts such as sausage patties, eggs and thick slices of homemade bread, it's a cozy spot with outdoor seating to enjoy a midday brunch or laid-back night out with friends.

Malabar
Fusion $$

(Map p124; ☎01-440-5200; www.malabar. com.pe; Av Camino Real 101; mains S28-64; ☺12:30-4pm & 7:30-11pm Mon-Sat) With an Amazonian bent, chef Pedro Miguel Schiaffino's seasonal menu features deftly prepared delicacies such as crisp, seared *cuy* (guinea pig) and Amazonian river snails bathed in spicy chorizo sauce. Don't forgo the cocktails (the chef's father, a noted

pisco expert, consulted on the menu) or desserts, which are perhaps the lightest and most refreshing in Lima.

🍴 Miraflores

By far the most varied neighborhood for eating, Miraflores carries the breadth and depth of Peruvian cooking at every price range, from tiny *comedores* with cheap lunchtime *menús* to some of the city's most revered gastronomic outposts. Pavement cafes are ideal for sipping pisco sours and people-watching.

There are myriad cheap and informal eateries on the small streets east of Av José Larco, just off Parque Kennedy.

La Lucha Sanguachería
Sandwiches $

(Map p124; ☎01-241-5953; Benavides 308; sandwiches S12-21; ☺8am-1am Sun-Thu, to 3am Fri & Sat) This all-hours corner sandwich shop is the perfect fix for the midnight munchies. *Lechón a la leña* (roasted pork) is its specialty, but there's also roast chicken or ham served in fluffy rolls, and juices are blended on the spot.

El Pan de la Chola · Cafe $

(Map p124; 01-221-2138; Av La Mar 918; mains S8-25; 8am-10pm Mon-Sat, 9am-7pm Sun;) In South America, finding real, crusty whole-grain bread is rarer than striking gold. Enter this small brick cafe that bakes four scrumptious varieties, and serves organic coffee from the Peruvian Amazon, Greek yogurt and sweets.

There's European-style seating at big wooden tables; grab a sandwich or share the tasting plate with bread, olives, hummus and fresh cheese.

Ana Avellana · Bakery $

(Map p124; www.facebook.com/anaavellanalima; Mendiburu 1096; desserts S5-16; 8am-9pm Tue-Sat, to 7pm Sun;) A jolly light-blue exterior invites you inside to gaze at Ana Avellana's sweet and savory creations. A dense flourless chocolate cake or luscious Borgoña grape pie is a great pairing for an Americano as you sit on one of the comfy sofas. It's a hit, partially because of the decent quality options, from quinoa-bread sandwiches filled with roast beef or turkey satisfy those with savory cravings.

El Bodegón · Bistro $$

(Map p124; 01-444-4704; www.elbodegon.com. pe; Av Tarapaca 197; mains S28-39; noon-midnight Mon-Sat, 11am-9pm Sun) Dimly lit with polished hardwood and offering snappy service, this corner taverna feels more Buenos Aires than Lima; we're just thankful it's here. This Gastón Acurio enterprise recaptures home-style Peruvian eating. It's worth sharing several dishes to spread your good fortune. Standouts include a creamy roasted cauliflower served whole and an ultra-delectable *rocoto relleno* (stuffed pepper) with a nutty, rich sauce.

Mercado 28 · Food Hall $$

(Map p124; 981-370-730; www.mercado28. pe; Av Vasco Núñez de Balboa 755; mains S12-30; 8am-10pm) This open 2nd-floor market houses more than a dozen restaurant stands attracting a mostly millennial crowd for cheap, informal dining. It's a hit, partially because of the decent quality options, from gourmet burgers to street chicken and poke bowls. In the center of it all, an island bar stocked with beer on tap, cocktails and wine holds it all together.

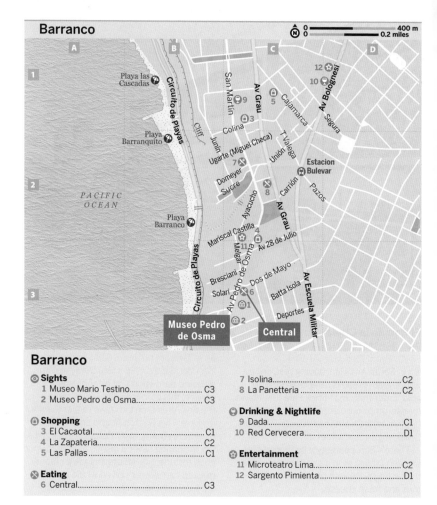

Barranco

Sights

IK Peruvian $$$

(Map p124; ☑01-652-1692; www.ivankisic.pe; Elías Aguirre 179; mains S45-75; ☺6-11pm Mon-Sat) Combining ancestral traditions with the Peruvian vanguard of molecular gastronomy is a tall order, but most feel that IK pulls it off with style. The restaurant is a tribute to a well-known local chef and its restorative atmosphere of living plants, natural sounds and light projections bring something new to the dining experience. Dishes are well balanced and meticulously presented.

Pescados Capitales Ceviche $$$

(Map p124; ☑01-421-8808; www.pescados-capitales.com; Av La Mar 1337; mains S39-70; ☺12:30-5pm) On a street once lined by clattering auto shops, this industrial-contemporary destination serves some of the finest ceviche around. Try the 'Ceviche Capital,' a mix of flounder, salmon and tuna marinated with red, white and green onions, bathed in a three-chili crème. A nine-page wine list offers a strong selection of Chilean and Argentinean vintages.

La Mar
Seafood $$$

(Map p124; ☑01-421-3365; www.lamarcebicheria.com; Av La Mar 770; mains S39-79; ☺noon-5pm Mon-Fri, 11:45am-5:30pm Sat & Sun) A good-time *cevichería* with outstanding service and wonderful ceviche and *tiraditos,* alongside a light and fresh *chifon chaufa* (fried rice). This Gastón Acurio outpost is not much more than a polished cement patio bursting with VIPs. Try the delicious riff on a bloody Mary – the sublime bloody *locho*, seafood shells and all. Desserts deliver too. It does not take reservations.

✪ Barranco

Even as Barranco has gone upscale in recent years, with trendy restaurants serving fusion fare of all types, the neighborhood still holds on to atmospheric, local spots where life is no more complicated than ceviche and beer.

A number of informal restaurants serving *anticuchos* and cheap *menús* line Av Grau around the intersection with Unión.

La Panetteria
Bakery $

(Map p127; ☑01-469-8260; www.facebook.com/lapanetteriabarranco; Av Grau 369; mains S8-22; ☺8am-9pm Tue-Sun; ☏) One of the neighborhood favorites, this bakery serves up a wide variety of breads, from traditional baguettes and French rolls, to playful experiments such as pesto or *aji* (Peru's slightly spicy pepper) loaves and gorgeous pastries. It's busy on weekends with the brunch crowd (eggs aren't on the menu but are available).

Café Tostado
Peruvian $$

(☑01-247-7133; Av Nicolás de Pierola 222; mains S10-38; ☺12:30-9pm Mon-Sat, 7:30am-6pm Sun) Call it a cultural experience. This barely converted auto-repair shop long ago transformed into a bastion of traditional cooking, with long wooden tables and an open kitchen surrounded by scarred iron pots and drying noodles. Daily specials rotate, but the sought-after signature dish is rabbit, which feeds up to three people.

Isolina
Peruvian $$$

(Map p127; ☑01-247-5075; www.isolina.pe; Av San Martín 101; mains S35-78; ☺noon-10pm Mon & Tue, to 11pm Wed-Fri, 9am-5pm Sat, 9am-11pm Sun) Go old school. This is home-style *criollo* (spicy Peruvian fare with Spanish and African influences) food at its best. Isolina doesn't shy away from tripe and kidneys, but also offers loving preparations of succulent ribs, *causa escabeche-da* (whipped potato dishes with marinated onions) and vibrant green salads on the handwritten menu. Family-sized portions come in old-fashioned tins, but you could make a lighter meal of starters such as marinated clams or ceviche.

🍷 DRINKING & NIGHTLIFE

Lima is overflowing with establishments of every description, from rowdy beer halls to high-end lounges to atmospheric old bars.

Dada
Cocktail Bar

(Map p127; www.dada.com.pe; Av San Martín 154; ☺7pm-1am Tue & Wed, to 3am Thu-Sat) This chic mansion with themed rooms and a gorgeous patio is Barranco's newest hot spot. You know those locales that are described not as a place but a feeling, perhaps like hugging a friend? That's Dada. Come well dressed and well funded. The cocktails here are not cheap, but they are delicious. Live performances of calypso, jazz and rock.

Museo del Pisco
Bar

(Map p122; ☑99-350-0013; www.museodelpisco.org; Jirón Junin 201, Lima Centro; ☺10am-midnight) The 'educational' aspect of this wonderful bar might get you in the door, but it's the congenial atmosphere and outstanding original cocktails that will keep you here. We loved the *asu mare* – a pisco martini with ginger, cucumber, melon and basil. A sister bar to the popular original in Cuzco, this one occupies the Casa del Oidor, a 16th-century *casona*.

Red Cervecera
Beer Garden

(Map p127; ☑01-396-7944; www.redcervecera.com; Av Francisco Bolognesi 721, Barranco;

LGBT+ Lima

Like in other Latin American countries, the LGBT+ community in Lima does not have a substantial public presence. While social acceptance has grown exponentially, Peru is a conservative Catholic country and the generational gap in acceptance is palpable.

Thousands participate in the city's Gay Pride march, **Marcha del Orgullo Lima** (www.facebook.com/marchadelorgullolima), at the end of June or beginning of July. **Gay Lima** (http://lima.gaycities.com) lists the latest LGBT+ and gay-friendly spots in the capital and social media apps can prove helpful for meeting locals.

Marcha del Orgullo Lima
CARLOS GARCIA GRANTHON/FOTOHOLICA PRESS/LIGHTROCKET VIA GETTY IMAGES ©

⊗11am-8pm Mon, to 1am Tue-Thu, to 3am Fri & Sat; ⚑⚑) A great stop for beer connoisseurs and amateurs alike. A well-stocked store at the entrance provides all the ingredients and equipment you'll need to brew up your own craft beer, while the bar toward the back serves up house brews and more on tap.

Huaringas Lounge
(Map p124; ☎01-243-8151; Bolognesi 460; ⊗7pm-midnight Mon-Thu, to 2:30am Fri & Sat) A popular Miraflores bar and lounge located inside the **Las Brujas de Cachiche** (Map p124; ☎01-444-5310; www.brujasdecachiche.com.pe; mains S44-80; ⊗noon-midnight Mon-Sat, to 4pm Sun) restaurant, Huaringas serves a vast array of cocktails, including a well-recommended passion-fruit sour. On busy weekends, there are DJs.

Nuevo Mundo Draft Bar Craft Beer
(Map p124; ☎01-241-2762; Calle Manuel Bonilla 103, Miraflores; ⊗noon-1am Mon-Thu, to 3am Fri & Sat, 5pm-1am Sun) Nuevo Mundo was one of the first craft breweries to come out of Lima, and it's now a major player on the pub scene, with a wide range of national craft brews on tap. Heavily decorated in what locals call '*chicha*' art (think neon palettes and loud phrases), this is a casual place for happy hour or to catch a soccer game.

⭐ ENTERTAINMENT

Microteatro Lima Theatre
(Map p127; ☎01-252-8092; www.microteatrolima.com; Jirón Batallón Ayacucho 271) A rotating roster of directors and actors changes weekly at this theater, offering up plays of just 15 minutes, performed in a 15-sq-meter room in front of 15 audience members. A lively bar makes this a great and unique outing. Plays are in Spanish.

Sargento Pimienta Club
(Map p127; ☎01-247-3265; www.sargentopimienta.com.pe; Av Bolognesi 757, Barranco; admission from S15; ⊗10pm-4am Tue & Thu-Sat) A reliable spot in Barranco whose name means 'Sergeant Pepper.' The club hosts various theme nights and occasional live bands.

Jazz Zone Club
(Map p124; ☎01-241-8139; www.jazzzoneperu.com; Av La Paz 656, Miraflores; cover from S8; ⊗3pm-midnight) A variety of jazz, folk, *cumbia* (Colombian salsa-like dance and musical style), flamenco, comedy and other acts at this intimate, well-recommended club on the eastern side of Miraflores.

ℹ INFORMATION

DANGERS & ANNOYANCES

Like any large Latin American city, Lima is a land of haves and have-nots, which has made stories about crime here the stuff of legend. Yet the city has greatly improved since the lawless 1980s and most travelers have a safe visit. Nonetheless, stay aware.

The most common offenses are thefts, such as muggings. Do not resist robbery. You are unlikely to be physically hurt, but it is nonetheless best to keep a streetwise attitude.

Increased police and private security in Miraflores and in the cliff-top parks make them some of the city's safest areas. Barranco is mostly safe and pedestrian-friendly but has seen some evening robberies at a few restaurants and bars. Security may increase by the time you read this, but it doesn't hurt to go out with the minimum of your belongings and leave the rest in a hotel safe. The most dangerous neighborhoods are San Juan de Lurigancho, Los Olivos, Comas, Vitarte and El Agustino.

MEDICAL SERVICES

There are a number of clinics with emergency services and some English-speaking staff. Consultations start in the vicinity of S80 and climb from there, depending on the clinic and the doctor. Treatments and medications incur an additional fee, as do appointments with specialists.

Pharmacies abound in Lima. **Botica Fasa** (Map p124; ☎01-619-0000; cnr Av José Larco 129, Miraflores; ⏰7am-11pm Mon-Sat, to 10pm Sun) and **InkaFarma** (Map p124; ☎01-315-9000, deliveries 01-314-2020; www.inkafarma.com.pe; Alfredo Benavides 425, Miraflores; ⏰24hr) are well-stocked chains – open 24 hours; they often deliver free of charge.

Clínica Anglo-Americana (Map p124; ☎01-616-8990; www.clinicaangloamericana.pe; Calle Alfredo Salazar 350; ⏰24hr) A renowned (but expensive) hospital. There's a walk-in center in La Molina, near the US embassy, and a branch in San Isidro.

Clínica Good Hope (Map p124; ☎01-610-7300; Malecón Balta 956; ⏰8:30am-8pm Mon-Fri, to 1pm Sun) Quality care at good prices; there is also a dental unit.

MONEY

Banks are plentiful and most have 24-hour ATMs, which tend to offer the best exchange rates.

For extra security use ATMs inside banks (as opposed to on the street or in supermarkets); cover the key pad as you enter your passcode; and graze the whole keypad to prevent infrared tracing of passwords. Avoid making withdrawals late at night.

Palacio Arzobispal, Plaza de Armas (p50)

MEHDI33300/SHUTTERSTOCK ©

TOURIST INFORMATION

iPerú (☏01-574-8000; www.peru.travel/iperu; Aeropuerto Internacional Jorge Chávez; ⏱24hr) The government's reputable tourist bureau dispenses maps, offers good advice and can help handle complaints. The **Miraflores office** (Map p124; ☏01-445-9400; www.peru.travel/iperu; LarcoMar; ⏱11am-1pm & 2-8pm) is tiny but is very useful on weekends. There's another branch in **San Isidro** (Map p124; ☏01-421-1627; www.peru.travel/iperu; Jorge Basadre 610; ⏱9am-6pm Mon-Fri).

ⓘ GETTING THERE & AWAY

AIR

Lima's Aeropuerto Internacional Jorge Chávez (p17) is stocked with the usual facilities plus a pisco boutique.

Avianca (Map p124; ☏01-511-8222; www.avianca.com; Av José Pardo 831, Miraflores; ⏱8:30am-7pm Mon-Fri, 9am-2pm Sat) Flies to Cuzco, Arequipa, Juliaca and Trujillo.

LC Perú (p309) Flies from Lima to Huaraz, Iquitos and Huancayo (Jauja) on smaller turbo-prop aircraft.

BUS

There is no central bus terminal; each company operates its ticketing and departure points independently. Some companies have several terminals, so always clarify from which point a bus leaves when buying tickets. The busiest times of year are Semana Santa (the week before Easter Sunday) and the weeks surrounding Fiestas Patrias (July 28–29), when thousands of *limeños* (inhabitants of Lima) make a dash out of the city and fares double. At these times, book well ahead.

Near the airport, the **Gran Terminal Terrestre** (Terminal Plaza Norte; ☏945-018-248; www.granterminalterrestre.com; cnr Av Tomás Valle & Av Túpac Amaru, Plaza Norte Panamericana Norte; ⏱6am-midnight), the city's largest bus terminal, has buses to international destinations as well as smaller subsidiaries to northern and southern Peru.

Cruz del Sur (☏01-225-3748; www.cruzdelsur.com.pe; Av Javier Prado Este 1109) One of the

From left: Monasterio de San Francisco (p51); Av Javier Prado; Huaca Pucllana (p53)

biggest companies, serving the coast – as well as inland cities such as Arequipa, Cuzco and Huaraz.

Oltursa (Map p124; ☑01-708-5000; www. oltursa.pe; Av Aramburu 1160, Surquillo) The main terminal for this very reputable company is located a short distance from San Isidro. Travels to Arequipa, Nazca, Paracas and Trujillo.

 GETTING AROUND

GETTING TO & FROM THE AIRPORT

The airport resides in the port city of Callao, about 12km west of downtown or 20km north-west of Miraflores. As you come out of customs, inside the airport to the right is the official taxi service: **Taxi Green** (☑01-484-4001; www. taxigreen.com.pe; Aeropuerto Internacional Jorge Chávez; ⊘24hr).

Fast and safe, **Airport Express** (☑958-130-950, 01-446-5539; www.airportexpresslima.com; Aeropuerto Internacional Jorge Chávez; one-way S25; ⊘7am-midnight; 🛜) has hourly service with seven stops throughout Miraflores.

BUS

The trans-Lima electric express bus system, **El Metropolitano** (www.metropolitano.com.pe), is the fastest and most efficient way to get into the city center. Routes are few, though coverage is expanding to the northern part of the city. Ruta Troncal (S2.50) goes through Barranco, Miraflores and San Isidro to Plaza Grau in the center of Lima. Users must purchase a *tarjeta intelligente* (cards S4.50) that can be credited for use.

Alternatively, traffic-clogging caravans of minivans hurtle down the avenues with a *cobrador* (ticket taker) hanging out the door and shouting out the stops. Look for the destination placards taped to the windshield. Your best bet is to know the nearest major intersection or landmark close to your stop (eg Parque Kennedy) and tell that to the *cobrador* – they'll let you know whether you've got the right bus. *Combis* are generally slow and crowded, but startlingly cheap: fares run from S1 to S3, depending on the length of your journey.

TAXI

Lima's taxis lack meters, so negotiate fares before getting in. Fares vary depending on the

Miraflores (p52)

length of the journey, traffic conditions, time of day (evening is more expensive) and your Spanish language skills. Registered taxis or taxis hailed outside a tourist attraction charge higher rates. As a (very) rough guide, a trip within Miraflores costs around S8 to S10. From Miraflores to Central Lima is S20 to S25, to Barranco from S10 to S12, and San Isidro from S15 to S20. You can haggle over fares – though it's harder during rush hour. If there are two or more passengers be clear on whether the fare is per person or for the car.

The majority of taxis in Lima are unregistered (unofficial); indeed, surveys have indicated that no less than one vehicle in seven here is a taxi. During the day, it's usually not a problem to use either. At night, for safety it is important to use registered taxis, which are traceable by the license number painted on their side. Taxis should also have checkers, a rectangular authorization sticker with the word SETAME on the upper left corner of the windshield and may have yellow paint.

Easy Taxi (☏01-716-4600; www.easytaxi.com/pe) Download the app for fast service and cost estimates from your smartphone.

Taxi Móvil (☏01-422-6890)

Taxi Real (☏01-215-1414; www.taxireal.com)

Where to Stay

If arriving at night, it's worth contacting hotels in advance to arrange for airport pickup; even budget hostels can arrange this – sometimes for a few dollars less than the official airport service.

Neighborhood	Atmosphere
Lima Centro	There is good-value lodging with proximity to some of the most storied attractions, but keep in mind that it's mainly alive during the day and can feel abandoned at night, so take taxis after dark.
San Isidro	San Isidro is tranquil with top-notch restaurants, but little atmosphere. Accommodations are unapologetically upscale.
Miraflores	Overlooking the ocean, this neighborhood's pedestrian-friendly streets teem with cafes, restaurants, hotels, high-rises, banks, shops and nightclubs that pump everything from disco to *cumbia*. There are many quiet blocks, too.
Barranco	This coastal neighborhood is cluttered with restaurants and bustling bars, its graceful mansions converted into hotels of every price range. It's a short drive or a long walk to neighboring Miraflores.

PARACAS & THE ISLAS BALLESTAS

In this Chapter

Paracas & the Islas Ballestas at a Glance...

Nicknamed the 'poor man's Galápagos,' the Islas Ballestas nonetheless make for a memorable excursion. The only way to see them is on a boat tour – and while the tours do not disembark onto the islands (they are protected), they do get you startlingly close to the wildlife.

The region's other essential business is a sojourn around the bald, deserted Península de Paracas. Birds and sea mammals are the lures here, but this is also one of Peru's most important archaeological sites.

Paracas & the Islas Ballestas in One Day

Start the day with breakfast at your hotel, the most common way to fuel up before a wildlife-spotting **boat tour** (p72) of the Islas Ballestas which will last till lunchtime or beyond. Chill in the afternoon and in the evening. Don't miss the local seafood at a restaurant such as **As de Oro's** (p77) in Pisco or **Inti-Mar** (p76) just outside Paracas, which sells fresh scallops right on the bay.

Paracas & the Islas Ballestas in Two Days

The second day can be devoted to exploring the **Reserva Nacional de Paracas** (p74), the vast national park that spans the Península de Paracas. Start at the **Museo Julio C Tello** (p74) and work your way south. Take it easy afterwards, exploring the lively town of El Chaco (known as Paracas) or doing sweet nothing on its long beaches.

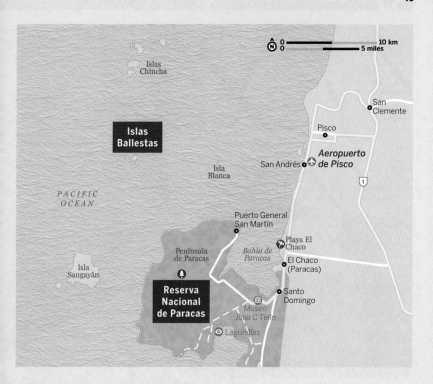

Arriving in Paracas & the Islas Ballestas

Boat Tours The only way to get near the Islas Ballestas. Depart from El Chaco (Paracas).

Air A new airport in Pisco has an infrequent service to Cuzco.

Bus A few buses run daily between Lima and Pisco or Paracas (the El Chaco beach district); some continue to Nazca, Ica and Arequipa. Bus companies include Cruz del Sur (www.cruzdelsur.com.pe) and Oltursa (www.oltursa.com.pe).

Where to Stay

The evolving but rundown town of Pisco may tout itself as an alternative to the beach resort of El Chaco (Paracas), but the latter makes for a much better base for trips to Reserva Nacional de Paracas and the Islas Ballestas, with a better location and choice of facilities.

Sea lion

KAYWIEGAND/GETTY IMAGES ©

Islas Ballestas

Protruding out of the Pacific Ocean, the Islas Ballestas are home to an astonishing number of sea lions, birds and fish. A boat tour will bring you as close to the action as possible – dodging guano bombs is part of the fun.

Great For...

☑ **Don't Miss**

Pointing your eyes (and lens) down at crabs and starfish.

Mystery Glyph

On the outward boat journey to the Islas Ballestas, which takes about 30 minutes, you will stop just offshore to admire the famous three-pronged Candelabra geoglyph, a giant figure etched into the sandy hills in the distance, more than 150m high and 50m wide. No one knows exactly who made the glyph, or when, or what it signifies, but theories abound.

Birds & Dolphins

In general, a further hour is spent cruising around the islands' arches and caves and watching herds of noisy sea lions sprawl on the rocks. The most common guano-producing birds in this area are the guanay cormorant, the Peruvian booby and the Peruvian pelican, seen in boisterous colonies several thousand strong.

Birds nesting on a rocky outcrop

❶ Need to Know

Tours S35-40, park entrance islands only S11, islands & peninsula S17

✕ Take a Break

Back on shore, grab a bite to eat at one of the many waterfront restaurants near the dock in El Chaco.

★ Top Tip

None of the small boats have a cabin, so dress to protect yourself against the wind, spray and sun.

You'll also see cormorants, Humboldt penguins and, if you're lucky, dolphins.

Bird Poo War

In the history of war, the 1864–66 skirmish between Spain and its former colonies of Peru and Chile might seem like a strange one: its primary motivation was guano, or, to put it less politely, bird poo. Although an unpleasant substance if dropped on your head, guano has long been a vital contributor to the Peruvian economy, and a resource worth protecting. In the early 19th century, German botanist Alexander von Humboldt sent samples of it to Europe, where British farmers found it to be 30 times more efficient than cow dung as a fertilizer. By the 1850s a rapidly industrializing Britain was importing 200,000 tons of guano annually. Suddenly the white droppings that covered Peru's bird-filled Pacific islands were worth the lion's share of the GDP. Spain understood as much in 1864 when, in an act of postcolonial petulance, it occupied the guano-rich Chincha Islands in an attempt to extract reparations from Peru over a small domestic incident in Lambayeque. Peru didn't hesitate to retaliate. A protracted naval war ensued that dragged in Chile, before the islands and their precious bird poo were wrenched back from Spain in 1866.

In the conflict-free present, the industry remains lucrative. Layers of sun-baked, nitrogen-rich guano still cover the Islas Ballestas, as well as the nearby Chincha Islands.

Preparation

The sea can get rough, so sufferers of motion sickness should take medication before boarding boats to Islas Ballestas. Wear a hat (cheap ones are sold at the harbor), as it's not unusual to receive a direct hit of guano (droppings) from the seabirds.

Playa La Mina

Reserva Nacional de Paracas

This vast desert reserve occupies most of the Península de Paracas and houses remote beaches backed by dramatic arid landscapes and plenty of wonderful wildlife.

Great For...

☑ Don't Miss

Check out Playa Yumaque which has excellent birdwatching and often attracts dolphins.

Museo Julio C Tello

Right next to the park visitor center, in front of the Paracas Necropolis burial grounds on Cerro Colorado, this recently expanded **museum** (Reserva Nacional de Paracas; admission S7.50; ⊙8am-4pm Tue-Sun) features interesting archaeological exhibits from the mysterious culture that once dominated the area.

While many top artifacts from the area have been moved to Ica's Museo Regional de Ica and Lima's Museo Larco, it's still well worth a visit. There's a fine collection of textiles, a display of some of the elongated skulls that were used to differentiate the upper classes of the society, pottery and re-creations of Paracas dwellings. Information panels are in Spanish and English.

❶ Need to Know

Carr Punta Pejerrey, Km 27; peninsula only S11, islands & peninsula S17

✕ Take a Break

There are basic food shacks in Lagunillas but better options in El Chaco.

★ Top Tip

Energetic travelers can walk or cycle into the reserve from El Chaco.

Lagunillas

Turkey vultures feast on the washed-up remains of yesterday's marine carcasses on the lonely beach at **Lagunillas** (Reserva Nacional de Paracas), 5km south of the visitor centre, where a bunch of almost-identical, salt-of-the-sea restaurants with fishing boats moored in front constitute 'the village.' It's a picturesque spot that looks better from a distance than up close.

Playa La Mina

This beach is a short drive or walk south of Lagunillas on a dirt road and has gentle waters that make it the best swimming area in the reserve. Vacationing Peruvians flock here in summer (January to March) when it can get fairly crowded. If it's busy

you may find the odd mobile drinks concession set up.

Playa Yumaque

Wildlife aficionados will want to check out this beach, which has excellent birdwatching and often attracts dolphins.

Punta Arquillo

Just before the Lagunillas turnoff, a spur road branches off the main La Mina road and heads to the southwest for a few kilometers to a parking area near this clifftop lookout. It has grand views of the ocean, with a sea-lion colony on the rocks below and plenty of seabirds gliding by.

Other seashore life around the reserve includes flotillas of jellyfish (swimmers beware), some of which reach about 70cm in diameter with trailing stinging tentacles of 1m. They are often washed up on the shore, where they quickly dry to form mandala -like patterns on the sand. Beachcombers can also find sea hares, ghost crabs and seashells along the shoreline, and the Andean condor occasionally descends to the coast in search of rich pickings.

El Chaco (Paracas)

The Paracas Peninsula's main village, El Chaco – often referred to as 'Paracas' – is the main embarkation point for trips to the Islas Ballestas and the Reserva Nacional de Paracas. Its natural attractions and long beaches stand out from many south coast destinations, and many travelers spend at least two or three nights here, allowing for a day tour to the islands, beachtime and an extended foray across the peninsula.

✪ ACTIVITIES

Paracas offers pretty great kitesurfing with limited chop, easy shallow access and good winds. Most outfitters are located at 'Kite Point' south of town near the Hilton.

For private classes expect to pay around S190 for one hour or S1020 for a six-hour course. Group classes are cheaper.

A professionally run kite school offering classes and equipment rental, **Kite Club** (☏994-831-021; www.kiteclubparacas.com; Urbanización Santo Domingo; ⊙10am-5pm Wed-Sun) is in front of the Double Tree Hilton.

✪ EATING & DRINKING

Inti-Mar   Seafood $$
(www.inti-mar.com; Contiguo Puerto General San Martín, Punto Pejerrey; mains S25-45; ⊙10:30am-3:30pm) One of our favorite places to eat on the entire coast, this breezy spot on the far side of the bay is a working scallop farm. The fresh scallops served *natural* with lemon and olive oil are phenomenal.

Lobo Fino   Peruvian $$
(Av Libertadores s/n; mains S26-35, set menus S15-25; ⊙11am-10pm) On the southern edge of town, this place prepares quality Peruvian cuisine at fair prices. Excellent set menus come in two varieties: *criollo* and *marino*.

Misk'i   Bar
(Garcia Perez s/n; ⊙5pm-11pm) The best place to begin your evening in Paracas, this chilled-out resto-bar has great wood-fired pizzas (S14 to S52), salads and Mexican dishes (mains S16 to S26) in addition to an extensive list of cocktails and strong mixed drinks, all accompanied by a perpetual reggae soundtrack.

Fishing boats, El Chaco (Paracas)

DON MAMMOSER/SHUTTERSTOCK ©

ℹ️ GETTING THERE & AWAY

The fastest way to get to Paracas is via the new **airport** at Pisco, although at the time of writing Cuzco was the only destination with regular flights.

Several buses run daily between Lima and the El Chaco beach district of Paracas (S45 to S68, 3½ hours) before continuing to other destinations south.

Cruz del Sur (📞056-53-6636; www.cruzdelsur.com.pe; Av Libertadores s/n, Ingreso El Chaco) departs from its flash terminal on the northern edge of town and has the most frequent services with departures at 7:30am, 12:30pm, 1:30pm, 3pm, 4pm and 7:10pm. Also runs buses from Paracas to Ica and Nazca at 7:25am, 10:30am, 10:40am, 11:10am, 5:10pm and 5:40pm.

Oltursa (📞056-53-0726; www.oltursa.com. pe; Av Libertadores s/n) has one comfortable bus a day to Lima leaving the office on the main boulevard at 9:50am and one bus south to Ica, Nazca and Arequipa at 10:15am.

Pisco

The traditional gateway to the wild, windswept Paracas region, Pisco was crushed by the devastating 2007 earthquake that destroyed its infrastructure and some of its most attractive buildings – but not its spirit. Gritty resolve has seen the city rebound, but it's not a particularly traveler-friendly place and for visits to the Islas Ballestas and Reserva Nacional de Paracas, it has been surpassed by nearby El Chaco.

🍴 EATING & DRINKING

Only a few cafes in Pisco open early enough for breakfast before an Islas Ballestas tour, however most hotels include breakfast in their rates.

As de Oro's   Peruvian $$

(www.asdeoros.com.pe; San Martín 472; mains S21-46; ⏱noon-midnight Tue-Sun) Widely considered Pisco's best restaurant, the plush As de Oro's serves up spicy mashed potato with octopus, plaice with butter and capers, and grilled prawns with fried yucca and tartare sauce on the back porch.

 Tours of Islas Ballestas & the Reserve

From El Chaco, most island boat tours leave daily at 8am, 10am and noon, and cost around S35 to S40 per person. Afternoon land tours of the Península de Paracas cost around S20 to S25. Tours of the reserve can be combined with an Islas Ballestas tour to make a full-day excursion (S60). A busy local travel agency, **Paracas Explorer** (📞056-53-1487; www.paracasexplorer.com; Av Libertadores s/n; ⏱7am-7pm) has two offices on the same block and offers the usual island and reserve tours, as well as tours to Tambo Colorado (S200) and multiday trips that take you to Ica and Nazca (from US$200 per person).

It's also perfectly viable to use Pisco as a base for tours of the Paracas Peninsula and Islas Ballestas. Agencies dot the central area around the Plaza de Armas. **Aprotur Pisco** (📞056-50-7156; aproturpisco@hotmail.com; San Francisco 112; ⏱7am-10pm) organizes trips to all the local sights, including the Islas Ballestas (S70) and even the Nazca Lines (US$90 to US$200).

Taberna de Don Jaime   Bar

(📞056-53-5023; San Martín 203; ⏱4pm-2am) This clamorous tavern is a favorite with locals and tourists alike. It is also a showcase for artisanal wines and piscos.

ℹ️ GETTING THERE & AWAY

Pisco is 6km west of the Panamericana Sur, and only buses with Pisco as the final destination actually go there. If you're not on a direct bus to either Pisco or Paracas, ask to be left at the San Clemente turnoff on the Panamericana Sur, where fast and frequent *colectivos* wait to shuttle passengers to Pisco's Plaza de Armas (S1.50, 10 minutes) or Paracas (S10, 20 minutes).

Flores (📞056-79-6643; Pedemonte s/n) offers multiple daily departures from the center of Pisco north to Lima and south to Ica and Arequipa.

NAZCA

Nazca at a Glance...

It's hard to say the word 'Nazca' without following it immediately with the word 'Lines,' a reference not just to the ancient geometric lines that crisscross the Nazca desert, but to the enigmatic animal geoglyphs that accompany them. Like all great unexplained mysteries, these immense etchings, thought to have been made by a pre-Inca civilization, attract a variable fan base of archaeologists, scientists, history buffs, New Age mystics, curious tourists, and pilgrims on their way to (or back from) Machu Picchu. Documented for the first time by scientist Paul Kosok in 1939, the Nazca Lines are the south coast's biggest attraction.

Nazca in One Day

Start the day with just a snack for breakfast – your stomach will thank you once you hit the dips and turns on the flights over the **Nazca Lines** (p82). Have brunch proper from one of the many international options in Nazca, then spend the afternoon with the fascinating archaeological finds at the **Museo Didáctico Antonini** (p84). In the evening, see the Nazca Lines explained in a projection on the dome of the **Nazca Planetarium** (p84).

Nazca in Two Days

On the second day, see more geoglyphs without the rush at the **Palpa Lines** (p85), the more abundant, but less famous cousin of the Nazca Lines. See them from a lookout, no overflight needed. Next, head on to the **Chauchilla Cemetery** (p85) to finish the afternoon getting close to ancient skeletons and mummies of the local desert from AD 1000.

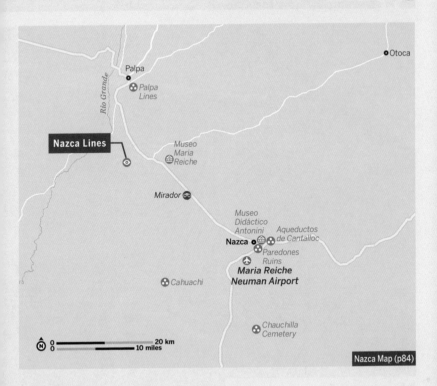

Nazca Map (p84)

Arriving in Nazca

Maria Reiche Neuman Airport A taxi from the airport to central Nazca, 4km away, costs about S6.

Bus Companies cluster at the west end of Calle Lima, near the *óvalo* (main roundabout) and about a block towards town on the same street.

Where to Stay

There are lots of hotels (and restaurants) in and around Callao and Bolognesi to the streets west of the Plaza de Armas.

Prices drop by up to 50% outside of peak season, which runs from May until August.

Spider geoglyph

Nazca Lines

The Nazca Lines – a set of carved glyphs so massive they can only be seen from the air – have long captured travelers' imaginations with their precision and scale.

Great For...

☑ Don't Miss

The intriguing owl-headed person, often referred to as an astronaut because of its goldfish-bowl shaped head.

Design

Spread over 500 sq km (310 sq mi) of arid, rock-strewn plain in the Pampa Colorada (Red Plain), the Nazca Lines are one of the world's great archaeological mysteries. Comprising over 800 straight lines, 300 geometric figures (geoglyphs) and 70 animal and plant drawings (biomorphs), the lines are almost imperceptible on the ground. From above, they form a striking network of stylized figures and channels, many of which radiate from a central axis.

The lines were made by the simple process of removing the dark sun-baked stones from the surface of the desert and piling them up on either side of the lines, thus exposing the lighter, powdery gypsum-laden soil below.

The figures are mostly etched out in single continuous lines, while the encompassing

'Astronaut' geoglyph

❶ Need to Know

Choose safety first – question any operator who charges less than US$80 for the standard 30-minute overflight.

✕ Take a Break

Eat after, not before, an overflight, as some twisting and turning is tummy challenging.

★ Top Tip

Morning overflights are best because the air is less turbulent.

geoglyphs form perfect triangles, rectangles or straight lines running for several kilometers across the desert.

The most elaborate designs represent animals, including a hummingbird, a spider, a 180m-long lizard, a monkey with an extravagantly curled tail, and a condor with a 130m (426ft) wingspan.

Mystery

Endless questions remain. Who constructed the lines and why? And how did they know what they were doing when the lines can only be properly appreciated from the air? Maria Reiche (1903–98), a German mathematician and long-time researcher of the lines, theorized that they were made by the Paracas and Nazca cultures between 900 BC and AD 600, with some additions by the Wari settlers from the highlands in the 7th century. She also claimed that the lines were an astronomical calendar developed for agricultural purposes, and that they were mapped out through the use of sophisticated mathematics (and a long rope).

A slightly more surreal suggestion from explorer Jim Woodman was that the Nazca people knew how to construct hot-air balloons and that they did, in fact, observe the lines from the air.

Water Worship

A more down-to-earth theory, given the value of water in the sun-baked desert, was suggested by anthropologist Johann Reinhard, who believed that the lines were involved in mountain worship and a fertility/water cult. Recent work by the Swiss-Liechtenstein Foundation (SLSA; www.slsa.ch) agrees that they were dedicated to the worship of water, and it is thus ironic that their theory about the demise of the Nazca culture suggests that it was due not to drought, but to destructive rainfall caused by a phenomenon such as El Niño.

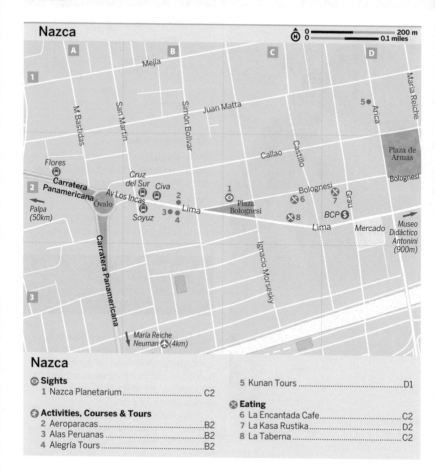

Nazca

◉ **Sights**

➕ **Activities, Courses & Tours**

❌ **Eating**

◎ SIGHTS

While many visitors head here just to fly over the Lines, there's more to see around Nazca. Most outlying sights can be visited on tours from Nazca, although individual travelers or pairs may have to wait a day or two before the agency finds enough people who are also interested in going.

Nazca Planetarium
Planetarium

(☎056-52-2293; DM Nazca Hotel, Bolognesi 147; admission S20; ⊗in English 7pm, in Spanish 8:15pm) This small planetarium is in the DM Nazca Hotel and offers scripted evening lectures on the Lines with graphical displays on a domed projection screen that last approximately 45 minutes. Call ahead or check the posted schedules for show times.

Museo Didáctico Antonini
Museum

(☎056-52-3444; Av de la Cultura 600; admission S15, plus camera S5; ⊗9am-7pm) On the east side of town, this excellent archaeological museum has an aqueduct running through the back garden, as well as interesting reproductions of burial tombs, a valuable collection of ceramic pan flutes and a scale model of the Lines.

Paredones Ruins
Ruins

(admission S10; ◷9am-6pm) The Paredones ruins, 2km southeast of town via Arica over the river, are not very well preserved (primarily because they were constructed from adobe rather than stone) although around 10% of the site has been reconstructed so it's possible to get an idea of how it once looked. Their position on a slope above the town is commanding, which is probably why the Incas used it as an administrative control center between the mountains and the coast.

Admission also covers entry to the nearby Cantalloc Aqueducts.

Aqueductos de Cantalloc
Archaeological Site

(admission S10; ◷9am-6pm) About 4km southeast of town are the 30-plus underground Cantalloc Aqueducts, many of which are still in working order and are essential in irrigating the surrounding fields. The impressive series of stone and wood channels and spiraling access ways were built by the Nazca between AD 200 and 900 and are considered one of the finest examples of pre-Hispanic engineering. Locals say the water here is still good to drink.

Museo Maria Reiche
Museum

(admission S5; ◷8:30am-5:30pm) When Maria Reiche, the German mathematician and long-term researcher of the Nazca Lines, died in 1998, her house, which stands 5km north of the *mirador* (lookout) along Panamericana Sur, was made into a small museum. Though disappointingly scant on information, you can see where she lived, amid the clutter of her tools and obsessive sketches in addition to a tattooed mummy.

Cahuachi
Ruins

(◷9am-4pm) FREE A dirt road travels 25km west from Nazca to Cahuachi, the most important known Nazca center, which is still undergoing excavation. It consists of several pyramids, a graveyard and an enigmatic site called Estaquería, which may have been used as a place of mummification. Tours from Nazca take three hours, cost S50 to S130 per person, and may include a side trip to Pueblo Viejo, a nearby pre-Nazca residential settlement, or sandboarding on nearby dunes.

Chauchilla Cemetery
Archaeological Site

(admission S8; ◷8am-5:30pm) The most popular excursion from Nazca, this cemetery, 28km south of Nazca, will satisfy any urges you have to see ancient bones, skulls and mummies. Dating back to the Ica-Chincha culture around AD 1000, the mummies were originally scattered haphazardly across the desert, left by ransacking tomb-robbers. Now they are seen carefully rearranged inside a dozen or so tombs, though cloth fragments and pottery and bone shards still litter the ground outside the demarcated trail.

Palpa Lines
Archaeological Site

Like Nazca, Palpa is surrounded by perplexing geoglyphs, the so-called Palpa Lines, which are serially overshadowed by the more famous, but less abundant, Nazca Lines to the south. The Palpa Lines display a greater profusion of human forms including the Familia Real de Paracas, a group of eight figures on a hillside.

Cerro Blanco
Sand Dune

Stand down all other pretenders. Cerro Blanco, 14km east of Nazca, is the highest sand dune in Peru and one of the tallest in the world: 2078m above sea level and 1176m from base to summit. That makes it higher than the tallest mountain in England and numerous other countries. If Huacachina's sand didn't irrevocably ruin your underwear, this could be your bag.

Due to the dune's height and steepness it's best to organize an excursion from Nazca. Trips leave at about 4am to avoid the intense heat. The arduous climb to the top of the dune (buggies can't climb this behemoth) takes approximately three hours. Going down is counted more in minutes with some clear runs of up to 800m. Many agencies in Nazca offer this trip, including Kunan Tours (p86).

⊙ TOURS

Most people fly over the Lines then leave, but there's more to see around Nazca. If you take one of the many local tours, they typically include a torturously long stop at a potter's and/or gold-miner's workshop for a demonstration of their techniques (tips for those who show you their trade are expected, too).

Hotels tirelessly promote their own tours but it's well worth wandering around town to shop around.

Aerodiana Scenic Flights
(☑014-47-6824; www.aerodiana.com.pe; Aeropuerto Maria Reiche Neuman) Nazca Lines flightseeing. Offers flights from both Pisco Airport and Nazca.

Alas Peruanas Scenic Flights
(☑056-52-2444; www.alasperuanas.com; Lima 168) Nazca Lines flightseeing.

Alegría Tours Adventure
(☑056-52-2497; www.alegriatoursperu.com; Hotel Alegría, Lima 168; ⊙7am-10pm) Behemoth agency offers all the usual local tours, plus off-the-beaten-track and sandboarding options. The tours are expensive for one person, so ask to join up with other travelers to receive a group discount. Alegría can arrange guides in Spanish, English, French and German in some cases.

Kunan Tours Tours
(☑056-52-4069; www.kunantours.com; Arica 419) Based out of the **Kunan Wasi Hotel** (s/d/tr S70/90/120; @ 🛜), this comprehensive travel company offers all the Nazca tours, plus excursions to the Islas Ballestas, Huacachina and Chincha.

⊗ EATING

West of the Plaza de Armas, Bolognesi is stuffed full of foreigner-friendly pizzerias, restaurants and bars.

La Taberna Peruvian $
(Lima 321; mains S14-35, menú S10-20; ⊙noon-10pm; 🍴) It's a hole-in-the-wall place, and the scribbles covering every inch of wall are a testament to its popularity. Try the spicy fish topped with sauce and mixed shellfish

Chauchilla Cemetery (p85)

CHATEAUDEDE/GETTY IMAGES ©

challengingly named *Pescado a lo Macho,* or choose from a list of vegetarian options. Daily changing *menús* are good value.

La Kasa
Rustika   Peruvian, International $$
(Bolgnesi 372; mains S18-40; ⊘7am-11pm) One of the best eateries on the main strip, La Kasa Rustika has a wide menu of Peruvian flavors and international dishes served on an inviting open terrace. Take your pick from steak, seafood, pasta and pizza. Portions are large, prices reasonable and service top-notch.

La Encantada Cafe   International $$
(☑056-52-4216; Bolgnesi 282; mains S20-60; ⊘10am-10:30pm) A top spot on the 'Boule-vard' (Bolgnesi), La Encantada sparkles in Nazca's dusty center with bright and modern dining areas, great coffee and courteous and friendly waitstaff. The exten-sive menu mixes Europhile flavors (pasta etc) with Peruvian favorites.

🛈 INFORMATION

BCP (Lima 495) Has a Visa/MasterCard ATM and changes US dollars.

iPerú (☑016-16-7300 ext 3042; Aerodromo Maria Reiche Neuman; ⊘7am-4pm) Helpful government-run tourism office based at the airfield.

🛈 GETTING THERE & AWAY

Nazca is a major destination for buses on the Panamericana Sur and is easy to get to from Lima, Ica or Arequipa. Bus companies cluster at the west end of Calle Lima, near the *óvalo* (main roundabout).

Most long-distance services leave in the late afternoon or evening. **Cruz del Sur** (☑0801-11111; www.cruzdelsur.com.pe; Av Los Incas) and **Civa** (☑056-52-4390; www.civa.com.pe; Lima 155; ⊘6am-2am) have a few luxury buses daily to Lima. Intermediate points such as Ica and Pisco are more speedily served by smaller, *económico* (cheap) bus companies, such as **Flores** (Panamericana s/n) and **Soyuz**

 Overflights Overview

Bad publicity wracked the Nazca Lines in 2010 when two small aircraft carrying tourists on *sobrevuelos* (overflights) crashed within eight months of each other causing a total of 13 fatalities. The crashes followed an equally catastroph-ic 2008 accident that killed five French tourists, along with another incident when a plane was forced to make an emergency landing on the Panamerica-na Sur in 2009.

In reaction to the incidents some changes have been made. All planes now fly with two pilots, more thor-ough safety inspections have been implemented, and prices have gone up to ensure that companies don't cut corners with poorly maintained aircraft or over-filled flights.

Nonetheless, it still pays to put safety before price when choosing your over-flight company. Question anyone who offers prices significantly lower than the other companies and don't be afraid to probe companies on their safety records and flight policies. **Aeroparacas** (☑016-41-7000; www.aeroparacas.com; Lima 169) is one of the better airline companies.

(☑056-52-1464; San Martín 142). These buses will also drop you at Palpa (S3, one hour).

To go direct to Cuzco, several companies, including Cruz del Sur and Civa, take the paved road east via Abancay.

AREQUIPA

In this Chapter

Arequipa at a Glance...

*Peru's second-largest city is only one-tenth of Lima's size, but pugnaciously equal
to it in terms of cuisine, historical significance and confident self-awareness.
Guarded by three volcanoes, the city enjoys a resplendent, if seismically precarious,
setting. Fortunately, the city's architecture, an ensemble of baroque buildings
grafted out of the sillar (white volcanic rock), has so far withstood most of what
nature has thrown at it. In 2000 the city's central core earned a well-deserved
Unesco World Heritage listing, and the sight of the gigantic cathedral, with ethereal
El Misti rising behind it, is worth a visit alone.*

Arequipa in Two Days

Spend the morning discovering the
sillar wonders of **La Catedral** (p98)
and the buildings around the **Plaza de
Armas** (p98). Make plans for your tour
of El Misti with one of the ample tour
operators nearby, then walk the narrow
corridors of **Monasterio de Santa
Catalina** (p94). Day two is all about
climbing **El Misti** (p92).

Arequipa in Four Days

Start day three in nearby **Yanahuara**
(p103) and its *picanterías,* spy El Misti
from afar at the *mirador,* and stop for
a pisco (Peruvian grape brandy) at a
bar along Calle San Francisco. On day
four, see 'Juanita, the Ice Maiden' at
Museo Santuarios Andinos (p98),
then blur the lines between shopping
and sightseeing at the **Claustros de la
Campañía** (p102). Finish on a high with
top-notch Peruvian cuisine.

Arequipa Map (p100)

Arriving in Arequipa

Rodríguez Ballón International Airport Located about 8km northwest of the city center.

Terminal Terrestre The main bus terminal, located on Av Andrés, under 3km south of the city center.

Terrapuerto Bus Terminal The smaller of the two bus terminals is next door to the main terminal, also on Av Andrés.

Where to Stay

Anywhere within about three blocks of Plaza de Armas makes for a convenient base to explore the city, especially north, nearest Monasterio de Santa Catalina.

Peaceful San Lazaro, on the western end of Calle Llosa, has a cute square and a village vibe.

There are plenty of budget options along Av Puente Grau near the corner with Calle Jerusalén.

Converted *casonas* (large houses) are beautiful and have thick, sound-insulated walls along with inner courtyards to cushion you from street noise and car exhaust.

S FORSTER/SHUTTERSTOCK ©

El Misti

Looming 5822m (19,101ft) above Arequipa, the city's guardian volcano is the most popular climb in the area. Misti's sulfurous crater hisses gas, and there are spectacular views from the summit.

Great For...

☑ Don't Miss

Lingering in Reserva Nacional Salinas y Aguada Blanca to spot vicuñas and trek old Inca trails.

El Misti is within one of southern Peru's finest protected reserves, Reserva Nacional Salinas y Aguada Blanca (p116), along with Chachani mountain and the volcano Pichu Pichu. El Misti is technically one of the easiest ascents of any mountain of this size in the world, but it's hard work nonetheless and you normally need an ice ax and, sometimes, crampons. The view from the summit makes the climb worth it. On a clear day you can see as far out as the Pacific Ocean.

Planning

The optimum time to climb El Misti is between July and November, especially in the later months when things start to warm up.

COPYRIGHT ALENGEL/GETTY IMAGES ©

ℹ Need to Know

Misti is best climbed between July and November, with the later months being the least cold.

✕ Take a Break

Although most guides provide meals, come prepared with plenty of water and snacks.

★ Top Tip

Misti is a dormant volcano. Go with a guide and check volcanic activity before hiking.

Routes

The ascent can be approached by many routes, some more worn-in than others, most of which can be done in two days, to allow enough time to acclimatize to the altitude. No route is clearly marked and at least one (notably the Apurímac route) is notorious for robberies, so taking a guide is highly recommended. Prices depend on group size and transportation method: bank on between S190 and S270 per person including private transportation, guide, meals and all equipment.

One popular route, starting from Chiguata, is a hard eight-hour uphill slog on rough trails to base camp (4500m/14,763ft); from there to the summit and back takes eight hours, while the sliding return from base camp to Chiguata takes three hours or less. The most common method to reach the mountain is hiring a driver in a 4WD for around S250, who will take you up to 3300m and pick you up on the return.

The Aguada Blanca route is restricted to a handful of official tour operators and allows climbers to arrive at 4100m before starting to climb.

What's Nearby?

If you're more interested in photo ops of El Misti without the huff and puff, the peaceful neighborhood of Yanahuara (p103) makes a diverting short trip from Arequipa's city center. The plaza there has a *mirador* (lookout) with wonderful views of El Misti and Arequipa.

Monasterio de Santa Catalina

Even if you've overdosed on colonial edifices, this convent shouldn't be missed. Occupying a whole block and guarded by imposing high walls, it is one of the most fascinating religious buildings in Peru.

Santa Catalina is not just a religious building – the 20,000-sq-m complex is almost a citadel within the city. It was founded in 1580 by a rich widow, doña María de Guzmán.

The best way to visit is to hire one of the informative guides, available for S20 from inside the entrance (in the southeast corner). Guides speak Spanish, English and other languages. The tours last about an hour, after which you're welcome to keep exploring by yourself, until the gates close. Alternatively, you can wander around on your own without a guide, soaking up the meditative atmosphere and getting slightly lost.

Great For...

☑ **Don't Miss**

Climbing the narrow stairs next to Zocodober Sq for a rooftop view of El Misti and Arequipa.

Novice Cloister

After passing under the *silencio* (silence) arch you will enter the Novice Cloister,

ℹ️ Need to Know

📋054-22-1213; www.santacatalina.org.pe; Santa Catalina 301; admission S40; ⏰9am-5pm, to 7:30pm Tue & Wed, last entry 1hr before closing

✕ Take a Break

Stop by next door for Italian specialties at **La Trattoria del Monasterio** (📋054-20-4062; www.latrattoriadelmonasterio.com; Santa Catalina 309; mains S23-50; ⏰noon-3pm & 7-11pm Mon-Sat, noon-3pm Sun; 🖊️).

★ Top Tip

Catalina opens two evenings a week to allow traipsing through the shadowy grounds by candlelight.

marked by a courtyard with a rubber tree at its center. After passing under this arch, novice nuns were required to zip their lips in a vow of solemn silence and resolve to a life of work and prayer for four years, during which time their wealthy families were expected to pay a dowry of 100 gold coins per year. Afterwards they could choose between taking their vows and entering into religious service, or leaving the convent – although the latter would have brought shame upon their family.

Orange Cloister

Graduated novices passed onto the Orange Cloister, named for the orange trees clustered at its center that represent renewal and eternal life. This cloister allows a peek into the Profundis Room, a mortuary where dead nuns were mourned.

Continuing, Córdova St is flanked by cells that served as living quarters, housing one or more nuns, along with a handful of servants. Toledo St leads you to the communal washing area where servants washed in mountain runoff.

Great Cloister

Heading down Burgos St toward the cathedral's sparkling *sillar* tower, visitors may enter the musty darkness of the communal kitchen.

Just beyond, Zocodober Sq was where nuns gathered on Sundays to exchange handicrafts such as soaps and baked goods. Continuing on, to the left is the cell of legendary Sor Ana, a nun renowned for her eerily accurate predictions about the future.

Finally, the Great Cloister is bordered by the chapel on one side and the art gallery, which used to serve as a communal dormitory, on the other.

Architecture Walking Tour

The star of Arequipa's architecture may be its unique *sillar*, but it isn't the only feature. Jump from baroque to *churrigueresque* (an elaborate and intricately decorated Spanish style), and from ornate to the austere living quarters of nuns.

Start Plaza de Armas
End Casa Ricketts
Length 1km; three hours

Take a Break ...
Chicha (p127) serves Inca-Spanish cuisine.

5 Pass treasure-laden antique stores on the way to **Monasterio de Santa Catalina** (p94) and its fascinating, sprawling interior.

4 Head back behind La Catedral. Turn right on Calle Santa Catalina and then take the first left down Moral to the baroque **Casa de Moral** (☎054-21-4907; Moral 318; admission S5; ⊗ 9am-5pm Mon-Sat).

Classic Photo: La Catedral with El Misti in the background.

1 Start in the **Plaza de Armas** (p118), Arequipa's main square. Its centerpiece is **La Catedral** (p118), Peru's widest cathedral.

6 Head east along Zela to the **Iglesia de San Francisco** (054-22-3048; Zela 202; admission S10; 9am-noon & 3-6pm Mon-Sat). Witness the giant crack left by an earthquake in the cupola.

7 Finish with a pisco or meal in one of the many bars and restaurants along Calle San Francisco.

3 Take a peek at the small gallery and interior courtyards of ornate **Casa Ricketts** (054-21-5060; San Francisco 108; 9am-6pm Mon-Fri, to 1pm Sat), the city's most splendid working bank.

2 Check out the Jesuit **Iglesia de La Compañía** (p98). Next door is the ornate **Claustros de la Compañía** (p102), an outdoor museum with boutique shops.

0 — 100 m
0 — 0.05 miles

⊙ SIGHTS

Iglesia de La Compañía   Church

(www.jesuitasaqp.pe; Moral cnr Álvarez Thomas;
⊘9-11am & 3-6pm) **FREE** If Arequipa's cathedral seems *too* big, an interesting antidote
is this diminutive Jesuit church on the
southeast corner of the Plaza de Armas.
Proving that small can be beautiful, its
facade is an intricately carved masterpiece
of the *churrigueresque* style hatched in
Spain in the 1660s (think baroque and then
some). The equally detailed altar, completely covered in gold leaf, takes the style
further and will be eerily familiar to anyone
who has visited Seville cathedral in Spain.

La Catedral   Cathedral

(☎054-23-2635; ⊘7-10am & 5-7pm Mon-Sat,
11am-noon Sun) **FREE** This beautiful building
on the Plaza de Armas stands out for its
stark white *sillar* and massive size – it's
the only cathedral in Peru that stretches
the length of a plaza. It also has a history
of rising from the ashes. The original structure, dating from 1656, was gutted by fire in
1844, rebuilt and then flattened by the 1868

earthquake. Most of what you see now has
been rebuilt since then. A 'museum' tour is
worthwhile.

Museo Santuarios Andinos   Museum

(☎054-28-6613; www.ucsm.edu.pe/museo-san-
tuarios-andinos; La Merced 110; adult S20, child
5-17 S10; ⊘9am-6pm Mon-Sat, to 3pm Sun)
There's an escalating drama to this theatri-
cally presented museum, dedicated to the
preserved body of a frozen 'mummy,' and
its compulsory guided tour (free, but a tip
is expected at the end). Spoiler: the climax
is the vaguely macabre sight of poor Juanita, the 12-year-old Inca girl sacrificed to the
gods in the 1450s and now eerily preserved
in a glass refrigerator. Tours take about an
hour and are conducted in Spanish, English
and French.

Plaza de Armas   Square

Arequipa's main plaza, unblemished by
modern interference, is a museum of the
city's *sillar* architecture – white, muscular and aesthetically unique. Impressive
colonnaded balconies line three sides.
The fourth is given over to Peru's widest

Basilica, La Catedral

LEVI BIANCO/GETTY IMAGES ©

cathedral, a humongous edifice with two soaring towers. Even this is dwarfed by the dual snowcapped sentinels of El Misti and Chanchani, both visible from various points in the central park.

Museo de la Catedral   Basilica

(☑054-21-3149; www.museocatedralarequipa. org.pe; Santa Catalina, Plaza de Armas; admission & tour S10; ☺10am-5pm Mon-Sat) A must for visitors who want to see more of Arequipa's cathedral, the included 45-minute bilingual tour of this 'museum' is actually a peek at the inner workings of the basilica, with an explanation of the impressive 1000-pipe church organ and the symbology and colors employed in religious paintings and ornaments. The rooftop views of Arequipa and its *sillar* buildings are a bonus.

Callejón del Solar   Neighborhood

(enter from Bolognesi or San Agustín) This magical neighborhood lane is Arequipa's most picturesque with radiant white *sillar* houses – people really live here – and pavers, trellis-covered park benches and pots spilling over with flowers. It could easily pass as the tidy set for 'Arequipa: The Stage Production' but has somehow managed to stay off the tourist radar. At night teenagers and lovers are drawn to the privacy of this city oasis; some gates are locked.

⊕ ACTIVITIES

Arequipa is the center for a slew of outdoor activities dotted around the high country to the north and east of the city. Trekking, mountaineering and river running are the big three, but there are plenty more.

Naturaleza Activa   Adventure Sports

(☑968-969-544; naturactiva@yahoo.com; Santa Catalina 211; ☺office 11am-7pm Mon-Sat) With a full range of trekking, climbing and mountain-biking options on offer, this is a favorite of those seeking adventure tours. A major advantage over going to an agency is that the people you speak to at Naturaleza Activa are actually the qualified guides, not salespeople, so can answer your questions

 Juanita – the Ice Maiden

In 1992 local climber Miguel Zárate was guiding an expedition on Nevado Ampato (6288m) when he found curious wooden remnants, suggestive of a burial site, exposed near the icy summit. In September 1995 he returned with American mountaineer and archaeologist Johan Reinhard and together they discovered a statue and other offerings and, some distance from the collapsed burial site, the bundled mummy of an Inca girl.

The girl had been wrapped and almost perfectly preserved by the icy temperatures for about 500 years. It was apparent from the remote location of her tomb and from the care and ceremony surrounding her death (as well as the crushing blow to her right eyebrow) that this 12- to 14-year-old girl had been sacrificed to the gods at the summit. For the Incas, mountains were gods who could kill by volcanic eruption, avalanche or climatic catastrophes. These violent deities could only be appeased by sacrifices from their subjects, and the ultimate sacrifice was that of a child.

After being carried down the mountain and undergoing a battery of scientific examinations at the Universidad Católica in Arequipa, the mummy (dubbed 'Juanita, the Ice Maiden') was given her own museum, Museo Santuarios Andino, in 1998.

Museo Santuarios Andinos
SAIKO3P/SHUTTERSTOCK ©

with genuine knowledge. Guides speak English, French and German.

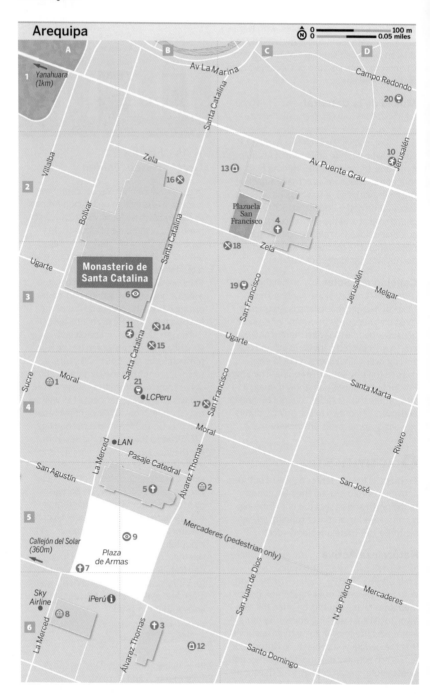

Arequipa

N 0 ———— 100 m
0 ———— 0.05 miles

Yanahuara
(1km)

A   B   C   D

Av La Marina

Campo Redondo

20

Santa Catalina

Av Puente Grau

Jerusalén

10

Zela

13

16

Villalba

Bolívar

Plazuela
San
Francisco

4

Ugarte

Zela

18

**Monasterio de
Santa Catalina**

19

Melgar

Jerusalén

6

Santa Catalina

San Francisco

11

14

15

Ugarte

Santa Marta

Sucre

Moral

1

21

LCPeru

San Francisco

17

Moral

Rivero

La Merced

LAN

Pasaje Catedral

Alvarez Thomas

San Agustín

5

2

San José

Callejón del Solar
(360m)

9

Mercaderes (pedestrian only)

San Juan de Dios

N de Piérola

Mercaderes

Plaza
de Armas

7

Sky
Airline

iPerú

8

3

La Merced

Alvarez Thomas

12

Santo Domingo

Arequipa

Carlos Zárate
Adventures   Adventure Sports
(☏054-20-2461; www.zarateadventures.com; Jerusalén 505A) This highly professional company offers various treks, and climbs all the local peaks. Founded in 1954 by Carlos Zárate, the great-grandfather of climbing in Arequipa, it's now run by one of his sons, experienced guide Carlos Zárate Flores. Another of Zárate's sons, Miguel, was responsible, along with archaeologists, for unearthing 'Juanita the Ice Maiden' (p99) atop Nevado Ampato in 1995.

COURSES

Want to learn to speak Spanish? Immersion is the best way and Arequipa provides plenty of opportunities for class time, while practicing with the locals in the evenings. Book with a recommended agency and you'll be reading Arequipa-born novelist Mario Vargas Llosa in the original before you know it.

If you recognize the name Gastón Acurio and concur that Peru is the gastronomical capital of Latin America, you may be inspired to enroll in an Arequipa cooking course.

Peruvian Cooking
Experience   Cooking
(☏054-213-975; www.peruviancookingexperi ence.com; San Martín 116, Vallecito; 3hr course US$23.50; ⊙11am & 3pm Mon-Sat) A popular option for Peruvian cooking lessons, where you can study the art of ceviche (raw seafood marinated in lime juice) preparation or even opt for vegetarian recipes. Courses are available in Spanish and English. Maximum group size is six. It's based out of the **Casa de Avila** (☏054-21-3177; www.casa deavila.com; s/d/tr incl breakfast S151/188/271; @⊛) hotel four blocks southwest of Plaza de Armas.

ROCIO   Language
(☏054-22-4568; www.spanish-peru.com; Ayacucho 208) This language school with accommodation options charges US$6 per hour for an individual Spanish class, while small group lessons cost US$116 per 20-hour week. Ring bell number 21 at the communal entrance.

⊕ TOURS

The Association of Mountain Guides of Peru warns that many guides are uncertified and untrained, so climbers are advised to go well-informed about medical and wilderness-survival issues. Most agencies sell climbs as packages that include transportation, so prices vary widely depending on the size of the group and the mountain, but the cost for a guide alone is around US$85 per day.

If you're nervous about hiking without guides or want to tackle more untrammeled routes, there are dozens of tour

Juice stalls, Mercado San Camilo

companies based in Arequipa that can arrange guided treks.

🔒 SHOPPING

Claustros de la Compañía
Shopping Center

(118 General Morán; ⊗most stores 9am-9pm) One of South America's most elegant shopping centers, with a wine bar, ice-cream outlet, numerous alpaca-wool shops and chic cafes and restaurants. Its ornate double courtyard is ringed by cloisters held up by *sillar* columns, etched with skillful carvings. Couples often dot the upper levels enjoying the romantic setting and southerly views.

Fundo El Fierro
Craft Market

(San Francisco 200; ⊗9am-1:30pm & 3-8:30pm Mon-Thu, to 9pm Fri & Sat) The city's primary craft market occupies a beautiful colonial *sillar* courtyard next to the Iglesia de San Francisco. Garments, paintings, handmade crafts and jewelry predominate, but you can also procure rare alpaca carpets from

Cotahuasi. There's an artisanal fair with special stalls held here in August.

🍴 EATING

Arequipa has a reputation for tasty local dishes like *rocoto relleno* (stuffed spicy red peppers), best enjoyed in the traditional, communal *picantería* (local restaurants). Trendy upscale spots line San Francisco north of the Plaza de Armas, while touristy outdoor cafes huddle together on Pasaje Catedral. Good, local eateries are in the busy Mercado on San Camilo southeast of the plaza.

Crepísimo
Crêperie $

(www.crepisimo.com; Alianza Francesa, Santa Catalina 208; mains S15-34; ⊗8am-11pm;) All the essential components of a great cafe – food, setting, service, ambience – come together at Crepísimo, located inside Arequipa's French cultural center. In this chic colonial setting, the simple crepe is offered with 100 different types of filling, from Chilean smoked trout to South American fruits and ample vegetarian options, while casual waitstaff serve you Parisian-quality coffee.

Tradición Arequipeña   Peruvian $
(☎054-42-6467; www.tradicionarequipena.com; Av Dolores 111, José Luis Bustamante y Rivero; meals S18-40; ☺11:30am-6pm Mon-Fri, to 8pm Sat, 8:30am-6pm Sun) This locally famous restaurant has maze-like gardens, live *folklórica* and *criollo* (an upbeat coastal style) music, and does traditional Peruvian fare well, such as seabass ceviche. Sunday breakfast includes *adobo de cerdo,* a traditional slow-cooked pork dish. It's 2km southeast of the center; a taxi ride here costs about S5.

La Nueva Palomino   Peruvian $$
(☎054-25-2393; Leoncio Prado 122; mains S22-69; ☺noon-5pm Mon-Sat, 7:30am-noon Sun; ☂🅿🅗) An unmissable local favorite, this long-running *picantería* has old-world formal service but a casual atmosphere that turns boisterous even during the week when family groups descend to eat generous servings of local specialties and drink copious amounts of *chicha de jora* (fermented corn beer) in the courtyard. Solo diners will fill up on the excellent *rico-to relleno* (meat-stuffed peppers) alone.

Zig Zag   Peruvian $$
(☎054-20-6020; www.zigzagrestaurant.com; Zela 210; mains S36-50; ☺noon-11pm; 🅿) Up-scale but not ridiculously pricey, Zig Zag is a Peruvian restaurant with European inflections. It inhabits a two-story colonial house with an iron stairway designed by Gustave Eiffel (blimey, that bloke must have been busy). The menu classic is a meat selection served on a unique volcano-stone grill with various sauces. The fondues are also good.

Cevichería Fory Fay   Ceviche $$
(Álvarez Thomas 221; mains S20-35; ☺10am-4:30pm) This small and to-the-point place serves only the best ceviche and nothing else. Pull up a chair at a rickety table and crack open a beer – limit three per person at this family-oriented joint, though.

🔭 A Stroll Through Yanahuara

This tranquil **neighborhood** (cnr Cuesta del Angel & Av Lima) makes for a pleasant, walkable excursion, with a *mirador* (lookout) as its centerpiece providing excellent views of Arequipa and El Misti through arches inscribed with poetry. To get here, go west on Puente Grau over the namesake bridge, and take the first right along Francisco Bolognesi hugging the park. Take the first left on Cuesta del Ángel and continue four blocks to Plaza Yanahuara with its church and *mirador*.

CHRISTIAN VINCES/SHUTTERSTOCK ©

Salamanto   Peruvian $$$
(☎979-394-676; www.salamanto.com; San Francisco 211; mains S48-57, 5-course tasting menus S85; ☺12:30-3:30pm & 6:30-10:30pm Mon-Sat; ☂) The innovative, wonderfully plated contemporary Peruvian creations at Salamanto bolster Arequipa's reputation as a foodie destination. The five-dish degustation is unmissable with mushroom and pistachio mousse, trout carpaccio, and alpaca steak with pisco (Peruvian grape brandy) mustard dazzling on artful slabs of stone. There are only three wines (Argentinian and Peruvian) to choose from but they have been carefully chosen.

Chicha   Peruvian, Fusion $$$
(☎054-28-7360; www.chicha.com.pe; Santa Catalina 210; mains S44-69; ☺noon-11pm Mon-Sat, to 8pm Sun; ☂🅿) Peru's most famous chef, Gastón Acurio, owns this

Arequipa Nights

The nocturnal scene in Arequipa is pretty slow midweek but takes off on weekends, when anyone who's anyone can be seen joining the throng on the corner of San Francisco and Ugarte sometime after 9pm. Many of the bars there offer happy-hour specials worth enjoying. The 300 block has the highest concentration of places to compare fashion notes.

experimental place where the menu closely reflects Peru's Inca-Spanish roots. River prawns are a highlight in season (April to December), but Acurio prepares Peruvian staples with equal panache, along with tender alpaca burgers and earthy pastas. Staff can help pair food with pisco cocktails and wines by the glass.

DRINKING & NIGHTLIFE

Chelawasi Public House
Microbrewery

(www.facebook.com/chelawasi; Campo Redondo 102; beers S15-18; ⊙4-11pm Mon-Fri, from noon Sat) Arequipa's first craft-beer bar is a modern but unpretentious pub in the village-like San Lázaro area. The burgers, wings and hand-cut fries are excellent for pacing yourself. New to craft beer? Chelawasi's friendly Canadian-Peruvian owners will step you through the best beers from Peru's microbreweries, with bonus local travel advice, or a chat with other solo drinkers.

Casona Forum
Club

(www.casonaforum.com; San Francisco 317; ⊙nightclubs 9pm-late Thu-Sat, bars & restaurant from 7pm daily) A seven-in-one excuse for a good night out in a *sillar* building incorporating a pub (Retro), pool club (Zero), sofa bar (Chill Out), restaurant (Terrasse) and nightclubs (Forum, Club 80s and Latino Salsa Club).

Museo del Pisco
Cocktail Bar

(www.museodelpisco.org; cnr Santa Catalina & Moral; drinks S16-32, tastings per person S37; ⊙5pm-midnight Sun-Thu, to 1am Fri & Sat) The name says 'museum,' but the designer slabs of stone and glass, plus the menu of more than 100 pisco varieties, says cocktail bar. Identify your favorite with a tasting of three mini craft piscos, explained in English by knowledgeable staff. Then mix your own (S26) behind the bar. Pace yourself with gourmet burgers and hummus.

INFORMATION

iPerú (☏054-22-3265, 24hr hotline 574-8000; iperuarequipa@promperu.gob.pe; Portal de la Municipalidad 110, Plaza de Armas; ⊙9am-6pm Mon-Sat, to 1pm Sun) Excellent government-supported source for objective information on local and regional attractions with English-speaking staff. There is also an office at the **airport** (☏054-44-4564; 1st fl, Main Hall, Aeropuerto Rodríguez Ballón; ⊙10am-7:30pm).

🛈 GETTING THERE & AWAY

AIR

Arequipa's **Rodríguez Ballón International Airport** (Aeropuerto Internacional Alfredo Rodríguez Ballón; AQP; ☏054-34-4834; Cerro Colorado) is about 8km northwest of the city center.

LAN (☏054-20-1100; Santa Catalina 118C; ⊙office 9am-7pm, to 2pm Sat) has daily flights to Lima and Cuzco. **LCPeru** (☏054-21-4746; www.lcperu.pe; Moral 225; ⊙office 9am-7pm Mon-Fri, to 1pm Sat) also offers daily flights to Lima. **Sky Airline** (☏054-28-2899; www.skyairline.cl; La Merced 121) flies to Santiago in Chile.

BUS

Most bus companies have departures from the Terminal Terrestre or the smaller Terrapuerto bus terminal, located together on Av Andrés Avelino Cáceres, less than 3km south of the city center (take a taxi for S7). Check in advance which terminal your bus leaves from and keep a close watch on your belongings while you're waiting

Chupe de camarones (shrimp chowder)

there. There's a S1.50 departure tax from either terminal, paid separately at a booth. Both terminals have shops, restaurants and left-luggage facilities. The more chaotic Terminal Terrestre also has a global ATM.

Dozens of bus companies have desks at the Terminal Terrestre so shop around. Prices range between super-luxury **Cruz del Sur** (📞054-42-7375; www.cruzdelsur.com.pe) and **Ormeño** (📞054-42-3855; www.grupo-ormeno.com.pe/destinos.html) with 180-degree reclining 'bed' seats.

🛈 GETTING AROUND

TO & FROM THE AIRPORT

An official taxi from downtown Arequipa to the airport costs around S15 to S20.

TAXI

You can often hire a taxi with a driver for less than renting a car from a travel agency. Local taxi companies include **Tourismo Arequipa** (📞054-45-8888; www.facebook.com/taxiturismo arequipa) and **Taxitel** (📞054-20-0000; www.taxitel.com.pe). A short ride around town costs about S5, while a trip from the Plaza de Armas out to the bus terminals costs about S7. Whenever possible, try to call a recommended company to ask for a pickup as there have been numerous reports of travelers being scammed or even assaulted by taxi drivers.

CAÑÓN DEL COLCA

Cañón del Colca at a Glance...

It's not just the vastness and depth of the Colca Canyon that make it so fantastical, it's also the shifts in its scenery, from the ancient terraced farmland of Yanque and Chivay to the steep-sided canyon proper beyond Cabanaconde. Of course, one shouldn't turn a blind eye to the vital statistics. The Colca is the world's second-deepest canyon, a smidgen shallower than the Cotahausi, and twice as deep as the more famous Grand Canyon in the US. But, more than that, it is replete with history, culture, ruins, tradition and – rather like Machu Picchu – intangible Peruvian magic.

Cañón del Colca in Two Days

The classic tour from Arequipa stops to spot wild vicuñas (threatened, wild relatives of alpacas) and lofty mountain peaks in the **Reserva Nacional Salinas y Aguada Blanca** (p116), then finishes in **Chivay**, with restaurant performances. Start day two early to catch kids dancing in the square at **Yanque**, making stops in the **Cañon del Colca** and visiting **Cruz del Cóndor** (p113) to see the condors glide over the canyon.

Cañón del Colca in Four Days

With more time, continue from Cruz del Cóndor to the true canyon experience of **Cabanaconde**. Descend on a two-hour hike to the greenery of **Sangalle**, cooling off with a swim at the pools, then spending the night at some simple lodgings under a blanket of stars. On day four, hike back up and return to Chivay.

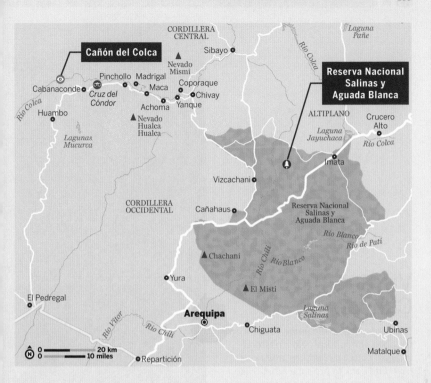

Arriving in Cañón del Colca

Bus & Car Chivay is the gateway (and resting point) to the region on most standard classic tours from Arequipa.

Where to Stay

Though it's a tiny town, Chivay has plenty of budget guesthouses to choose from. The most convenient are on Siglo XX, off the plaza.

In Yanque, a number of simple, family-run guesthouses have joined together in a local development project; they are scattered around town, and offer lodging from S15 per night.

Accommodation options are limited in Cabanaconde.

Cruz del Cóndor viewpoint (p112)

Visiting the Canyon

The canyon has been embellished with terraced agricultural fields, pastoral villages, colonial churches, and ruins that date back to pre-Inca times. Hike it, bike it, raft it or zip line it, just keep your eyes peeled for the emblematic condors.

Great For...

Cañón del Colca

Nevado Coropuna
Huambo
Río Colca
Chivay
Lagunas Mucurca
Reserva Nacional Salinas y Aguada Blanca
Arequipa

ℹ Need to Know

June to September is your best chance of seeing Andean condors gliding above the canyon.

★ **Top Tip**

Locals bearing birds or llamas, urging you to take photos, expect a one sol tip.

Despite its depth, the Cañón del Colca is geologically young. The Río Colca has cut into beds of mainly volcanic rock, which were deposited less than 100 million years ago along the line of a major fault in the earth's crust. Though cool and dry in the hills above, the deep valley and generally sunny weather produce frequent updrafts on which soaring condors often float by at close range.

Viscachas (burrowing rodents closely related to chinchillas) are also common around the canyon rim, darting furtively among the rocks. Cacti dot many slopes and, if they're in flower, you may be lucky enough to see tiny nectar-eating birds braving the spines to feed. In the depths of the canyon it can be almost tropical, with palm trees, ferns, and even orchids in some isolated areas.

Boleto Turístico

To access sites in the Cañón del Colca you need to purchase a *boleto turístico* (tourist ticket; S70) from a booth on the Arequipa road just outside Chivay. If you are taking an organized tour, the cost of the tour usually does not include this additional fee, and you will be asked for this in cash by your guide at the booth.

Pinchollo

An active geothermal area set amid wild greenery and a pockmarked landscape lies about 30km from Chivay starting in Pinchollo, a simple mud-brick village. Though it's not very clearly marked, a rough four-hour trail climbs toward Hualca Hualca (a snowcapped volcano of 6025m) up to a bubbling geyser that used to erupt dramatically before an

Coporaque (p114)

earthquake contained it. Ask around for directions, or just head left uphill in the direction of the mountain, then follow the water channel to its end.

Cruz del Cóndor

Some much hyped travel sights are anticlimactic in the raw light of day, but this is *not* one of them. No advance press can truly sell the **Cruz del Cóndor** (Chaq'lla; Carr al Colca; admission with boleto turístico), a famed viewpoint, also known locally as Chaq'lla, about 50km west of Chivay. A large family of Andean condors nests by the rocky outcrop

> ### ☑ Don't Miss
> Non-commercialized Coporaque, which has the valley's oldest church and gorgeous views of canyon slopes covered in terraced fields.

and, weather and season permitting, they can be seen between approximately 8am and 10am gliding effortlessly on thermal air currents rising from the canyon, swooping low over onlookers' heads. It's a mesmerizing scene, heightened by the spectacular 1200m drop to the river below and the sight of **Nevado Mismi** reaching over 3000m above the canyon floor on the other side of the ravine.

Recently it has become more difficult to see the condors, mostly due to air pollution, including from travelers' campfires and tour buses. The condors are also less likely to appear on rainy days, so it's best to visit during the dry season; they are unlikely to emerge at all in January and February. You won't be alone at the lookout; expect a couple of hundred people for the 8am 'show' in season. Afterwards, it is possible to walk 12.5km from the viewpoint to Cabanaconde.

Sangalle

You've only half-experienced Colca if you haven't descended into the canyon by foot (the only method anywhere west of Madrigal). The shortest route is the spectacular two- to three-hour hike from Cabanaconde down to flower-filled Sangalle (known as 'the Oasis') at the canyon's base.

Sangalle lives up to its nickname, and is surrounded by mountain walls topped with a blanket of stars at night. Here there are camping grounds and four very similar hostels comprised of basic bungalows.

Upper Canyon

The Upper Canyon (really still a valley at this stage as it heads northeast) has a colder and harsher landscape than the terraced fields around Chivay and Yanque, and is only lightly visited, meaning you can see handsome traditional villages without any crowds.

> ### ✕ Take a Break
> Small towns and Cruz del Cóndor itself have home-cooked meals, plus coca-leaf tea to help with the altitude.

Pierced by a single road which plies north-east through the village of Tuti to Sibayo, the grassy terrain is inhabited by livestock while the still-young river is ideal for river running and trout fishing. **Tuti** is a tourist-lite village situated only 19km northeast of Colca-hub Chivay. With an economy centered on broad-bean cultivation and clothes-making, it is surrounded by some interesting sights all connected by hiking trails.

North Side

The first town north of the canyon from Chivay, **Coporaque** has the valley's oldest church and not a lot else, unless you count the splendiferous views of canyon slopes covered in terraced fields. To really enjoy it, stay at La Casa de Mamayacchi, a charming hut-like inn built with traditional materials that presides over the valley views.

A one-hour walk from Coporaque will take you to a bridge where you can cross south to Yanque, or continue along the Northern Canyon through sleepy towns. **Ichupampa** has a humble church; the church in **Lari** is geometrically pleasing, with impressive straight slabs of white holding up a 'half orange' cupola. Around Lari are the 'enchanted' valley lakes of **Hañinch'iwa**, home to a great variety of native birds.

The last village on the canyon's north side reachable by road (unpaved by this point) is **Madrigal**, a bucolic backwater perfect for a slow unflustered digestion of traditional Colca life. You can forge west on foot from here to two nearby archaeological sites: the **Fortaleza de Chimpa**, a walled Collagua citadel atop a hill, and the **Pueblo Perdido Matata**, some long-abandoned ruins.

'El Clásico' Trek

Short on time? Confused by the complicated web of Colca paths? Couldn't stand the crowds on the Inca Trail? What you need is 'El Clásico,' the unofficial name for a circular two- to three-day hike that incorporates the best parts of the mid-lower Colca canyon below the Cruz del Cóndor and Cabanaconde.

Start by walking out of Cabanaconde on the Chivay road. At the San Miguel viewpoint (p121), start a long 1200m descent into the canyon on a zigzagging path. Cross the Río Colca via a bridge and enter the village of **San Juan de Chuccho**. Accommodations are available here at the **Casa de Rivelino** (San Juan de Chuccho; r without bathroom S10), with bungalows with warm water and a simple restaurant. Alternatively, you can ascend to the charming village of **Tapay**. Camping or overnight accommodations are available at **Hostal Isidro** – it's owned by a guide and has a shop, satellite phone and rental mules.

On day two descend to the **Cinkumayu Bridge** before ascending to the villages of **Coshñirwa** and **Malata**. The latter has a tiny **Museo Familiar**, basically a typical local home where the owner will explain about the Colca culture. From Malata, descend to the beautiful **Sangalle** oasis (crossing the river again), with more

Condor

overnight options, before ascending the lung-stretching 4km trail back to Cabanaconde (1200m of ascent).

Though it's easy to do solo, this classic trek can be easily organized with any reputable Arequipa travel agency. In Chivay, Marco Antonio through D&M Travel Adventure (p119) charges S100 per person for a tour and one night in Sangalle.

Source of the Amazon Trek

It is surprisingly easy to hike to the Amazon's source (marked inauspiciously by a wooden cross) from the Cañón del Colca. Paths ply north from the villages of Lari or Tuti. It's a two-day out-and-back hike from the latter village, though some people prefer to undertake a three-day route starting in Lari and ending in Tuti, thus making a complete circuit of Nevado Mismi.

Alternatively, in the dry season, it is possible to get a 4WD to within 30 minutes' hike of the Apacheta cliff. Carlos Zárate Adventures (p101) in Arequipa organizes memorable guided hikes. Those going it solo should come equipped with maps, food, tents and cold-weather clothing.

★ **Did You Know?**

The wingspan of an Andean condor can measure up to 3.3m.

★ **Top Tip**

A cup of *mate de coca* (coca-leaf tea) is said to cure altitude sickness and is perfectly legal in Peru – though be careful not to bring any back to your home country where it is likely illegal because of the cocaine-like qualities.

DANIELE FALLETTA/GETTY IMAGES ©

Reserva Nacional Salinas y Aguada Blanca

One of southern Peru's finest protected reserves, Reserva Nacional Salinas y Aguada Blanca is a vast Andean expanse of dozing volcanoes and brawny wildlife forging out an existence against the odds several kilometers above sea level.

Great For...

☑ Don't Miss

Chewing coca leaves en route. Not only does it help combat the high altitudes, it's a traditional experience.

The paved road from Arequipa climbs northeast past volcanoes El Misti and Chachani to this national reserve, which covers 367,000 hectares at an average elevation of 4300m. As most travelers speed through on the way to the canyons, this is where their heads may tingle at high altitude as they note the rocky and extraterrestrial landscape turn sparse of vegetation, and criss-crossed with darting vicuñas. Get out here to trek on old Inca trails.

Only a handful of llama herders roam the national reserve, giving a chance for high-altitude loving *tarucas envinados* (Andean deer), guanacos and flamingos to thrive without human interference.

ℹ Need to Know

☎054-25-7461; ⊘24hr `FREE`

✕ Take a Break

Be sure to stock up snacks and water as stops are few and far between.

★ Top Tip

Vicuñas are unmissable but startle easily, so you'll need a camera with a good zoom lens.

Paso de Patopampa

The highest point on the road between Arequipa and Chivay is this almost lifeless pass which, at 4910m, is significantly higher than Europe's Mt Blanc and anywhere in North America's Rocky Mountains. If your red blood cells are up to it, disembark into the rarefied air at the **Mirador de los Volcanes** to view a muscular consortium of eight snowcapped volcanoes including El Misti (5822m) and Chachani (6075m).

Hardy ladies in traditional dress discreetly ply their wares at the *mirador* (lookout) during the day – this must be the world's highest shopping center. It's also usually the last tour-bus stop from Arequipa heading into canyon country.

Pampa de Toccra

This high plain that lies between El Misti/ Chachani and the Colca Canyon has an average height of around 4300m and supports plentiful bird and animal life. You're almost certain to see vicuñas on the roadside in the Zona de Vicuñas on the approach to **Patahuasi** (Hwy 34A). At a boggy and sometimes icy lake, waterfowl and flamingos reside in season. Nearby is a bird-watching *mirador*.

Accessing the Reserve

Nearly every visitor stops through the reserve on a classic tour from Arequipa, or merely passes by on a public bus without any chance of getting out. Car hire is not recommended for inexperienced drivers on the sharp turns here. Book a longer tour or car with driver in Arequipa, if you want to spend any real time here.

There are no accommodations available in this harsh environment.

Chivay

Behold the most accessible and popular segment of the Cañón del Colca, a landscape dominated by agriculture and characterized by some of the most intensely terraced hillsides on earth. The greenery and accessibility has led to this becoming the canyon's busiest region with the bulk of the business centered in the small town of Chivay. The Canyon's unashamedly disheveled nexus, this traditional town has embraced tourism without (so far) losing its unkempt high-country identity. Long may it continue!

◎ SIGHTS

Astronomical Observatory   Observatory

(Planetario; ☏054-53-1020; www.casa-andina. com; Casa Andina, cnr Huayna Cápac & Garcilazo de la Vega; admission S20; ⊗presentations in English 8pm) No light pollution equals excellent Milky Way vistas. The Casa Andina hotel six blocks southwest of the Plaza de Armas has a tiny observatory which holds nightly sky shows in Spanish and English. The price includes a 30-minute explanation and chance to peer into the telescope. It is open daily but often closes between January and March, when it is hard to catch a night with clear skies.

❸ ACTIVITIES

Chivay is a good starting point for canyon hikes, both short and long. The view-embellished 7km path to **Corporaque** on the north side of the canyon starts on the north edge of town. Fork left on the La Calera Hot Springs road, cross the Puente Inca, and follow the fertile fields to the village. Rather than retracing your steps, you can head downhill out of Corporaque past some small ruins and descend to the orange bridge across the Río Colca toward Yanque. From Yanque, on the southern bank, you can catch a passing bus or *colectivo* (shared transportation) for the 7km return to Chivay (or you can walk along the road). For a quicker sojourn rent a mountain bike in Chivay.

Chivay

To penetrate further west it's possible to continue on up the northern side of the canyon from Corporaque to the villages **Ichupampa**, **Lari** and, ultimately, **Madrigal**. Occasional *combis* (minibuses) run to these villages from the streets around the main market area in Chivay. Another option is to pitch northeast from near the Puente Inca and follow a path along the river to the villages of Tuti and Sibayo.

Colca Zip-Lining   Adventure Sports
(☏95-898-9931; www.colcaziplining.com; 2/4/6 rides S50/100/150; ⊙from 9am Mon-Sat, from 10:30am Sun) Four-ride sessions last one hour and instructors speak English.

La Calera
Hot Springs   Thermal Baths
(admission S5-15; ⊙5am-6pm) If you've just arrived from Arequipa, you can acclimatize by strolling 3km here and examining the canyon's (surprisingly shallow) slopes alfresco while lying in the naturally heated pools. The setting is idyllic and you'll be entertained by the whooping zip liners as they sail overhead. Free basic padlocked lockers are available.

TOURS

D&M Travel Adventure   Cultural
(☏054-48-0083; Plaza de Armas; ⊙10am-7pm) Runs tours all across the canyon country. It's right next to the police station on Chivay's Plaza de Armas.

⊗ EATING

There are no fancy eating options in Chivay. Tour groups tend to head to a (perfectly fine) buffet restaurant for lunch and one with a show for dinner. For *menús* (set meals), in the market is where to eat with the locals for as little as S5, while traveler-geared restaurants around the plaza offer good *menús* for S12 to S20.

Innkas   Peruvian $
(Plaza de Armas 705; mains S12-20; ⊙8am-11pm; 🛜) Maybe it's the altitude, but the *lomo*

People of the Canyon

The local people of Cañón del Colca are descendants of two groups that originally occupied the area, the Cabanas and the Collagua. These two groups used to distinguish themselves by performing cranial deformations, but nowadays use distinctively shaped hats and intricately embroidered traditional clothing to denote their ancestry. In the Chivay area at the east end of the canyon, the white hats worn by women are usually woven from straw and are embellished with lace, sequins and medallions. At the west end of the canyon, the hats have rounded tops and are made of painstakingly embroidered cotton.

HADYNYAH/GETTY IMAGES ©

saltado (strips of beef stir-fried with onions, tomatoes, potatoes and chili) here tastes worthy of star chef Gastón Acurio. The sweet service is backed up by even sweeter cakes and great coffee. In an old building with cozy window nooks warmed by modern gas heaters (and boy do you need 'em).

El Balcon
De Don Zacarias   Buffet $$
(cnr Av 22 de Agosto & Trujillo; buffet S35; ⊙11am-3pm; 🛜⚠) There are buffets galore catering to captive tour-group diners but this large restaurant on a corner of the Plaza de Armas stands out for the freshness of dishes such as alpaca steaks and the abundance of meat-free options such as *pastel de papa andina* (potato lasagna) and stuffed eggplant.

Digging Deeper: Cañón del Cotahuasi

While the Cañón del Colca has stolen the limelight for many years, it is actually this remote canyon, 200km northwest of Arequipa as the condor flies, that is the deepest known canyon in the world. Cañón del Cotahuasi is around twice the depth of the Grand Canyon, with stretches dropping down below 3500m. While the depths of the ravine are only accessible to experienced river runners, the rest of the fertile valley is rich in striking scenery and trekking opportunities. The canyon also shelters several traditional rural settlements that currently see only a handful of adventurous travelers.

The main access town for hikes in Cañón del Cotahuasi is appropriately named **Cotahuasi** (population 3800).

Trekking trips of several days' duration can be arranged in Arequipa; some can be combined with the **Toro Muerto petroglyphs** and, if you ask, they may return via a collection of dinosaur footprints on the west edge of the canyon.

If going solo, the 420km bus journey from Arequipa to Cotahuasi, much of which is on unpaved roads, takes 10 hours if the going is good. **Reyna** (☏054-43-0612; www.reyna.com. pe) operates buses (S30) that leave Arequipa at 7am and 5pm.

ⓘ INFORMATION

Caja Arequipa (Av Salaverry 506) Bank with 24-hour ATM accepting international cards.

ⓘ GETTING THERE & AWAY

The bus terminal is a 10- to 15-minute walk from the central Plaza de Armas. There are at least nine daily departures to Arequipa (S13, three hours), the best with Reyna and Andalucia, and four daily with Milagros to Cabanaconde (S8, 2½ hours, from 7:30am), stopping at towns along the southern side of the canyon and at the Cruz del Cóndor.

Traveling onward to Cuzco from Chivay is possible on Monday, Wednesday and Friday with the tourist-geared **4M Express** (☏95-974-6330; http://busperu4m.com; Av Siglo XX 118; Chivay to Puno US$50, to Cuzco US$65).

To get to Puno, take a daily direct tourist bus with the luxurious 4M Express or comfortable **Rutas del Sur** (☏95-102-4754; chivay@rutasur peru.com; Av 22 de Agosto s/n; Chivay to Puno US$35).

Yanque

Of the Cañón del Colca's dozen or so villages, Yanque, 7km west of Chivay, has the prettiest and liveliest main square, and sports its finest church (from the exterior, at least): the Iglesia de la Inmaculada Concepción, whose ornate baroque doorway has a look that's almost *churrigueresque* (an elaborate and intricately decorated Spanish style). Local children in traditional costume dance to music in the main square most mornings at around 7am for tips, catching tourists on their way to the Cruz del Cóndor.

◎ SIGHTS & ACTIVITIES

Pop into the **Colca Lodge** (☏054-28-2177; www.colca-lodge.com; Fundo Puye s/n, Yanque; d/ste incl breakfast S594/735; ❄🛜♨) to relax in the thermal baths (nonguests S35 including one meal in the lodge restaurant).

Museo Yanque   Museum
(☏054-38-2038; www.ucsm.edu.pe/museo-de-yanque; Arequipa 212; admission S7; ◷9am-6pm)
This university-run museum is unexpectedly comprehensive for a small village, explaining the culture of the Cañón del Colca in conscientious detail. Exhibits include information on Inca fabrics, cranial deformation, local agriculture, ecclesial architecture and a mini-exposé on Juanita, the 'Ice Maiden' (p99) now on display in Arequipa. It's opposite the church on the plaza.

Baños Chacapi   Thermal Baths
(Av Chacapi; admission S10; ◷4am-7pm) These hot springs, a more basic version of La Calera (p119) in Chivay, are a 30-minute walk down to the river from the plaza. The early-bird opening time is mainly for locals, many of whom don't have hot water in their houses.

❶ GETTING THERE & AWAY

Buses from Chivay's bus station stop here on their way to Cabanaconde.

Cabanaconde

The narrow lower canyon that runs roughly from Cabanaconde down to Huambo is the Colca at its deepest. Only approximately 20% of Cañón del Colca visitors get as far as ramshackle Cabanaconde (most organized itineraries turn around at the Cruz del Cóndor). For those who make it, the attractions are obvious – fewer people, more authenticity and greater tranquility. Welcome to the *true* canyon experience.

The Colca is significantly deeper here with steep, zigzagging paths tempting the fit and the brave to descend 1200m to the eponymous river. Fruit trees can be found around Tapay and Sangalle, but otherwise the canyon supports no real economic activity. There are no ATMs in Cabanaconde; be sure to bring some cash.

◎ SIGHTS & ACTIVITIES

Local guides can be hired by consulting with your hostel or the *municipalidad* (town hall) in Cabanaconde. The going rate for guides is S30 to S60 per day, depending on the type of trek, season and size of the group. Ask at **Pachamama** (☏054-76-7277, 959-316-322; www.pachamamahome.com; San Pedro 209) about guided tours for anywhere in the canyon – highly recommended for safety and not getting lost.

Mirador de San Miguel   Viewpoint
(Cabanaconde; ◷24hr) **FREE** The spectacular views here are a highlight of Cabanaconde, taking in the mountain range, with the villages resembling specks of white dust clinging to its ragged surface, and the canyon below, including the blue-green postage stamp of 'the Oasis.' The descent to the Colca Canyon starts here, but even if you don't make it down, it's worth visiting this *mirador*.

❶ GETTING THERE & AWAY

Buses for Chivay (S5, 2½ hours) and Arequipa (S17, five hours) via the Cruz del Cóndor leave Cabanaconde from the main plaza (6am, 11am, 11:30am, 1:30pm and 10pm) with three companies, including **Andalucía** (☏054-44-5089) and **Reyna** (☏054-43-0612; www.reyna.com.pe).

LAKE TITICACA

In this Chapter

Lake Titicaca at a Glance...

In Andean belief, Titicaca is the birthplace of the sun. In addition, it's the largest lake in South America and the highest navigable body of water in the world. Enthralling, and in many ways singular, the shimmering deep-blue Lake Titicaca is the longtime home of highland cultures steeped in the old ways. Pre-Inca Pukara, Tiwanaku and Collas all left a mark on the landscape. Today, the region is a mix of crumbling cathedrals, desolate altiplano (Andean plateau) and checkerboard fields backed by high Andean peaks. Ancient holidays are marked with riotous celebrations where elaborately costumed processions and brass bands start a frenzy that lasts for days.

Lake Titicaca in Two Days

Spend the first day exploring the floating reed islands of **Islas Uros**, continue on to some great walks on **Isla Taquile**, then head back to Puno to check out **Catedral de Puno** (p132), where you can have dinner nearby. Spend day two exploring the *chullpas* (funerary towers) at **Sillustani** (p128) and visiting a local home as evening falls.

Lake Titicaca in Four Days

On the third day head along the road toward Bolivia and stay in a homestay at a south-shore community of Lake Titicaca, such as **Luquina Chico**. Explore the miniature funerary towers there in the late afternoon. On the fourth day you can continue on to Bolivia or head back to Puno to peruse the archaeological finds in the **Museo Carlos Dreyer** (p132).

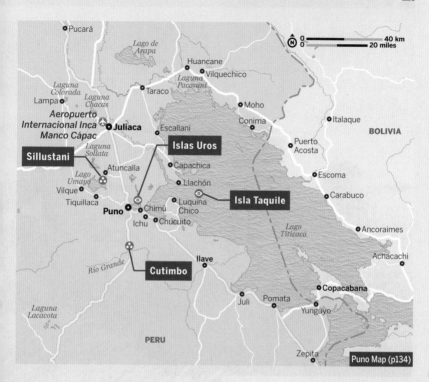

Pucará
Lago de Arapa
Huancane
Vilquechico
Laguna Pacosani
Laguna Colorada
Laguna Chacas
Taraco
Lampa
Moho
Aeropuerto Internacional Inca Manco Cápac
Juliaca
Escallani
Conima
Italaque
BOLIVIA
Puerto Acosta
Laguna Sollata
Islas Uros
Sillustani
Atuncalla
Capachica
Escoma
Lago Umayo
Llachón
Vilque
Tiquillaca
Luquina Chico
Isla Taquile
Carabuco
Puno
Chimú
Ichu
Chucuito
Lago Titicaca
Ancoraimes
Achacachi
Río Grande
Ilave
Cutimbo
Laguna Lacacota
Juli
Pomata
Yunguyo
Copacabana
PERU
Zepita
Puno Map (p134)

0 — 40 km
0 — 20 miles

Arriving in Lake Titicaca

Aeropuerto Internacional Inca Manco Cápac The region's only airport is one hour from Puno, the gateway to Titicaca.

Bus and Car Overland crossings from the southeast side of the lake are usually through Copacabana in Bolivia to the border post at Yunguyo.

Where to Stay

In Puno, pedestrianized Calle Lima between Parque Pino and Plaza de Armas is the most active and safest street. Staying anywhere within three blocks of here is the most convenient and secure. Calle Lima and Arequipa can suffer from nighttime bar or traffic noise, so try to avoid street-facing rooms.

There are homestays on many of the islands, which include the option of a home-cooked meal while staying with a local family.

Reed boat

TRAVELERPIX/GETTY IMAGES ©

Islas Uros

These extraordinary floating islands are Lake Titicaca's top attraction. Their uniqueness is due to their construction, created entirely with the buoyant totora *reeds that grow abundantly in the shallows of the lake.*

Great For...

☑ **Don't Miss**

A taste test of the reeds, which resemble sugar cane without any sweetness.

The lives of the Uros people are interwoven with the *totora* reeds. Partially edible, the reeds are also used to build homes, boats and crafts. The islands are constructed from many layers of the *totora*, which are constantly replenished from the top as they rot from the bottom, so the ground is always soft and springy.

Some islands also have elaborately designed versions of traditional tightly bundled reed boats on hand and other whimsical reed creations, such as archways and even swing sets. Be prepared to pay for a boat ride (S10) or to take photographs.

Intermarriage with the Aymara-speaking indigenous people has seen the demise of the pure-blooded Uros, who nowadays all speak Aymara. Always a small tribe, the Uros began their unusual floating existence

❶ Need to Know

Boat tours take you to the islands, which are 7km east of Puno.

✖ Take a Break

Snacks and drinks are sold by island inhabitants, but there are no restaurants as such.

★ Top Tip

Handicrafts sold on the islands are an important livelihood for inhabitants, who sometimes see little tour money.

centuries ago in an effort to isolate themselves from the aggressive Colla and Inca.

The popularity of the islands has led to aggressive commercialization in some cases. The most traditional reed islands are located further from Puno through a maze of small channels, only visited by private boat. Islanders there continue to live in a relatively traditional fashion and prefer not to be photographed.

Homestays

There are now more than a handful of upmarket homestays on Islas Uros with accommodations ranging from elegant huts to luxury rooms with floor to ceiling windows to maximize lake views. Check if boat transfer and any cultural activities are included in rates.

An outstanding option is staying in the reed huts of Isla Khantati with **Cristina Suaña** (☏951-472-355, 951-695-121; uroskhan tati@hotmail.com; Isla Khantati; per person full board S180), an Uros native with a boundless personality, who has built a number of impeccable semi-traditional huts (with solar power, outhouses and shady decks) which occupy half the tiny island. The hyper-relaxed pace means a visit here is not ideal for those with little time on their hands. The tariff is steep but includes top-notch accommodations, three meals, fishing and ample cultural activity.

Getting There & Away

Getting to the Uros is easy – there's no need to go with an organized tour, though you will miss out on the history lesson given by the guides. Ferries leave from the port for Uros (return trip S10) at least once an hour from 6am to 4pm. The community-owned ferry service visits two islands, on a rotation basis. Ferries to Taquile and Amantaní can also drop you off in the Uros.

Sillustani

RAFAL CICHAWA/SHUTTERSTOCK ©

Chullpas

The ancient Colla people who once dominated the Lake Titicaca area buried their nobility in imposing chullpas (funerary towers), which can be seen scattered widely around the hilltops of the region.

The Colla were a warlike, Aymara-speaking tribe, who later became the southeastern group of the Inca. Their *chullpas* housed the remains of complete family groups, along with plenty of food and belongings for their journey into the next world. Their only opening was a small hole facing east, just large enough for a person to crawl through, which would be sealed immediately after a burial. Nowadays nothing remains of the burials, but the *chullpas* are well preserved.

Sillustani

The most impressive towers are at **Sillustani** (adult/child S15/2), where the tallest reaches a height of 12m. The afternoon light is the best for photography, though the site can get busy at this time.

Great For...

☑ Don't Miss

Lago Umayo (partially encircling Sillustani), home to a wide variety of plants and Andean water birds.

Carving detail, Cutimbo

❶ Need to Know

Sillustani tours leave at 2:30pm daily (from S30; taxi S80); Cutimbo tours cost from US$59 (taxi S30).

✕ Take a Break

Tours often include visiting local families and eating boiled potato dipped in *arcilla* (edible clay).

★ Top Tip

A homestay means you can help your host family with farming and visit lesser-known archaeological sites.

The walls of the towers are made from massive coursed blocks reminiscent of Inca stonework, but are considered to be even more complicated. Carved but unplaced blocks, and a ramp used to raise them, are among the site's points of interest, and you can also see the makeshift quarry. A few of the blocks are decorated, including a well-known carving of a lizard on one of the *chullpas* closest to the parking lot.

Sillustani is partially encircled by the sparkling Lago Umayo (3890m), which is home to a wide variety of plants and Andean water birds, plus a small island with vicuñas (threatened, wild relatives of alpacas). Birders take note: this is one of the best sites in the area.

Cutimbo

Just over 20km from Puno, this dramatic site has an extraordinary position upon a table-topped volcanic hill surrounded by a fertile plain. Its modest number of well-preserved *chullpas*, built by the Colla, Lupaca and Inca cultures, come in both square and cylindrical shapes. You can still see the ramps used to build them. Look closely and you'll find several monkeys, pumas and snakes carved into the structures.

This remote place receives few visitors, which makes it both enticing and potentially dangerous for independent travelers – go in a group and keep an eye out for muggers.

Combis (minibuses) en route to Laraqueri (S3, 30 minutes) leave from the Terminal Zonal in Puno. You can't miss the signposted site, which is on the left-hand side of the road when facing towards Laraqueri – just ask the driver where to get off – from where it's another 20-minute walk uphill.

MAY_LANA/SHUTTERSTOCK ©

Isla Taquile

In the strong island sunlight, the deep, red-colored soil of Taquile contrasts with the intense blue of the lake and the glistening backdrop of Bolivia's snowy Cordillera Real.

Great For...

☑ **Don't Miss**

Fiesta de San Diego – a celebration with dancing and music from July 25 until early August.

Inhabited for thousands of years, Isla Taquile is a tiny 7-sq-km island with a population of about 2000 people. Taquile's lovely scenery is reminiscent of the Mediterranean, with several hills that boast Inca terracing on their sides and small ruins on top.

Taquile's People

Quechua-speaking islanders are distinct from most of the surrounding Aymara-speaking island communities and maintain a strong sense of group identity. They rarely marry non-Taquile people.

Handicrafts

Taquile has a fascinating tradition of handicrafts, and the islanders' creations are made according to a system of deeply ingrained social customs.

HADYNYAH/GETTY IMAGES ©

ℹ Need to Know

Ferries (round-trip S25; island admission S5) leave from the Puno port for Taquile from 7:35am.

✕ Take a Break

Consider eating in the Restaurante Comunál, Taquile's only community-run food outlet.

★ Top Tip

There are no roads or streetlights, so bring a flashlight for an overnight stay.

Men wear tightly woven woolen hats that resemble floppy nightcaps, which they knit themselves – only men knit, learning from the age of eight. These hats are closely bound up with social symbolism: men wear red hats if they are married and red and white hats if they are single, and different colors can denote a man's current or past social position.

Taquile women weave thick, colorful waistbands for their husbands, which are worn with roughly spun white shirts and thick, calf-length black pants. Women wear eye-catching outfits comprising multilayered skirts and delicately embroidered blouses. These fine garments are considered some of the most well-made traditional clothes in Peru, and can be bought in the cooperative store on the island's main plaza.

Visiting

Visitors are free to wander around, explore the ruins and enjoy the tranquility. The island is a wonderful place to catch a sunset and gaze at the moon, which looks twice as bright in the crystalline air, rising over the breathtaking peaks of the Cordillera Real.

A stairway of more than 500 steps leads from the dock to the center of the island. The climb takes a breathless 20 minutes if you're acclimatized – more if you're not.

Make sure you already have lots of small bills in local currency, as change is limited and there's nowhere to exchange dollars. You may want to bring extra money to buy some of the exquisite crafts sold in the cooperative store.

The *hospedajes* (small, family-owned inns) on Taquile offer basic accommodation for around S20 a night. Meals are additional (S10 to S15 for breakfast, S20 for lunch). Options range from a room in a family house to small guesthouses. As the community rotates visitors to lodgings, there is little room for choosing.

Puno

With a regal plaza, concrete block buildings and crumbling bricks that blend into the hills, Puno has its share of both grit and cheer. It serves as the jumping-off point for Lake Titicaca and is a convenient stop for those traveling between Cuzco and La Paz. But it may just capture your heart with its own rackety charm.

⊙ SIGHTS

Casa del Corregidor Historic Building

(☑051-35-1921; www.casadelcorregidor.pe; Deustua 576; ⊙9am-9pm Mon-Sat) FREE An attraction in its own right, this 17th-century house is one of Puno's oldest residences. A former community center, it now houses a fair-trade arts-and-crafts store and a cafe.

Museo Carlos Dreyer Museum

(Conde de Lemos 289; admission with English-speaking guide S15; ⊙9am-7pm Mon-Fri, to 1pm Sat) This small museum houses a fascinating collection of Puno-related archaeological artifacts and art from pre-Inca, Inca,

colonial and the Republic periods. Upstairs there are three mummies and a full-scale fiberglass *chullpa*.

It's around the corner from Casa del Corregidor. Guides tend to leave an hour before closing.

Catedral de Puno Church

(Ayacucho at Deustua; ⊙8am-noon & 3-6pm) FREE Puno's baroque cathedral, on the western flank of the Plaza de Armas, was completed in 1757. The interior is more spartan than you'd expect from the well-sculpted facade, except for the silver-plated altar, which, following a 1964 visit by Pope Paul VI, has a Vatican flag placed to its right.

Yavari Historic Site

(☑051-36-9329; www.yavari.org; Sesqui Centenario 962; admission by donation; ⊙8am-1pm & 3-5:30pm) The oldest steamship on Lake Titicaca, the famed *Yavari* has turned from British gunship to a museum and recommended bed and breakfast, with bunk-bed lodging and attentive service under the stewardship of its captain. And no, you

Plaza de Armas and Catedral de Puno

ROBERT CHG/GETTY IMAGES ©

don't have to be a navy buff reflecting on Titicaca. The *Yavari* is moored behind the Sonesta Posada Hotel del Inca, about 5km from the center of Puno. It's probably the most tranquil spot in Puno.

TOURS

Edgar Adventures   Cultural
(☑051-35-3444; www.edgaradventures.com; Lima 328; ☺office 7am-8pm) Longtime agency with positive community involvement. More unusual activities include kayaking on Lake Titiicaca and visiting remote areas.

All Ways Travel   Cultural
(☑051-35-3979; www.titicacaperu.com; Deustua 576, 2nd fl) Offers both classic and 'nontourist' tours of Islas Uros and Taquile, Sillustani and visiting rural communities in Llachón. It aims to be socially conscious.

Las Balsas Tours   Boating
(☑051-36-4362; www.balsastours.com; Lima 419, 2nd fl, No 213; ☺office 9am-noon & 3-8pm Mon-Sat) Offers classic tours on a daily basis.

Nayra Travel   Boating
(☑051-36-4774; www.nayratravel.com; Lima 419 No 105; ☺9am-8:30pm Mon-Sat) Local package-tour operator.

SHOPPING

Artesanías (handicrafts, from musical instruments and jewelry to scale models of reed islands), wool and alpaca sweaters, and other typical tourist goods are sold in every second shop in the town center. The prices are a bit better at the **Feria** (Av Costanera; ☺7am-5pm) at the port.

The hypermarket on Los Incas sells not only food but also pisco, electronics and home needs.

❌ EATING

To save a few soles, head a couple of blocks away. Many restaurants don't advertise their *menús* (set meals), which are cheaper

Tips for Tours

It pays to shop around for a tour operator. Agencies abound and competition is fierce, leading to touting in streets and bus terminals, undeliverable promises, and prices so low as to undercut fair wages. Several of the cheaper tour agencies have reputations for ripping off the islanders of Amantaní and Taquile, with whom travelers stay overnight and whose living culture is one of the main selling points of these tours.

Island-hopping tours, even with the better agencies, are often disappointing: formulaic, lifeless and inflexible, the inevitable result of sheer numbers and repetition. If you only have a day or two though, a reputable tour can give a good taster and insight you might not otherwise get. If you have time, seeing the islands independently is recommended – you can wander around freely and spend longer in the places you like.

Reed boats, Lake Titicaca
SAIKO3P/SHUTTERSTOCK ©

than ordering à la carte. The most commercial restaurants cater to visitors with a *menú turistico*, which often represents excellent value and great food, and is rarely the tourist trap you might fear. Locals eat *pollo a la brasa* (roast chicken) and economical *menús* on Tacna between Calles Puno and Libertad.

If you're feeling broccoli or sweet-and-sour deprived, head to Arbulú to fill up at a cheap and cheerful *chifa* (Chinese restaurant; meals S9 to S11). For self-catering, head to **Mercado Central** (Oquendo s/n;

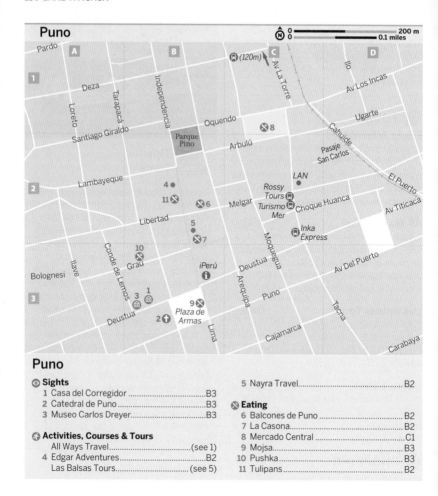

Puno

◎ Sights
1 Casa del Corregidor B3
2 Catedral de Puno B3
3 Museo Carlos Dreyer B3

⊕ Activities, Courses & Tours
All Ways Travel ....(see 1)
4 Edgar Adventures B2
Las Balsas Tours ....(see 5)

5 Nayra Travel..B2

⊗ Eating
6 Balcones de Puno B2
7 La Casona...B2
8 Mercado Central C1
9 Mojsa..B3
10 Pushka..B3
11 Tulipans..B2

⊙7am-9:30pm) (but be wary of pickpockets)
and the supermarket plaza across the road
on Los Incas.

Pushka   Peruvian $
(Grau 338; mains S8-15, ménus S8; 👪) It's hard
to imagine that just a couple of blocks
from Puno's busy tourist street there is
a large beer-garden-style restaurant. Yet
here it is, with kid's play equipment, astro-
turf and families enjoying excellent-value
ménus of Peruvian dishes that are of the
quality you'll find back on Calle Lima, but
without the frills.

La Table del Inca   Fusion $$
(📞994-659-357; www.fb.me/latabledelinca;
Ancash 239; mains S26-40, 3 courses with
wine S80; ⊙noon-2pm & 6-9:30pm Mon-Thu,
6-9:30pm Sat & Sun; 🛜) If you need a reason
to dress up, this fusion restaurant, a little
away from the noise, shows off paintings
by local artists on its walls, with colorful
plating. Peruvian dishes like lomo saltado
(stir-fried beef with potatoes and chili) hold
their own against Euro-Peruvian twists
such as quinoa risotto, alpaca carpaccio
with huacatay (a local aromatic herb), and
French desserts.

Mojsa   Peruvian $$

(📞051-36-3182; Lima 635; mains S22-30; ⊗noon-9:30pm; 🛜🍴) The go-to place for locals and travelers alike, Mojsa lives up to its name, which is Aymara for 'delicious.' Overlooking the plaza, it has a thoughtful range of Peruvian and international food, including innovative trout dishes and a design-your-own salad option. All meals start with fresh bread and a bowl of local olives. In the evening, crisp brick-oven pizzas are on offer.

Balcones de Puno   Peruvian $$

(📞051-36-5300; Libertad 354; mains S18-35; ⊗9am-10pm Mon-Sat) Dinner-show venue with traditional local food. The nightly show (7:30pm to 9pm) stands out for its quality and sincerity – no panpipe butchering of 'El Cóndor Pasa' here. Save room for dessert, a major focus of dining here. Reserve ahead for weekends.

La Casona   Peruvian $$

(📞051-35-1108; http://lacasona-restaurant.com; Lima 423, 2nd fl; mains S22-45; ⊗noon-9:30pm) A solid choice for upscale *criollo* (spicy Peruvian fare with Spanish and African influences) and international food, even if portions are on the small side. Trout comes bathed in garlic or chili sauce. There's also pasta, salad and soup.

Mareas Ceviche y Más   Ceviche $$

(www.fb.me/mareassocialpage; Cajamarca 448; mains S13-35; ⊗9am-4pm; 🛜) There are dozens of ways to do ceviche and seafood in this family-filled courtyard restaurant. If you can't decide between seafood pasta, squid fried rice, trout ceviche or ceviche *palteado* (with avocado), try a *combinado* (set combo) of ceviche, *chaufa* (fried rice) and battered fried fish.

Tulipans   Pizza $$

(📞051-35-1796; Lima 394; mains S15-30, menús S20; ⊗10am-10pm; 🛜) Highly recommended for its yummy sandwiches, big plates of meat and piled-high vegetables, this cozy spot is warmed by the pizza oven in the corner. It also has a selection of South American wines. The courtyard patio is attractive for warm days – whenever those happen! Pizzas are only available at night. Tulipans is inside La Casona Parodi.

🍷 DRINKING & NIGHTLIFE

Central Puno's nightlife is geared toward tourists, with lively bars scattered around the bright lights on Lima (where touts hand out free-drink coupons), the Plaza de Armas and Parque Pino, where live bands sometimes play on weekend evenings.

ℹ️ INFORMATION

iPerú (📞051-36-5088; Plaza de Armas, Lima at Deustua; ⊗9am-6pm Mon-Sat, to 1pm Sun) Patient, English-speaking staff offer good advice here. An excellent first port of call on arrival in Puno. Other useful iPerú offices are at the Terminal Terrestre and Juliaca airport.

ℹ️ GETTING THERE & AWAY

AIR

The nearest airport is in Juliaca, about an hour away. Hotels can book you a comfortable, safe shuttle bus for S15 or you can book directly with **Rossy Tours** (📞051-36-6709; www.rossytours.com; Tacna 308; ⊗office 9am-8pm). The earliest bus is timed to give you just enough time to check in for the earliest flight, so there is no need to stay in Juliaca. There is a **LAN** (📞051-36-7227; Tacna 299) office in Puno.

BUS

The **Terminal Terrestre** (📞051-36-4737; Primero de Mayo 703), three blocks down Ricardo Palma from Av El Sol, houses Puno's long-distance bus companies.

Buses leave for Cuzco every two to three hours from 4am to 10pm, and for Arequipa every three to four hours from 2am to 10pm. **Cruz del Sur** (📞in Lima 01-311-5050; www.cruzdelsur.com.pe; Terminal Terrestre) has the best services to both. **Turismo Mer** (📞051-36-7223; www.turismomer.com; Tacna 336; ⊗office 8am-1pm

Fiestas & Folklore

The folkloric capital of Peru, Puno boasts as many as 300 traditional dances and celebrates numerous fiestas throughout the year. Although dances often occur during celebrations of Catholic feast days, many have their roots in precolonial celebrations, usually tied in with the agricultural calendar. The dazzlingly ornate and imaginative costumes worn on these occasions are often worth more than an entire household's everyday clothes. Styles range from strikingly grotesque masks and animal costumes to glittering sequined uniforms.

Seeing street fiestas can be planned, but it's often simply a matter of luck. Some celebrations are localized to one town, whilst the whole region lets loose for others. Ask at the tourist office in Puno about any fiestas in the surrounding area while you're in town. Many countrywide fiestas are celebrated here, too.

If you plan to visit during a festival, either make reservations in advance or show up a few days early, and expect to pay premium rates for lodgings.

Traditional dance, Puno
JERSSON TELLO/SHUTTERSTOCK ©

& 3-8pm) buses to Cuzco are also comfortable. **Civa** (☏051-365-882; www.civa.com.pe; Terminal Zonal) goes to Lima and Arequipa.

The most enjoyable way to get to Cuzco is via **Inka Express** (☏051-36-5654; www.inkaexpress.com; Tacna 346; ⊙office 8am-7pm Mon-Fri,

9am-1pm & 4-7pm Sat & Sun); its luxury buses with panoramic windows depart every morning at 6.50am.

TRAIN

There are two train services to Cuzco. The sumptuous Belmond Andean Explorer train is an overnight sleeper service with three meals and cocktails included, coming at a hefty cost for five-star-hotel-like pampering. The cheaper PeruRail Titicaca service is a day trip.

Andean Explorer trains depart from Puno's **train station** (☏051-36-9179; www.perurail.com; Av La Torre 224; ⊙train station office 6:30am-noon & 4-6pm Mon-Fri, 6:30am-2:30pm Sat) at noon on Wednesdays, arriving at Cuzco around 7:40am the next day. Tickets cost from US$480 per person.

PeruRail Titicaca trains depart Mondays, Thursdays and Saturdays at 7:30am, and arrive in Cuzco at 5:50pm the same day. Tickets are US$260.

Reservations can be made online at www.perurail.com.

Juliaca

The region's only commercial airport makes Juliaca, the largest city on the altiplano, an unavoidable transit hub. The city bustles with commerce (and contraband) due to its location near the Bolivian border. Daytime muggings and drunks on the street are not uncommon. Since Juliaca has little to offer travelers, it is advisable to while away some hours in nearby Lampa or move on to Puno.

Hotels, restaurants, *casas de cambio* (foreign-exchange bureaus) and internet cafes abound along San Román, near Plaza Bolognesi. ATMs and banks are nearby on Nuñez.

Getting There & Away

The **airport** (Inca Manco Capac International Airport; JUL; ☏051-32-4248) is 2km west of town. **LATAM** (☏051-32-2228; San Roman 125; ⊙office 8am-7pm Mon-Fri, to 4pm Sat) has daily flights to/from Lima, Arequipa and Cuzco. **Avianca** (☏051-827-4951; www.avianca.com; Centro Comercial Real Plaza, Tumbes 391, Local LC-105; ⊙11am-8pm Mon-Fri, to 6pm Sat & Sun) also flies to Lima.

Lampa

The **Terminal Terrestre** (San Martín at Av Miraflores) houses long-distance bus companies. Buses leave for Cuzco every two hours from 5am to 11pm, and for Arequipa every two hours from 2:30am to 11:30pm.

Lampa

This charming little town, 36km northwest of Juliaca, is known as La Ciudad Rosada (the Pink City) for its dusty, pink-colored buildings. A significant commercial center in colonial days, it still shows a strong Spanish influence and its church is worth visiting for oddities such as its replica of Michelangelo's *Pietà* sculpture (there is another at the town hall). It's an excellent place to kill a few hours before flying out of Juliaca, or to spend a quiet night.

⊙ SIGHTS

Iglesia de Santiago Apostol   Church
(Plaza de Armas, Lampa; tour S10; ⊗9am-12:30pm & 2-4pm) Worth seeing and the pride of locals, this lime-mortar church includes fascinating features, such as a life-sized sculpture of *The Last Supper*; Santiago (St James) atop a real stuffed horse, returning from the dead to trample the Moors; creepy catacombs; secret tunnels; a domed tomb topped by a wonderful copy of Michelangelo's *Pietà*; and hundreds of skeletons arranged in a ghoulishly decorative skull-and-crossbones pattern. It truly has to be seen to be believed. Excellent Spanish-speaking guides are on hand daily.

Lampa Municipalidad   Notable Building
(⊗8am-4pm Mon-Fri) FREE In the small square beside the Plaza de Armas, the town hall is recognizable by its murals depicting Lampa's history – past, present and future. Inside there's a gorgeous courtyard, a replica of the *Pietà* (a second one is in the church) and a museum honoring noted Lampa-born painter Víctor Humareda (1920–86).

Museo Kampaq   Museum
(✐951-820-085; cnr Ayacucho & Ugarte; suggested donation S5; ⊗8am-6pm Mon-Fri) Staff at the shop opposite this museum,

Staying Healthy at Altitude

Ascend to nearly 4000 meters direct from the coast and you run a real risk of getting *soroche* (altitude sickness). Plan on spending some time in elevation stops such as Arequipa (2350m) or Cuzco (3326m) first to acclimatize, or take it very easy after arriving in Puno. Higher-end hotels (and even some buses) offer oxygen, but this is a temporary fix; your body still needs to acclimatize at its own pace.

High altitude makes for extreme weather conditions. Nights get especially cold, so check if your hotel provides heating. During the winter months of June to August (the tourist high season), temperatures can drop well below freezing. Meanwhile, days are very hot and sunburn is a common problem.

two blocks west of the Plaza de Armas, will give you a Spanish-language guided tour of the museum's small but significant collection. It includes pre-Inca ceramics and monoliths, plus one mummy. They may also show you a unique vase inscribed with the sacred cosmology of the Incas.

🛈 GETTING THERE & AWAY

Combis (minibuses) for Lampa (S2.50, 30 minutes) leave when full from Huáscar (five blocks north of Plaza Bolognesi along San Romàn) in Juliaca. If you have time to kill after checking in at Juliaca airport, get a taxi to drop you off in Lampa (S8, 35 minutes). There is no direct public transportation to/from Puno.

Pucará

More than 60km northwest of Juliaca, the sleepy village of Pucará is famous for its celebrations of **La Virgen del Carmen** (The Virgin of Carmen; Plaza de Armas; ☺Jul 16) and its earth-colored pottery – including the ceramic *toritos* (bulls) often seen perched on the roofs of Andean houses for good luck. Local workshops are open to the public and offer ceramics classes. The pre-Inca site Kalasaya lies above town, with some of its monoliths on show in the central Museo Lítico Pucará.

◎ SIGHTS

Kalasaya   Ruins
(Complejo Arqueológico de Pucará; admission S10; ☺9am-4pm) These pre-Inca ruins are spread out across a large area above the town and consist of nine pyramid-like structures, the largest of which gives the site its name. Kalasaya is a short way up Lima, west of the main plaza. Just S10 gets you into Kalasaya and the Museo Lítico Pucará at the Plaza de Armas, though there's nobody to check your ticket at the ruin.

The Kalasaya pyramid is constructed from stone monoliths and human head sculptures jut out from its walls. Other carved creatures include serpents and pumas. The center was used for offerings to the gods and Pucará culture became the central force in the Lake Titicaca region by 200 BC.

Museo Lítico Pucará   Museum
(Lima; admission S10; ☺8:30am-5pm Tue-Sun) The Museo Lítico Pucará displays a surprisingly good selection of anthropomorphic monoliths from the town's pre-Inca site, Kalasaya. The museum is next to the Plaza de Armas.

ⓘ GETTING THERE & AWAY

Buses to Juliaca (S3.50, one hour) run from 6am to 8pm from Jr 2 de Mayo.

South Shore Towns

Ichu

Ten kilometers out of Puno, this rural community, spread across a gorgeous green valley, is home to little-known Inca ruins – Centro Ceremonial Tunuhuire. With superb views, it's a great place for a hike.

Leave the Panamericana at Ichu's second exit (after the service station) and head inland past the house marked 'Villa Lago 1960.' Walk 2km, bearing left at the junction, aiming for the two small, terraced hills you can see in the left of the valley.

After bearing left at a second junction (you'll pass the school if you miss it), the road takes you between the two hills. Turn left again and head straight up the first one. Fifteen minutes of stiff climbing brings you to the top, where you'll be rewarded with the remains of a multi-layered temple complex, and breathtaking 360-degree views.

This can be done as an easy half-day trip from Puno, arranged by private tour. Take plenty of water and food as there's no store.

Chucuito

Quiet Chucuito's claim to fame is the outlandish **Templo de la Fertilidad** (Inca Uyu; Trucos; admission S8; ⊘9am-4:30pm); its grounds are populated with large stone phalluses. The underappreciated, real appeal of Chucuito is staying near a secluded part of Lake Titicaca and eating in the main plaza further uphill from the main road, which has two attractive colonial churches, **Santo Domingo** and **Nuestra Señora de la Asunción**.

With its location so close to Puno, despite feeling a world away, weekends are very popular with nostalgic visitors from the big smoke who want a taste of *pueblo* (village) life.

Santo Domingo, Chucuito

From left: Ceramic *torito* (bull), Pucará; Templo de la Fertilidad (p139) , Chucuito; San Juan de Letrán, Juli

Luquina Chico

This tiny community, 53km east of Puno on the Chucuito Peninsula, is stunning. If you want to relax in a rural community, Luquina Chico also boasts the best standard of homestay accommodations of any community around the lake. The community is making economic strides thanks to tourism.

Sweeping views of Puno, Juliaca and all the islands of the lake can be taken in from the headland's heights or the fertile flats by the lake. A lagoon forms in the wet season, attracting migrating wetland birds.

Chullpitas (miniature burial towers) are scattered all around this part of the peninsula. They are said to house the bodies of gentiles, little people who lived here in ancient times, before the sun was born and sent them underground.

Ask around town about renting kayaks. Edgar Adventures (p133) in Puno can also get you here on a mountain bike; a somewhat grueling but extremely scenic three-hour ride along the peninsula.

Juli

Sleepy Juli is a tourist-friendly stop. It's called Peru's *pequeña Roma* (little Rome) on account of its four colonial museum-like churches from the 16th and 17th centuries, which are slowly being restored. Churches are most likely to be open on Sundays, though opening hours here should not be taken as gospel. It's worth hammering on the door if one seems closed.

The imposing 1557 church of **Nuestra Señora de la Asunción** (Cusco; admission S5; ☺8:30am-5pm) has an expansive courtyard approach that may awaken an urge to oratory. Its interior is airy, and the pulpit is covered in gold leaf.

Other churches nearby include **Santa Cruz**, which has lost half its roof and remains closed for the foreseeable future, but its skeleton and facades are visible. The 1560 stone church of **San Pedro**, on the main plaza, is in the best condition, with carved ceilings and a marble baptismal font. Mass is celebrated here every Sunday at 8am.

Dating from 1570, the adobe baroque church of **San Juan de Letrán** (Jr San Juan;

CHRIS SALOMON/ALAMY STOCK PHOTO ©

admission S5; ⊘8:30am-5pm) contains richly framed *escuela cuzqueña* (Cuzco School) paintings that depict the lives of saints. It's two blocks north of the Plaza de Armas.

Pomata

Just beyond Juli, the road to Pomata runs along the south shore of Lake Titicaca, 105km from Puno. As you arrive, you'll see Dominican church **Templo de Pomata**

Santiago Apóstolo (Plaza de Armas; admission S2) – totally out of proportion with the town it dominates, in terms of both size and splendor – dramatically located on top of a small hill. Founded in 1700, it is known for its windows made of translucent alabaster and its intricately carved baroque sandstone facade. Look for the puma carvings – the town's name means 'place of the puma' in Aymara.

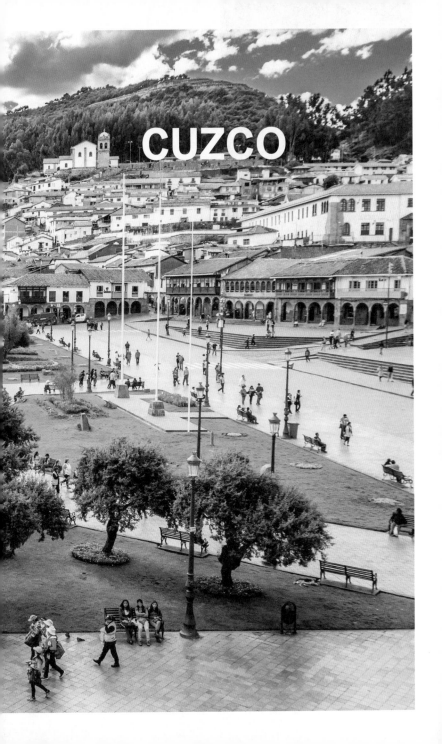

CUZCO

Cuzco at a Glance...

Cosmopolitan Inca capital Cuzco (also Cusco, or Qosq'o in Quechua) thrives with a measure of contradiction. Ornate cathedrals squat over Inca temples, massage hawkers ply the narrow cobblestone streets, a woman in traditional skirt and bowler hat offers bottled water to a pet llama, while the finest boutiques sell alpaca knits for small fortunes. The foremost city of the Inca Empire is now the undisputed archaeological capital of the Americas, as well as the continent's oldest continuously inhabited city. Few travelers to Peru will skip this premier South American destination, also the gateway to Machu Picchu.

Cuzco in Two Days

Visit the city's many museums. **Museo Quijote** (p163) is highly recommended for fine art; **El Museo de Arte Popular** (p164) for folksy art, and the **Museo Inka** (p161) and the **Museo Machu Picchu** (p161) for preconquest Peruvian artifacts. On the second day, see relics left by the Incas and Spanish conquistadors at **Qorikancha** (p150) and **La Catedral** (p157).

Cuzco in Four Days

Start day three with a *jugo* (fruit juice) in **Mercado San Pedro** (p170). Then follow the **walking tour** up through arty San Blas to the impressive fortress of **Sacsaywamán** (p152). Day four can be spent on one of the many nearby hikes, or pop back to San Blas to visit the **artisan workshops** (p170) and pick up some local textiles.

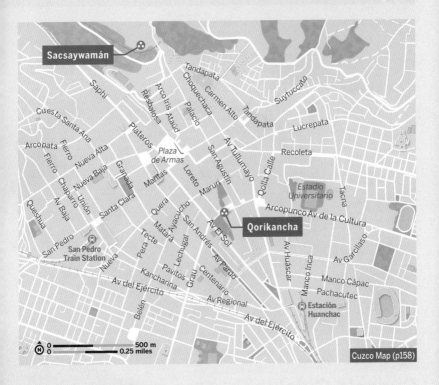

Cuzco Map (p158)

Arriving in Cuzco

Aeropuerto Internacional Alejandro Velazco Astete Official taxis from the airport to addresses near the city center cost S30 to S40. Plans are pending to build an airport in the Sacred Valley near Chinchero.

Terminal Terrestre The bus terminal lies around 2km out of town towards the airport; a taxi is about S30.

Where to Stay

Many of Cuzco's guesthouses and hotels are located in colonial buildings with interior courtyards, which can echo resoundingly with noise from other guests or the street outside. Old stone buildings are notorious for having poor wi-fi connections – often it can only be accessed in a lobby. Many places that offer breakfast start serving as early as 5am to accommodate those heading out on tour. For this reason, early check-ins and check-outs are the rule. For more information on the best neighborhood to stay in, see p179.

Alpaca steak

ANASTASIYA KOTELNYK/SHUTTERSTOCK ©

Cuzco's Cuisine

Cuzco's location, nearly dropping off the eastern edge of the Andes, gives it access to an unbelievable range of crops, from highland potatoes and quinoa to avocados and ají picante (hot chili).

Great For...

☑ **Don't Miss**

Sampling flavorsome *cuy* (guinea pig) – correctly prepared it makes an exceptional feast.

Cuzco Specialties

Sunday lunch with a country stroll is a Cuzco ritual. Locals head to the villages south of town: **Tipón** is the place to eat *cuy*, **Saylla** is the home of *chicharrón* (deep-fried pork) and **Lucre** is renowned for duck.

Look for the following foods in local restaurants, on the street and at festivals:

Anticucho Beef heart on a stick, punctuated by a potato, is the perfect evening street snack.

Caldo de gallina Healthy, hearty chicken soup is the local favorite to kick a hangover.

Cañazo Rustic bootleg versions of this potent sugarcane alcohol have long been the life of the village party. New distillery Caña Alta in Ollantaytambo produces a high-quality artisan version to make exquisite cocktails.

Fried *cuy* (guinea pig)

BY ELIUKOVA, OKSANA/GETTY IMAGES ©

Choclo con queso Huge, pale cobs of corn are served with a teeth-squeaking chunk of cheese in the Sacred Valley.

Cuy Guinea pig, raised on grains at home – what could be more organic? The faint of heart can ask for it served as a fillet (without the head and paws).

Grilled alpaca Lean and flavorful, this tender, high-protein meat has gone mainstream in upscale restaurants.

Lechón Suckling pig with plenty of crackling, served with tamales (corn cakes).

The Guinea Pig's Culinary Rise

Love it or loathe it, *cuy* is an Andean favorite that's been part of the local culinary repertoire since pre-Inca times. And before you dredge up childhood memories of cuddly mascots in protest, know that these rascally rodents were gracing Andean dinner plates long before anyone in the West considered them worthy pet material.

It's believed that *cuy* may have been domesticated as early as 7000 years ago in the mountains of southern Peru, where wild populations of *cuy* still roam today. Direct evidence from Chavín de Huántar shows that they were certainly cultivated across the Andes by 900 BC.

Cuy are practical animals to raise and have adapted well over the centuries to survive in environments ranging from the high Andean plains to the barren coastal deserts. You'll often see them scampering around Andean kitchens in true free-range style. *Cuy* are the ideal livestock alternative: they're high in protein, feed on kitchen scraps, breed profusely and require much less room and maintenance than traditional domesticated animals.

Inti Raymi, Plaza de Armas

Festivals & Events

Cuzco and the surrounding highlands celebrate many lively fiestas and holidays. Between them they provide riveting manifestations of both Andean and Catholic culture.

Great For...

☑ **Don't Miss**

June's Inti Raymi, Cuzco's drawcard festival.

El Señor de los Temblores

This procession through the Plaza de Armas takes place on Holy Monday, the Monday before Easter. It dates to the earthquake of 1650. El Señor de los Temblores' crucifix of the savior (now charred with soot) is considered the patron saint of Cuzco, responsible for saving the city from further earthquake damage.

Crucifix Vigil

On May 2 to 3, a Crucifix Vigil is held on all hillsides with crosses atop them.

Corpus Christi

Held on the ninth Thursday after Easter, Corpus Christi usually occurs in early June and features fantastic religious processions and celebrations in the cathedral.

The Q'oyoriti Pilgrimage

Incredibly elaborate costumes, days of dancing, repetitive brass-band music, fireworks and sprinklings of holy water: welcome to one of Peru's lesser-known, but most intense, festivals, Q'oyoriti (Star of the Snow).

Held at the foot of Ausangate the Tuesday before Corpus Christi, in late May or early June, this is a dizzy, delirious spectacle, yet no alcohol is involved or even allowed. Offenders are whipped by anonymous men dressed as *ukukus* (mountain spirits) with white masks that hide their features.

At 6384m, Ausangate is the Cuzco department's highest mountain and the most important *apu* (sacred deity) in the area. The subject of countless legends, it's the *pakarina* (mythical place of sacred origin)

of llamas and alpacas, and controls their health and fertility.

Q'oyoriti is a pilgrimage – the only way in is by trekking three or more hours up a cold mountain, arriving around dawn. The sight of a solid, endless line of people quietly wending their way up or down the track and disappearing around a bend in the mountain is unforgettable, as is Q'oyoriti's eerie, otherworldly feel.

Many *cuzqueños* (inhabitants of Cuzco) believe that if you attend Q'oyoriti three times, you'll get your heart's desire.

Inti Raymi

Cuzco's most important festival is **Inti Raymi** (Festival of the Sun; ⊙24 Jun). Visitors from throughout Peru and the world join the whole city celebrating in the streets with dancing and parades. The festival culminates in a re-enactment of the Inca winter-solstice festival at Sacsaywamán. Despite its commercialization, it's still worth seeing the pageantry in the city and at Sacsaywamán.

Qorikancha during the Inti Raymi festival

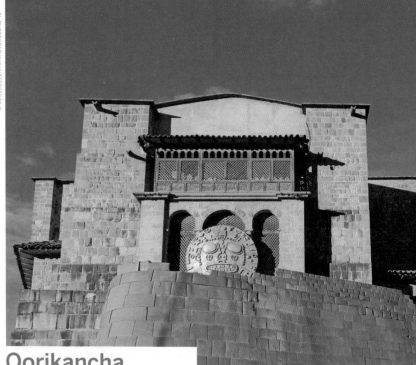

Qorikancha

Built in the mid-15th century during the reign of the 10th inca (king), Túpac Yupanqui, Qorikancha was once the richest temple in the Inca empire; all that remains today is the masterful stonework.

Great For...

☑ Don't Miss

Paintings outside the courtyard depicting God's guard dogs (*dominicanus* in Latin) holding torches.

Post-conquest, Francisco Pizarro gave Qorikancha to his brother Juan who bequeathed it to the Dominicans. It remains in their possession today and forms the base of the colonial church and convent of Santo Domingo. Its site is a bizarre combination of Inca and colonial architecture, topped with a roof of glass and metal.

In Inca times, Qorikancha (Quechua for 'Golden Courtyard') was literally covered with gold. The temple walls were lined with some 700 solid-gold sheets, each weighing about 2kg. There were life-sized gold and silver replicas of corn, which were ceremonially 'planted' in agricultural rituals. Also reported were solid-gold treasures such as altars, llamas and babies, as well as a replica of the sun, which was lost. Within months of the arrival of the first

MARKTUCAN/SHUTTERSTOCK ©

ℹ Need to Know

☏084-24-9176; Plazoleta Santo Domingo; admission S15 or boleto turístico; ⊗8:30am-5:30pm Mon-Sat, 2-5pm Sun

✕ Take a Break

Head to Pampa de Castillo near Qorikancha, where local workers lunch on Cuzco classics.

★ Top Tip

If you visit only one site in Cuzco, make it these Inca ruins.

conquistadors, this incredible wealth had all been looted and melted down.

Rituals

Various religious rites took place in the temple. It is said that the mummified bodies of several previous *incas* were kept here, brought out into the sunlight each day and offered food and drink, which was then ritually burnt. Qorikancha was also an observatory where high priests monitored celestial activities. Most of this is left to the imagination of the modern visitor, but the remaining stonework ranks with the finest Inca architecture in Peru.

Architecture

Once inside the site, the visitor enters a courtyard. The octagonal font in the middle was originally covered with 55kg of solid gold. Inca chambers lie to either side of the courtyard. The largest, to the right, were said to be temples to the moon and the stars, and were covered with sheets of solid silver. The walls are perfectly tapered upward and, with their niches and doorways, are excellent examples of Inca trapezoidal architecture. The fitting of the individual blocks is so precise that in some places you can't tell where one block ends and the next begins.

Opposite these chambers, on the other side of the courtyard, are smaller temples dedicated to thunder and the rainbow. Three holes have been carved through the walls of this section to the street outside, which scholars think were drains, either for sacrificial *chicha* (fermented corn beer), blood or, more mundanely, rainwater.

TEREKHOV IGOR/SHUTTERSTOCK ©

Sacsaywamán

This immense ruin of both religious and military significance is 2km from Cuzco. The long Quechua name means 'Satisfied Falcon,' though tourists will inevitably remember it by the mnemonic 'sexy woman.'

Sacsaywamán feels huge, but only about 20% of the original structure remains. Soon after the conquest, the Spaniards tore down many walls and used the blocks to build their own houses, leaving the largest and most impressive rocks, especially the main battlements.

Rebel Base

In 1536 the fort was the site of one of the most bitter battles of the Spanish conquest. More than two years after Pizarro's entry into Cuzco, the rebellious Manco Inca recaptured the lightly guarded Sacsaywamán and used it as a base to lay siege to the conquistadors in Cuzco. Manco was on the brink of defeating the Spaniards when a desperate last-ditch attack by 50 Spanish cavalry led by Juan Pizarro, Francisco's brother, succeeded in retaking Sacsaywamán and

Great For...

☑ Don't Miss

Arriving at dawn (though not alone, for safety) to have the site almost to yourself.

⊗ Need to Know

The *boleto turístico* (tourist ticket) for entry to **Sacsaywamán** (boleto turístico adult/student S130/70; ⊙7am-5:30pm) is valid for 10 days and covers 16 other sites.

✕ Take a Break

Bring snacks and water as there are no decent food stalls near the site.

★ Top Tip

To walk up to the site from the Plaza de Armas takes 30 to 50 minutes; make sure you're acclimatized before attempting it.

effective defense mechanism that forced attackers to expose their flanks.

Five Thousand Warriors

Opposite is the hill called Rodadero, with retaining walls, polished rocks and a finely carved series of stone benches known as the Inca's Throne. Three towers once stood above these walls. Only the foundations remain, but the 22m diameter of the largest, Muyuc Marca, gives an indication of how big they must have been. With its perfectly fitted stone conduits, this tower was probably used as a huge water tank for the garrison. Other buildings within the ramparts provided food and shelter for an estimated 5000 warriors. Most of these structures were torn down by the Spaniards and later inhabitants of Cuzco.

putting an end to the rebellion. Manco Inca survived and retreated to the fortress of Ollantaytambo, but most of his forces were killed. Thousands of dead littered the site after the Incas' defeat, attracting swarms of carrion-eating Andean condors. The tragedy was memorialized by the inclusion of eight condors in Cuzco's coat of arms.

Zigzag Fortifications

The site is composed of three different areas, the most striking being the magnificent three-tiered zigzag fortifications. One stone, incredibly, weighs more than 300 tons. It was the ninth *inca,* Pachacutec, who envisioned Cuzco in the shape of a puma, with Sacsaywamán as the head, and these 22 zigzagged walls as the teeth of the puma. The walls also formed an extremely

Walking Tour: Cuzco

At every turn Cuzco's architecture exhibits the collision of the city's Inca and colonial past. There are refreshments everywhere, and small supermarkets near Plaza de Armas.

Start Plaza de Armas
End Sacsaywamán
Length 4km; three hours

2 As you pass through **Plaza Regocijo**, there is a beautiful building on your left, once a hotel that now houses restaurants and chic boutiques.

3 Calle Garcilaso is named for the Inca chronicler Garcilaso de la Vega, whose childhood home now houses the **Museo Histórico Regional** (p162).

4 On Sundays, Quechua-speaking country folk meet in **Plaza San Francisco**. Drop in to the **church and museum of San Francisco** (p161).

5 If it's open, peek inside the **church and convent of Santa Clara**. The mirrors were used in colonial times to entice curious indigenous people into the church.

Take a Break...
Get a juice from a stall at **Mercado San Pedro** (p170).

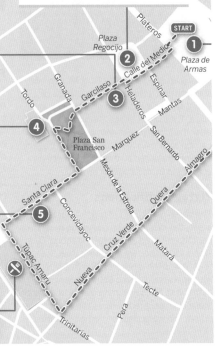

10 Last, forge uphill to **Sacsaywamán** (p152).

Classic Photo: Plaza San Blas.

9 From **Plaza San Blas**, Cuzco's bohemian HQ, head along **Tandapata** for the classic cobblestone experience.

1 Start from the stunning **Plaza de Armas** (p156).

8 The **Museo de Arte Religioso** (p161) is housed in the former palace of the sixth *inca*, Roca. Its wall on Hatunrumiyoc is home to the **12-sided stone**.

7 The east wall of **Loreto**, a walkway with Inca walls on both sides, is one of the best and oldest in Cuzco, belonging to the Acllahuasi (House of the Chosen Women). Post conquest, it became part of the **closed convent of Santa Catalina** (p162).

6 The **Palacio de Justicia** is a big white building with llamas mowing the back garden.

0 — 200 m
0 — 0.1 miles

2 ROSEMARY CALVERT/GETTY IMAGES © 6 ALEXANDREFAGUNDES/GETTY IMAGES © 9 SAMOSP/SHUTTERSTOCK ©

◉ SIGHTS

While the city is sprawling, areas of interest to visitors are generally within walking distance, with some steep hills in between. The center of the city is the Plaza de Armas, while traffic-choked Av El Sol nearby is the main business thoroughfare. Walking just a few blocks north or east of the plaza will lead you to steep, twisting cobblestone streets, little changed for centuries. The flatter areas to the south and west are the commercial center.

The alley heading away from the northwest side of the Plaza de Armas is Procuradores (Tax Collectors), nicknamed 'Gringo Alley' for its tourist restaurants, tour agents and other services. Watch out for predatory touts. Beside the hulking cathedral on the Plaza de Armas, narrow Calle Triunfo leads steeply uphill toward Plaza San Blas, the heart of Cuzco's eclectic, artistic *barrio* (neighborhood).

A resurgence of indigenous pride means many streets have been signposted with new Quechua names, although they are still commonly referred to by their Spanish names. The most prominent example is Calle Triunfo, which is signposted as Sunturwasi.

◉ Central Cuzco

Plaza de Armas   Plaza
In Inca times, the plaza, called Huacaypata or Aucaypata, was the heart of the capital. Today it's the nerve center of the modern city. Two flags usually fly here – the red-and-white Peruvian flag and the rainbow-colored flag of Tahuantinsuyo. Easily mistaken for an international gay-pride banner, it represents the four quarters of the Inca empire.

Colonial arcades surround the plaza, which in ancient times was twice as large, also encompassing the area now called the Plaza Regocijo. On the plaza's northeastern side is the imposing cathedral, fronted by a large flight of stairs and flanked by the churches of **Jesús María** and **El Triunfo** (Triunfo s/n). On the southeastern side is the strikingly ornate church of La Compañía de Jesús (p161). The quiet pedestrian alleyway of Loreto, which has Inca walls, is a historic means of access to the plaza.

La Catedral

ARTMARIE/GETTY IMAGES ©

It's worth visiting the plaza at least twice – by day and by night – as it takes on a strikingly different look after dark, when it is all lit up.

La Catedral
Church

(Plaza de Armas; adult/student S25/12.50; ⏲10am-5:45pm) A squatter on the site of Viracocha Inca's palace, the cathedral was built using blocks pilfered from the nearby Inca site of Sacsaywamán. Its construction started in 1559 and took almost a century. It is joined by Iglesia del Triunfo (p156) (1536) to its right and **Iglesia de Jesús María** (1733) to the left.

The cathedral is one of the city's greatest repositories of colonial art, especially for works from the *escuela cuzqueña* (Cuzco school), noted for its decorative combination of 17th-century European devotional painting styles with the color palette and iconography of indigenous Andean artists. A classic example is the frequent portrayal of the Virgin Mary wearing a mountain-shaped skirt with a river running around its hem, identifying her with Pachamama (Mother Earth).

One of the most famous paintings of the *escuela cuzqueña* is *The Last Supper* by Quechua artist Marcos Zapata. Found in the northeast corner of the cathedral, it depicts one of the most solemn occasions in the Christian faith, but graces it with a small feast of Andean ceremonial food; look for the plump and juicy-looking roast *cuy* (guinea pig) stealing the show with its feet held plaintively in the air.

Also look for the oldest surviving painting in Cuzco, showing the entire city during the great earthquake of 1650. The inhabitants can be seen parading around the plaza with a crucifix, praying for the earthquake to stop, which it miraculously did. This precious crucifix, called **El Señor de los Temblores** (The Lord of the Earthquakes), can still be seen in the alcove to the right of the door leading into El Triunfo. Every year on Holy Monday, the Señor is taken out on **parade** (The Lord of the Earthquakes; ⏲Mar/Apr) and devotees throw *ñucchu* flowers at him – these resemble droplets

Cuzco's Boleto Turístico

To visit most sites in the region, you will need Cuzco's official *boleto turístico* (tourist ticket; adult/student S130/70), valid for 10 days. Among the 17 sites included are Sacsaywamán, Q'enqo, Pukapukara, Tambomachay, Piquillacta, Tipón, Museo de Arte Popular, Pisac, Ollantaytambo, Chinchero and Moray, as well as an evening performance of Andean dances and live music at the Centro Qosqo de Arte Nativo. While some inclusions are admitted duds, you can't visit any of them without it.

Three partial tickets (adult/student S70/35) cover the ruins immediately outside Cuzco, the museums in Cuzco, and the Sacred Valley ruins. They are valid for one day, except for the Sacred Valley option, which is valid for two.

Purchase *boletos turístico* from **DIRCETUR** (✆084-58-2030 ext 2000; www.dirceturcusco.gob.pe; Garcilaso s/n, Museo Historico Regional; ⏲7am-7:30pm Mon-Sat) or at the sites themselves, except for the Centro Qosqo de Arte Nativo. Students must show valid ID.

The *boleto circuito religioso* (religious circuit ticket; adult/student S30/15), also valid for 10 days, secures entry to Cuzco's churches, the Museo de Arte Religioso and Cuzco's most significant display of contemporary art at Museo Quijote. It's available at any of the sites.

Sacsaywamán
MATYAS REHAK/GETTY IMAGES ©

of blood and represent the wounds of crucifixion. The flowers leave a sticky residue

Cuzco

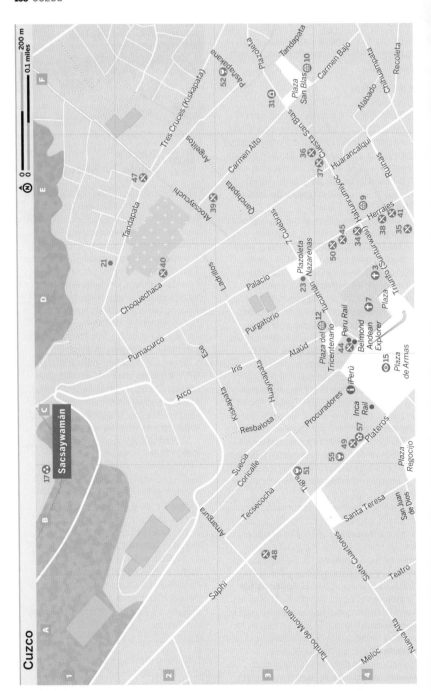

Sacsaywamán

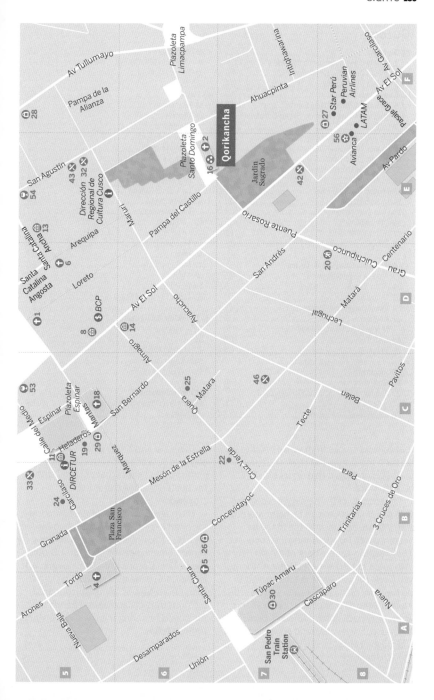

Cuzco

that collects smoke from votive candles lit beneath the statue: this is why he's now black. Legend has it that under his skirt, he's lily white.

The sacristy of the cathedral is covered with paintings of Cuzco's bishops, starting with Vicente de Valverde, the friar who accompanied Pizarro during the conquest. The crucifixion at the back of the sacristy is attributed to the Flemish painter Anthony van Dyck, though some guides claim it to be the work of the 17th-century Spaniard Alonso Cano. The original wooden altar is at the very back of the cathedral, behind the present silver altar, and opposite both is the magnificently carved choir, dating from the 17th century.

There are also many glitzy silver and gold side chapels with elaborate platforms and altars that contrast with the austerity of the cathedral's stonework.

The huge main doors of the cathedral are open to genuine worshippers between 6am and 10am. Religious festivals are a superb time to see the cathedral. During the feast of Corpus Christi, for example, it is filled with pedestals supporting larger-than-life statues of saints, surrounded by thousands of candles and bands of musicians honoring them with mournful Andean tunes.

Iglesia de La Compañía de Jesús   Church

(Plaza de Armas; admission S10; ⊙9am-5pm Mon-Sat, 9-10:30am & 12:45-5pm Sun) Built upon the palace of Huayna Cápac, the last *inca* to rule an undivided, unconquered empire, the church was built by the Jesuits in 1571 and reconstructed after the 1650 earthquake. Two large canvases near the main door show early marriages in Cuzco in wonderful period detail. Local student guides are available to show you around the church, as well as the grand view from the choir on the 2nd floor, reached via rickety steps. Tips are gratefully accepted.

The Jesuits planned to make this the most magnificent of Cuzco's churches. The archbishop of Cuzco, however, complained that its splendor should not rival that of the cathedral, and the squabble grew to a point where Pope Paul III was called upon to arbitrate. His decision was in favor of the cathedral, but by the time word had reached Cuzco, La Compañía de Jesús was just about finished, complete with an incredible baroque facade and Peru's biggest altar, all crowned by a soaring dome.

Museo de Arte Religioso   Museum

(cnr Hatunrumiyoc & Herrajes; admission S10; ⊙8am-6pm) Originally the palace of Inca Roca, the foundations of this museum were converted into a grand colonial residence and later became the archbishop's palace. The beautiful mansion is now home to a religious-art collection notable for the accuracy of its period detail, and especially its insight into the interaction of indigenous peoples with the Spanish conquistadors.

There are also some impressive ceilings and colonial-style tile work that's not original, having been replaced during the 1940s.

Museo Machu Picchu   Museum

(Casa Concha; ☑084-25-5535; Santa Catalina Ancha 320; adult/child S20/10; ⊙8am-7pm Mon-Fri, 9am-5pm Sat) This newish museum exhibits 360 pieces from Machu Picchu taken by Hiram Bingham's expeditions and recently returned by Yale University, including lithic and metals, ceramics and

bones. The collection shows the astounding array of fine handicrafts and ceramics acquired from throughout the vast Incan empire. There's also good background on the Bingham expeditions with informative documentaries (subtitled). Signs are in English and Spanish.

Museo Inka   Museum

(☑084-23-7380; http://museoinka.unsaac.edu. pe; Tucumán near Ataúd; admission S10; ⊙8am-6pm Mon-Fri, 9am-4pm Sat) The charmingly modest Museo Inka, a steep block northeast of the Plaza de Armas, is the best museum in town for those interested in the Incas. The restored interior is jam-packed with a fine collection of metal- and gold-work, jewelry, pottery, textiles, mummies, models and the world's largest collection of *queros* (ceremonial Inca wooden drinking vessels). There's excellent interpretive information in Spanish, and English-speaking guides are usually available for a small fee.

The museum building, which rests on Inca foundations, is also known as the Admiral's House, after the first owner, Admiral Francisco Aldrete Maldonado. It was badly damaged in the 1650 earthquake and rebuilt by Pedro Peralta de los Ríos, the count of Laguna, whose crest is above the porch. Further damage from the 1950 earthquake has now been fully repaired, restoring the building to its position among Cuzco's finest colonial houses. Look for the massive stairway guarded by sculptures of mythical creatures, and the corner window column that from the inside looks like a statue of a bearded man but from the outside appears to be a naked woman. The ceilings are ornate, and the windows give good views straight out across the Plaza de Armas.

Downstairs in the sunny courtyard, highland Andean weavers demonstrate their craft and sell traditional textiles directly to the public.

Iglesia San Francisco   Church

(Plaza San Francisco; museum admission S15; ⊙9am-6pm) More austere than many of Cuzco's other churches, Iglesia San Francisco dates from the 16th and 17th

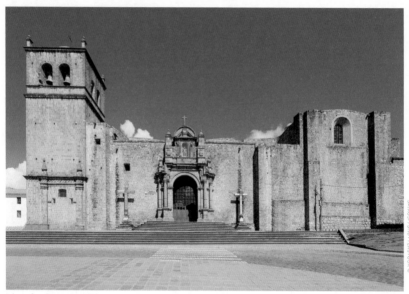

Iglesia San Francisco (p161)

centuries and is one of the few that didn't need to be completely reconstructed after the 1650 earthquake. It has a large collection of colonial religious paintings and a beautifully carved cedar choir.

The attached **museum** supposedly houses the largest painting in South America, which measures 9m by 12m and shows the family tree of St Francis of Assisi, the founder of the Franciscan order. Also of macabre interest are the two crypts, which are not totally underground. Inside are human bones, some of which have been carefully arranged in designs meant to remind visitors of the transitory nature of life.

Iglesia y Monasterio de Santa Catalina
Church

(Arequipa s/n; admission S8; ⊙8:30am-1pm & 2-5:30pm Mon-Sat) This convent houses many colonial paintings of the *escuela cuzqueña*, as well as an impressive collection of vestments and other intricate embroidery. The baroque side chapel features dramatic friezes, and many life-sized (and sometimes startling) models of nuns praying, sewing and going about their lives. The convent also houses 13 real, live contemplative nuns.

Museo Histórico Regional
Museum

(Garcilaso at Heladeros; boleto turístico adult/student S130/70; ⊙8am-5pm) This eclectic museum is housed in the colonial Casa Garcilaso de la Vega, the house of the Inca-Spanish chronicler who now lies buried in the cathedral. The chronologically arranged collection begins with arrowheads from the Preceramic Period and continues with ceramics and jewelry of the Wari, Pukara and Inca cultures. Admission is with the *boleto turístico* (tourist ticket) only, which is valid for 10 days and covers 16 other sites.

Templo y Convento de La Merced
Church

(☎084-23-1821; Mantas 121; admission S10; ⊙8am-12:30pm & 2-5:30pm Mon-Sat, cloister 8-11am) Cuzco's third most important colonial church, La Merced was destroyed in the 1650 earthquake, but was quickly rebuilt. To the left of the church, at the back of a small courtyard, is the entrance to the monastery and museum. Paintings based on the life of San Pedro Nolasco, who founded the order of La Merced in Barcelona in 1218, hang on the walls of the beautiful colonial **cloister**.

The church on the far side of the cloister contains the tombs of two of the most famous conquistadors: Diego de Almagro and Gonzalo Pizarro (brother of Francisco). Also on the far side of the cloister is a small religious museum that houses vestments rumored to have belonged to conquistador and friar Vicente de Valverde. The museum's most famous possession is a priceless solid-gold monstrance, 1.2m high and covered with rubies, emeralds and no fewer than 1500 diamonds and 600 pearls. Ask to see it if the display room is locked.

Museo Quijote   Museum

(Galería Banco la Nacion, Almagro s/n; ⊘9am-6pm Mon-Fri, to 1pm Sun) FREE Housed inside a bank, this privately owned museum of contemporary art houses a diverse, thoughtful collection of painting and sculpture ranging from the folksy to the macabre. There's good interpretive information about 20th-century Peruvian art history, some of it translated into English.

San Blas

Known as the artists' neighborhood, San Blas is nestled on a steep hillside next to the center. With classic architecture, its signature blue doors and narrow passageways without cars, it has become a hip attraction full of restaurants, watering holes and shops.

Museo de la Coca   Museum

(☑979-711-403; museodelacoca@hotmail.com; Plaza San Blas 618; admission S10; ⊘9am-7pm) A good primer on Andean culture, this is a wonderful and kitschy little museum that traces the uses of the coca leaf, from sacred ritual to its more insidious incarnations. Exhibits are labeled in both English and Spanish. Tips are suggested for guided visits.

⚠ Warning: Your Sacred Vision For Sale

Shamanic ceremonies may be native to the Amazon, but they have become a hot commodity in Cuzco and the Sacred Valley. The psychedelic properties of the San Pedro and *ayahuasca* plants have earned them fame and the interest of psychonauts who travel in search of these experiences.

Extremely powerful drugs, they can be highly toxic in the wrong hands. In 2018 a Canadian man was lynched in the Amazon region by an angry mob who believed he had killed a Shipibo healer. In 2015 a tourist fatally stabbed another traveler while both were under the drug's influence. In some cases, female guests have been attacked while under the influence as well.

Yet the commercial industry is insatiable. In Cuzco, San Pedro is offered alongside massages by street hawkers; *ayahuasca* ceremonies are advertised in hostels. It's important to note that these are not recreational drugs. A real shaman knows the long list of dos and don'ts for practitioners, and may screen participants. Ceremonies can require multiple days for preparation, fasting and extended rituals. Serious operations often use a medical questionnaire.

Many locals believe that it's a mockery to make these sacred ceremonies into moneymakers. While we don't recommend taking part, research your options and avoid casual opportunities if you do decide to participate.

Ayahuasca ceremony
BRIAN VAN TIGHEM/ALAMY STOCK PHOTO ©

From left: Ceiling panel, Iglesia de Santo Domingo; Hiking in the Cuzco region; The Inca Trail (p210)

⊙ Avenida Sol & Downhill

Iglesia de Santo Domingo   Church

The church of Santo Domingo is next door to Qorikancha (p151). Less baroque and ornate than many of Cuzco's churches, it is notable for its charming paintings of arch-angels depicted as Andean children in jeans and T-shirts. Opening hours are erratic.

Museo de Arte Popular   Museum

(☑084-25-8089; Basement, Av El Sol 103; admission S5; ⊘9am-6pm Mon-Sat, 8am-1pm Sun) Winning entries in Cuzco's annual Popular Art Competition are displayed in this engaging museum. This is where the artisans and artists of San Blas showcase their talents in styles ranging from high art to cheeky, offering a fascinating, humorous take on ordinary life amid the pomp and cir-cumstance of a once-grandiose culture.

Small-scale ceramic models depict drunken debauchery in a *picantería* (local restaurant), torture in a dentist's chair, carnage in a butcher shop, and even a caesarean section. There's also a display of photographs, many by renowned local photographer Martín Chambi, of Cuzco

from the 1900s to the 1950s, including striking images of the aftermath of the 1950 earthquake in familiar streets.

⊕ ACTIVITIES

Scores of outdoor outfitters in Cuzco offer trekking, rafting and mountain-biking adventures, as well as mountaineering, horseback riding and paragliding. Price wars can lead to bad feelings among locals, with underpaid guides and overcrowded vehicles. The cheaper tours usually take more guests and use guides with a more basic skill set.

⊕ Hiking

The department of Cuzco is a hiker's paradise. Ecosystems range from rainforest to high alpine environments in these enormous mountain ranges. Trekkers may come upon isolated villages and ruins lost in the undergrowth. Altitudes vary widely, it is essential to acclimatize properly before undertaking any trek.

Of course, most visitors come to hike the famed Inca Trail to Machu Picchu. Be

PICTUREGARDEN/GETTY IMAGES ©

aware that it's not the only 'Inca trail.' What savvy tourism officials and tour operators have christened the Inca Trail is just one of dozens of footpaths that the Incas built to reach Machu Picchu, out of thousands that crisscrossed the Inca empire. Some of these overland routes are still being dug out of the jungle by archaeologists. Many more have been developed for tourism, and an ever-increasing number of trekkers are choosing them.

Closer to Cuzco, multiday Sacred Valley trekking itineraries go well off the beaten track to little-visited villages and ruins.

Further afield, recommended treks include Lares and Ausangate and, for archaeological sites, Choquequirao and Vilcabamba.

Apus Peru   Hiking

(🔗084-23-2691; www.apus-peru.com; Cuichipun-co 366; ⏰9am-1pm & 3-7pm Mon-Sat) A rec-ommended outfitter for the Inca Trail and others, also offering conventional tours. Responsible and popular with travelers. The company joins the Choquequirao trek with the Inca Trail for a total of nine days of

spectacular scenery and an ever-more-impressive parade of Inca ruins, culminat-ing in Machu Picchu.

Alpaca Expeditions   Hiking

(🔗084-254-278; www.alpacaexpeditions.com; Heladeros 157, piso 2 No 24; ⏰9am-7:30pm Mon-Fri, 4:30-7:30pm Sat & Sun) ✈ A popular outfitter for the Inca Trail, Sacred Valley treks, Salkantay and Choquequirao, this is one of the few companies to prioritize hiring female guides and porters. Also uses portable bathrooms, plants trees and participates in trail cleanup.

Peru Eco Expeditions   Hiking

(🔗084-60-7516, 957-349-269; www.perueco expeditions.com; Urb San Judas Chico II D-13; ⏰9am-4pm Mon-Fri) ✈ A small luxury adventure travel company with custom expeditions ranging from day trips to lodge hikes and trips, such as the Inca Trail and Rainbow Mountain (with mountain biking or a cultural stop), throughout the region and in the Amazon. With sustainable tour-ism practices ranging from filtered water and 100% waste removal on treks to cultur-al sensitivity toward local communities.

Wayki Trek Hiking

(☎084-22-4092; www.waykitrek.net; Quera 239; ⏰9am-7pm Mon-Fri, to 1pm Sat) 🏃 A popular Inca Trail outfitter that earns rave reviews. It also does Choquequirao, Salkantay and Ausangate treks. ISO certified.

🌀 Rafting

Rafting (river running) isn't regulated in Peru – literally anyone can start a rafting company. On top of this, aggressive bargaining has led to lax safety by many cheaper rafting operators. The degree of risk cannot be stressed enough: there are deaths every year. Rafting companies that take advance bookings online are generally more safety conscious (and more expensive) than those just operating out of storefronts in Cuzco.

When choosing an outfitter, it's wise to ask about safety gear and guide training, ask about the quality of the equipment used (ie how old are the flotation devices) and check other traveler comments. It's essential to book a top-notch outfitter employing highly experienced rafting guides

with first-aid certification and knowledge of swift-water rescue techniques. Be wary of new agencies without a known track record.

In terms of locations, there are a number of rivers to choose from. Rivers further from Cuzco are days away from help in the event of illness or accident.

🌀 Mountain Biking

Mountain-biking tours are a growing industry in Cuzco, and the local terrain is superb. Rental bikes are poor quality and it is most common to find *rígida* (single suspension) models, which can make for bone-chattering downhills. Good new or secondhand bikes are not easy to buy in Cuzco either. If you're a serious mountain biker, consider bringing your own bike from home.

If you're an experienced rider, some awesome rides are quickly and easily accessible by public transport. Take the Pisac bus (stash your bike on top) and ask to be let off at **Abra de Ccorao**. From here, you can turn right and make your way back to Cuzco via a series of cart tracks and single track.

MATTHEW WILLIAMS-ELLIS/GETTY IMAGES ©

🍴 COURSES

Cuzco is one of the best places in South America to study Spanish. Shop around – competition is fierce and students benefit with free cultural and social activities. Salsa lessons and cooking nights are more or less ubiquitous.

The standard deal is 20 hours of classes per week, either individual or in groups of up to four people. Most schools will also let you pay by the hour or study more or less intensively.

Visit your school on a Friday to get tested and assigned to a group for a Monday start, or show up any time to start individual lessons. All schools can arrange family homestays and volunteer opportunities.

Excel Language Center   Language

(📞084-23-5298; www.excelspanishperu.info; Cruz Verde 336; ⏰8am-1pm & 4-9pm Mon-Fri, 9am-noon Sat) A Spanish-language program that has been highly recommended for its professionalism. Also offers lodging.

Marcelo Batata
Cooking Class   Cooking

(📞984-384-520; www.cuzcodining.com; Calle Palacio 135; 4hr course S297; ⏰2pm) If you've fallen for Peruvian cooking, this four-hour course is a worthwhile foray. A fully stocked market pantry demystifies the flavors of the region and the kitchen setup is comfortable. Includes appetizers, a pisco (Peruvian grape brandy) tasting and a main course. In English, Spanish or Portuguese. Accommodates vegetarians, and there's a private-course option.

🎫 TOURS

Cuzco has hundreds of registered travel agencies, so ask other travelers for recommendations. Many of the small agencies clustered around Procuradores and Plateros earn commissions selling trips run by other outfitters, which can lead to organizational mix-ups. If the travel agency also sells ponchos, changes money and has

🔭 The Ruins of Choquequirao

Remote, spectacular, and still not entirely cleared, the ruins of Choquequirao are often described as a mini–Machu Picchu. This breathtaking site at the junction of three rivers currently requires a challenging four-day hike to get there and back, though you will be happy if you budget more time for it.

Many see it as 'the next big thing' in Inca ruins tourism. In fact, the Peruvian government has already approved controversial plans to put in a tramway, the country's first, with a capacity of 3000 visitors daily. It would bring this remote attraction to within 15 minutes of the nearby highway. Conservationists worry about its potential impact.

For now, you can still go without the crowds. Most Cuzco trekking operators go. Travelers can also organize the walk on their own, but it is remote and its steepness makes it very challenging, especially if you're carrying a heavy pack.

Wall with image of a llama, Choquequirao
GLOWIMAGES/GETTY IMAGES ©

an internet cabin in the corner, chances are it's not operating your tour.

At tourist sites, freelance guides speak some English or other foreign languages. For more extensive tours at major sites, such as Qorikancha or the cathedral, always agree to a fair price in advance. Otherwise, a respectable minimum tip for a short tour is S5 per person in a small group and a little more for individuals.

Center for Traditional Textiles of Cuzco (p170)

Alain Machaca Cruz   Tours

(☎984-056-635; www.alternativeincatrails.com;
Belen s/n, Paruro) This independent guide
based outside Cuzco leads Laguna Yanahuara and multiday hikes to Choquequirao,
Vilcabamba and other areas. He also makes
recommended tours to the village of Paruro
where you can make *chicha* (fermented
corn beer) or see *cuy* (guinea pig) farms.
Quechua and English spoken. There's no
set office hours, contact ahead.

Andean Photo
Expeditions   . Tour

(☎960-724-103; www.andeanphotoexpeditions.
com; photo tour S248) Run by Peru enthusi-
asts, this highly personalized guide service
offers recommended photo tours in Cuzco
and Lima. It also specializes in off-the-
beaten-path trips, such as trips to Rainbow
Mountain via Cusipata with a homestay,
Ausangate mountain treks and jungle
trips. The co-owner is an accomplished
photographer with work in Cuzco galleries.
It offers services in multiple languages.

Crees   Ecotour

(☎084-26-2433, in UK 0-207-193-8759; www.
crees-manu.org; Urb Mariscal Garmarra B-5, Zona
1; ⊙9am-5pm Mon-Fri, to noon Sat) Crees runs
'voluntourism' trips into the Manu Area's
zona reservada in the Amazon Basin. It also
runs long-term volunteer projects (up to
16 weeks) where you'll be directly helping
communities in and around Manu – based
at Manu Learning Centre. It welcomes
queries at its office.

Culturas Peru   Adventure

(☎084-24-3629; www.culturasperu.com;
Tandapata 354-A; ⊙9am-5pm Mon-Fri) A
highly knowledgeable and reputable, locally
owned and run outfitter with sustainable
practices. Its two-day Inca Trail option is
popular.

Inkaterra   Adventure

(☎in Cuzco 084-24-5314, in UK 0-800-458-7506,
in US & Canada 1-800-442-5042; www.inkaterra.
com; Plazoleta Nazarenas 211; ⊙8am-6pm Mon-
Sat) This tour operator, also with an office in
Lima, manages two cracking lodges on the
Río Tamopata in the Amazon Basin:

Hacienda Concepción (📞in UK 0044-800-458-7506, in US 1-800-442-5042; www.inkaterra.com; s/d 3 days & 2 nights per person US$521/844) ✈ and **Inkaterra Reserva Amazonica** (www.inkaterra.com; s 3 days & 2 nights per person US$818-950, d US$1290-1478) ✈.

SAS Travel   Tours
(📞084-24-9194; www.sastravelperu.com; Calle Garcilaso 270; ⊙8am-8pm Mon-Sat) A direct operator with local owners. Offers high-end package tours to Machu Picchu, Inca Trail treks, jungle travel and Cuzco tours. While this outfitter charges more than the competition, traveler satisfaction is generally high.

SATO   Tours
(📞084-26-1505; www.southamericatravel sonline.com; Urbanización Quinta Jardín 288; ⊙9am-5pm Mon-Fri, to 1pm Sat) A reputable European agency working with local operators for trekking, hiking and rafting, also a last-minute specialist.

Travel & Healing   Outdoors
(📞084-22-7892; www.travelandhealing.com; Av La Cultura 2122, piso 3; ⊙8:30am-8pm Mon-Sat) Specializing in spiritual retreats, Ayahuasca ceremonies and Andean cultural wisdom, this outfitter takes a sincere spiritual approach to local tours and treks. Sometimes combined with yoga.

Virgin Estrella Taxi Tours   Tours
(📞974-955-374, 973-195-551) Reliable outfit offering taxi tours out of Cuzco, the Sacred Valley and the Southern Valley.

🔒 SHOPPING

The neighborhood of San Blas – the plaza itself, Cuesta San Blas, Carmen Alto and Tandapata – offers Cuzco's best shopping. Traditionally an artisan quarter, some workshops and showrooms of local craftspeople still remain here. Jewelry shops and quirky, one-off designer boutiques are a refreshing reminder that the local aesthetic is not confined to stridently colored ponchos and sheepskin-rug depictions of Machu Picchu.

🔭 More Ruins to Explore

The four ruins closest to Cuzco are Sacsaywamán, Q'enqo, Pukapukara and Tambomachay. They can all be visited in a day – far less if you're whisked through on a guided tour. If you only have time to visit one site, Sacsaywamán (p153) is the most important, and less than a 2km trek uphill from the Plaza de Armas in central Cuzco. The cheapest way to visit the sites is to take a bus bound for Pisac and ask the driver to stop at **Tambomachay** (📞84-227-037; boleto turístico adult/student S130/70; ⊙7:30am-5:30pm), the furthest site from Cuzco (at 3700m, it's also the highest). It's an 8km walk back to Cuzco, visiting all four ruins along the way. Alternatively, a taxi will charge roughly S70 to visit all four sites. Each site can only be entered with the *boleto turístico*. Local guides hang around offering their services, sometimes quite persistently. Agree on a price before beginning any tour. Robberies at these sites are uncommon but not unheard of. Cuzco's tourist police recommend visiting between 9am and 5pm.

Tambomachay

Cafe Ricchary   Coffee
(📞984-305-571; Concevidayoc 116; ⊙8:30am-8:30pm Mon-Sat) This tiny coffee seller near the San Pedro Market sells great local organic roasts, ground and whole bean, for very reasonable prices. You can also get a hot cup but there's only two stools to sit at.

The Lucky Toad

Ever wondered what the locals do to relax instead of whiling away the hours over a game of darts or pool in the local bar? Well, next time you're in a *picantería* (local restaurant) or *quinta* (house serving typical Andean food), look out for a strange metal *sapo* (frog or toad) mounted on a large box and surrounded by various holes and slots.

Men will often spend the whole afternoon drinking *chicha* (fermented corn beer) and beer while competing at this old test of skill in which players toss metal disks as close to the toad as possible. Top points are scored for landing one smack in the mouth.

Legend has it that the game originated with Inca royals, who used to toss gold coins into Lake Titicaca in the hopes of attracting a *sapo,* believed to possess magical healing powers and have the ability to grant wishes.

Sapo game
VICTORIA ZIKA/SHUTTERSTOCK ©

Center for Traditional Textiles of Cuzco
Arts & Crafts
(☎84-228-117; Av El Sol 603; ⏱7:30am-8pm) This nonprofit organization, founded in 1996, promotes the survival of traditional weaving. You may be able to catch a shop-floor demonstration illustrating different weaving techniques in all their finger-twisting complexity. Products for sale are high end.

Inkakunaq Ruwaynin
Arts & Crafts
(☎084-26-0942; inside CBC, Tullumayo 274; ⏱9am-7pm Mon-Sat) This weaving cooperative with quality goods is run by 12 mountain communities from Cuzco and Apurimac; it's at the far end of the inner courtyard.

Jerusalén
Books
(☎084-23-5428; Heladeros 143; ⏱10:30am-7:30pm Mon-Sat) Cuzco's most extensive public book exchange, plus used guidebooks, new titles and music for sale.

Mercado San Pedro
Market
(Plazoleta San Pedro; ⏱6am-7pm) Cuzco's central market is a must-see. Pig heads for *caldo* (soup), frogs (to enhance sexual performance), vats of fruit juice, roast *lechón* (suckling pig) and tamales are just a few of the foods on offer. Around the edges are typical clothes, spells, incense and other random products to keep you entertained for hours.

Taller Mendivil
Arts & Crafts
(☎084-63-7150; Plazoleta s/n; ⏱9am-7:30pm) A cramped but interesting artisan shop bursting with religious figures and ornate mirrors.

EATING

Cuzco's restaurant scene caters for a wide range of tastes and budgets, thanks to its international appeal.

For self-caterers, small, overpriced grocery shops are located near the Plaza de Armas, including **Gato's Market** (☎084-234-026; Santa Catalina Ancha 377; ⏱9:30am-11pm) and **Mega** (cnr Matará & Ayacucho; ⏱10am-8pm Mon-Sat, to 6pm Sun).

Central Cuzco
La Rabona
Bakery $
(Herrajes 146; mains S15-20; ⏱8am-8pm Mon-Sat, 10am-6pm Sun; 🛜🌱) Baking Cuzco's best multiseed and sourdough loaves (gold on a multiday trek), wonderful carrot cake and other baked goods including vegan

treats, this is a worthy stop for stocking up. It also serves espresso drinks, matcha tea and golden milk. Pressed juices, like the ginger-apple-beet combo, are liquid energy. Unfortunately, the downstairs seating is a little frumpy.

PER.UK
Cafe $$

(☎084-23-3978; Plateros 344; mains S38-60; ⊙noon-10:30pm; 🐾🥗) This love child of a Peruvian-British couple is a low-key cafe serving well-crafted Peruvian fusion dishes, plus pub burgers and oversized salads. Presentation is excellent and the service well above average. It's also kind to vegetarians and celiacs. The delicious *ají de gallina* (spicy chicken and walnut stew) could easily serve two.

Bojosan
Japanese $$

(☎084-24-6502; San Agustin 275; mains S20-26; ⊙12:30-10pm; 🐾🥗) This Tokyo-style noodle shop does right in so many ways. Take a stool and watch the cooks prepare your udon noodles from scratch. Oversized bowls have flavorful broth, you add the protein (duck, chicken and vegetarian options) and

a dash of authentic pepper mix. With bottled local artisan beers on offer. Run by the highly regarded Le Soleil (p173) next door.

Cicciolina
International $$

(☎084-23-9510; www.cicciolinacuzco.com; Triunfo 393, 2nd fl; mains S38-59; ⊙8am-11pm) On the 2nd floor of a lofty colonial courtyard mansion, Cicciolina may be Cuzco's best restaurant. The eclectic, sophisticated food is divine, starting with house-marinated olives, and continuing with crisp polenta squares with cured rabbit, huge green salads, charred octopus and satisfying mains like red trout in coconut milk, beetroot ravioli and tender lamb. With impeccable service and warmly lit seating.

La Bodega 138
Pizza $$

(☎084-26-0272; www.labodega138.com; Herrajes 138; mains S26-37; ⊙11am-10:30pm Mon-Fri, from 10am Sat & Sun; 🥗) Sometimes you are homesick for good atmosphere, uncomplicated menus and craft beer. In comes La Bodega, a fantastic laid-back enterprise run by a family in what used to be their home. Thin-crust pizzas are fired up in the adobe

Mercado San Pedro

CHRISTIAN VINCES/SHUTTERSTOCK ©

Cicciolina (p171)

oven, organic salads are fresh and abundant and the prices are reasonable. With weekend brunch. A true find. Cash only.

Limo   Seafood $$
(☑084-24-068; www.cuscorestaurants.com/ restaurant/limo; Portal de Carnes 236, 2nd fl; mains S20-60; ⊙11am-11pm Mon-Sat) If you must have seafood in Cuzco, make this elegant Nikkei restaurant the place. Don't skip the house pisco sour, tinged with ginger and garnished with a whole chili. *Tiraditos* (raw fish in a fragrant sauce) simply melt on the tongue. Other hits are the creamy potato *causas* and crunchy shrimp rolls with avocado and smoked pepper. With attentive service.

Marcelo Batata   Peruvian $$
(☑084-22-2424; www.cuscodining.com/ marcelo-batata; Palacio 121; mains S43-56; ⊙12:30-11pm) A sure bet for delectable Andean cuisine with a twist. Marcelo Batata innovates with traditional foods to show them at their best – like the humble *tarwi* pea, which makes a mean hummus. The chicken soup with *hierba Luisa* (a local

herb), is exquisite, alongside satisfying beet *quinotto* (like risotto), tender alpaca and twice-baked Andean potatoes that offer crispy-creamy goodness.

Mr Soup   International $$
(☑084-38-6073; Saphi 448; mains S20-28; ⊙noon-10pm Tue-Sun) Sometimes you just want a huge bowl of soup. Serving fairly authentic udon curry, Thai *tom kha* (coconut soup), Andean quinoa soup and others, this tiny shop does the trick. Recipes were sourced from families, which helps give them a homespun taste. For a bargain, go for the soup of the day (S15).

Uchu Peruvian
Steakhouse   Peruvian $$
(☑084-24-6598; www.cuscodining.com/uchu; Palacio 135; mains S48-57; ⊙12:30-10pm) With a cozy, cavernous ambience of low-lit adobe, dark tables and bright turquoise walls, this chic eatery offers meat (steak, alpaca or chicken) and fish cooked on hot volcanic stones at your table, served with delicious sauces. Starters are great – like the BBQ

ribs in a smoked elderberry sauce. Staff are knowledgeable and quick, a real treat.

Le Soleil
French $$$

(☎084-24-0543; www.restaurantelesoleilcusco. com; San Agustín 275; mains S38-89; ⊗12:30-3pm & 7-11:30pm Thu-Tue) Cuzco's go-to spot for traditional French cooking, this romantic white-linen restaurant delivers with cool precision. Start with trout in a tart mango ginger confit. The *duck à l'orange* cooked two ways is simply divine. You can also go for a tasting menu (from S145). There's a wonderful selection of French wines and lovely desserts – chocolate fondant being the obvious, happy choice.

Chicha
Peruvian $$$

(☎084-24-0520; Regocijo 261, 2nd fl; mains S30-65) A Gastón Acurio venture serving up haute versions of Cuzco classics in an open kitchen. Its riff on *anticuchos* (beef skewers) is a delectable barbecued octopus with crisp herbed potato wedges. Other contenders include *papas rellenas* (stuffed potatoes), curried alpaca with quinoa, and *chairo* (lamb and barley soup) served in a clay pot.

 San Blas

Monkey Cafe
Cafe $

(☎084-59-5838; Tandapata 300; mains S15-20; ⊗8am-8pm Wed-Mon) Cuzco's finest coffee shop is shoehorned into a tiny locale at the top of San Blas hill. All espresso drinks feature double shots made with Peruvian-origin roasts. There are also very tasty sweets and hearty breakfasts ranging from healthy to heart-stopping.

La Bohème Crepería
Crêperie $

(☎084-23-5694; www.labohemecusco.com; Carmen Alto 283; mains S10-17; ⊗8am-10pm; 🛜🍴) You can't go wrong with the authentic crepes in this French-owned cafe, crafted with fusion ingredients like caramelized onions, Andean cheese, mushrooms and béchamel. There's a little patio with great views and firelit evening ambiance. The set menu is a great deal. For dessert, try

 Cuzco's Legendary Origins

According to legend, in the 12th century, the first *inca* (king), Manco Capac, was ordered by the ancestral sun god Inti to find the spot where he could plunge a golden rod into the ground until it disappeared. At this spot – deemed the navel of the earth (*qosq'o* in the Quechua language) – he founded Cuzco, the city that would become the thriving capital of the Americas' greatest empire.

The Inca empire's main expansion occurred in the hundred years prior to the arrival of the conquistadors in 1532. The ninth *inca* (king), Pachacutec, gave the empire its first bloody taste of conquest, with unexpected victory against the more dominant Chanka tribe in 1438. His was the first wave of expansion that would create the Inca empire.

Pachacutec also proved himself a sophisticated urban developer, devising Cuzco's famous puma shape and diverting rivers to cross the city. He built fine buildings, including the famous Qorikancha temple and a palace on the present Plaza de Armas.

Pachacutec statue by Fausto Espinoza Farfán

its signature crepe with salted butter and caramel.

La Quinta Eulalia
Peruvian $$

(☎084-22-4951; Choquechaca 384; mains S25-54; ⊗12:30-4pm Tue-Sun) This Cuzco classic has been in business for over half a century and its courtyard patio is a score on a sunny day. The chalkboard menu features the tenderest roast lamb, alpaca and traditional sides like the phenomenal *rocotto relleno* (spicy peppers stuffed with beef, peas and carrots topped with dribbling cheese). Among the best places to order *cuy* (guinea pig).

Granja Heidi
Cafe $$

(📞084-23-8383; Cuesta San Blas 525, 2nd fl; mains S22-48; ⏰11:30am-9:30pm Mon-Sat; 🍽️) A cozy alpine cafe serving healthy fare that's consistently good, some of it provided from the small farm of the German owner. In addition to wonderful Peruvian fare (*rocoto relleno* is served vegetarian, with stuffed chili and peanuts), there are crepes and huge bowls of soups and salads. The lunchtime set menu (S28) is a good deal. Save room for dessert.

Jack's Café
Cafe $$

(📞084-25-4606; Choquechaca 509; mains S15-31; ⏰7am-11pm) A line often snakes out the door at this consistently good Western-style eatery with Aussie roots. With fresh juices blended with mint or ginger, strong coffee and eggs heaped with smoked salmon or roasted tomatoes, it's

easy to get out of bed. Also has nice cafe food, soups and good service.

✘ Avenida El Sol & Downhill

La Valeriana
Bakery $

(📞084-50-6941; Av El Sol 576; mains S8-22; ⏰7am-10pm Mon-Sat, 8am-9pm Sun; 📶) Facing the sacred garden, this ambient bakery sells truffled cupcakes, whole-wheat sandwiches and good veggie empanadas served on patterned china. There are also coffee drinks and refreshing juices blended with medicinal herbs. A fine stop to charge your batteries.

🍷 DRINKING & NIGHTLIFE

Limbus
Rooftop Bar

(📞084-431-282; www.limbusrestobar.com; Pasñapakana 133; ⏰8am-1am Mon-Sat, noon-midnight Sun) Billed as the best view in Cuzco, it's all that (even after climbing to the top of San Blas). Don't worry, if you come during peak hours you'll have plenty of time to catch your breath while you queue to get in. With gorgeous cocktails

From left: Ceviche; Cuzco sour cocktail; Selection of piscos (grape brandies); Museo del Pisco

and glass-walled panoramas, this was the hottest city spot when we visited.

Museo del Pisco
Bar

(☑084-26-2709; www.museodelpisco.org; Santa Catalina Ancha 398; mains S30-38; ⊗noon-1am) When you've had your fill of colonial religious art, investigate this pisco museum, where the wonders of the national drink are extolled, exalted and – of course – sampled. Opened by an enthusiastic expat, this museum-bar is Pisco 101, combined with a tapas lounge. Grab a spot early for show-stopping live music (9pm to 11pm nightly).

Chango
Club

(☑990-523-722; www.facebook.com/chango clubcusco; Tecsecocha 429; ⊗9pm-7am) Humming to a techno beat, this happening club with live DJs is the latest of Cuzco's all-night party places. There's also rock, reggae and salsa on rotation. Keep a close eye on your belongings, as there have been reports of pickpocketing.

Mundo Nuevo
Pub

(☑084-24-0594; Portal de Confituria 233; ⊗1pm-1am Tue-Sat, from 5pm Sun & Mon) With eye-popping views of the cathedral, this upstairs bar has a dozen Peruvian microbrews on draft. You could do far worse than watch the sunset on the plaza from here, cold quinoa beer in hand. You can also count on decent pub food and a cheerful atmosphere. With live music from Wednesday to Saturday.

Republica de Pisco
Bar

(☑084-24-4111; www.facebook.com/republica delpiscocusco; Plateros 354; ⊗5pm-2am) A wonderful, elegant bar with attentive bartenders and drinks that merit seconds. It's popular with locals and travelers alike. Check the Facebook site for events.

⭐ ENTERTAINMENT

Ukuku's
Live Music

(☑084-24-2951; Plateros 316; ⊗6pm-2am) The most consistently popular nightspot in town, Ukuku's plays a winning combination of crowd-pleasers – Latin and Western

BEN PIPE/ALAMY STOCK PHOTO

Centro Qosqo de Arte Nativo

rock, reggae, *reggaetón*, salsa and hip-hop – and often hosts live bands. Usually full to bursting after midnight with as many Peruvians as foreign tourists, it's good, sweaty, dance-a-thon fun. Happy hour is 8pm to 10:30pm.

Centro Qosqo de Arte Nativo
Performing Arts

(☎084-22-7901; www.centroqosqodeartenativo. com; Av El Sol 604) Has live nightly performances of Andean music and folk dancing at 6:45pm.

ℹ INFORMATION

DANGERS & ANNOYANCES

● Bags may be stolen from the backs of chairs in public places or from overhead shelves in overnight buses.

● Walk around with a minimum of cash and belongings. If you keep your bag in your lap and watch out for pickpockets in crowded streets, transport terminals and markets, you are highly unlikely to be a victim of crime in Cuzco.

● Avoid walking by yourself late at night or very early in the morning. Revelers returning late from bars or setting off for the Inca Trail before sunrise are particularly vulnerable to 'choke and grab' attacks.

MEDICAL SERVICES

Pharmacies abound along Av El Sol. Cuzco's medical facilities are limited; head to Lima for serious procedures.

Hospital Regional (☎084-23-9792, emergencies 084-22-3691; Av de la Cultura s/n; ☻24hr) Public and free, but wait times can be long and good care is not guaranteed.

MONEY

ATMs are found around the Plaza de Armas, at the airport, Huanchaq train station and the bus terminal. All accept Visa, most accept MasterCard.

BCP (☎01-458-1230; Av El Sol 189; ☻9am-6:30pm Mon-Thu, to 7:30pm Fri, to 1pm Sat) With an ATM.

TOURIST INFORMATION

iPerú (📞084-59-6159; www.peru.travel; Portal de Harinas 177, Plaza de Armas; ⊙9am-7pm Mon-Fri, to 1pm Sat) Efficient and helpful. Excellent source for tourist information for both the region and entire country. There's an adjoining section of guarded ATMs. Also has a branch at the **airport** (📞084-23-7364; ⊙6am-5pm).

GETTING THERE & AWAY

AIR

Cuzco's **Aeropuerto Internacional Alejandro Velasco Astete** (CUZ; 📞084-22-2611) receives national and international flights. Most arrivals are in the morning, as afternoon conditions make landings and takeoffs more difficult. If you have a tight connection, it's best to reserve the earliest flight available, as later ones are more likely to be delayed or canceled.

There are daily flights to Lima, Juliaca, Puerto Maldonado and Arequipa. Check in at least two hours ahead as overbooking errors are commonplace. During the rainy season, flights to Puerto Maldonado are often seriously delayed. Departure taxes are included in ticket prices.

Avianca (📞0800-18-2222; www.avianca.com; Av El Sol 602; ⊙8:30am-7pm Mon-Fri, 9am-2pm Sat) Service to/from Lima Monday to Saturday and direct flights to Bogota, Colombia.

LATAM (📞084-25-5555; www.latam.com; Av El Sol 627B; ⊙9am-7pm Mon-Fri, to 1pm Sat) Direct flights to Lima, Arequipa, Juliaca and Puerto Maldonado, as well as Santiago, Chile.

Peruvian Airlines (📞084-25-4890; www.peruvianairlines.pe; Av El Sol 627-A; ⊙9am-7pm Mon-Sat, to noon Sun) To Lima and La Paz, Bolivia.

Star Perú (📞01-705-9000; www.starperu.com; Av El Sol 627, oficina 101; ⊙9am-1pm & 3-6:30pm Mon-Sat, 9am-12:30pm Sun) Service to Lima.

Viva Air (📞call center 084-64-4004; www.vivaair.com) Low-cost airline with online booking.

BUS

All international services depart from the **Terminal Terrestre** (📞084-22-4471; Vía de Evitamiento 429), about 2km out of town toward the airport. Take a taxi (S30) or walk via Av El Sol.

To Bolivia, **Transporte Copacabana** (📞084-40-2953; www.transcopacabanasa.com.bo; Vía de Evitamiento 429, Terminal Terrestre; ⊙9am-6pm) offers daily services to Copacabana (10 hours) and La Paz, along with **Transporte Internacional Salvador** (📞084-23-3680; www.trans-salvador.com; Vía de Evitamiento 429, Terminal Terrestre; ⊙9am-7pm), via Desaguadero (12 hours). This is the quickest way to get to La Paz.

Ormeño (📞969-933-579; Vía de Evitamiento 429, Terminal Terrestre; ⊙9am-7pm) travels to Brazil.

Cruz del Sur (📞084-74-0444; www.cruzdelsur.com.pe; Av Industrial 121) and **CIVA** (📞084-24-9961; www.civa.com.pe; Vía de Evitamiento 429, Terminal Terrestre; ⊙9am-6pm) offer relatively painless services to Lima. Wari is the best of the cheaper options. Most buses to Lima stop in Nazca (13 hours) and Ica (16 hours). Cruz del Sur has its own terminal but tickets can be purchased at the Terminal Terrestre.

The most enjoyable way to get to Puno is via luxury tourist buses that take the Ruta del Sol. **Inka Express** (📞084-63-4838; www.inkaexpress.com; Av Alameda Pachacuteq 499; ⊙9am-1pm & 3-7pm Mon-Fri, 9am-1pm & 4-6pm Sat) and **Turismo Mer** (📞084-24-5171; www.turismomer.com; El Óvalo, Av La Paz A3; tourist service with entry fees S198; 🛜) go every morning.

Buses to Arequipa cluster around 6am to 7am and 7pm to 9:30pm.

Wari (📞084-22-2694; www.grupopalomino.com.pe; Vía de Evitamiento 429, Terminal Terrestre; ⊙9am-7pm) and **Expreso Los Chankas** (📞084-26-2909; Vía de Evitamiento 429, Terminal Terrestre; ⊙9am-6pm) depart every couple of hours through the day for Abancay and Andahuaylas (S70, nine hours). Change at Andahuaylas to get to Ayacucho via rough roads that get very cold at night.

TRAIN

Cuzco has two train stations. **Estación Huanchac** (Wanchaq; 📞084-58-1414; Av Pachacutec s/n; ⊙7am-5pm Mon-Fri, to midnight Sat & Sun), near the end of Av El Sol, serves Juliaca and Puno on Lake Titicaca. **Estación Poroy** (Calle Roldan s/n, Carr Cuzco-Urubamba), east of town, serves Ollantaytambo and Machu Picchu.

An exercise in old-fashioned romance, the **Belmond Andean Explorer** (☎084-58-1414; www.perurail.com; Estación Huanchac; to Puno/Arequipa from S5754/13,393; ☻7am-5pm Mon-Fri, to noon Sat) is a gorgeous luxury sleeper train with a glass-walled observation car. It travels across the altiplano to Puno and on to Arequipa. Weekly departures leave Thursdays, arriving at Puno the same evening and Arequipa on Saturday.

Peru Rail (☎084-58-1414; www.perurail.com; Estación Poroy; ☻7am-5pm Mon-Fri, to noon Sat) The flagship service to Aguas Calientes, with multiple departures daily from Estación Poroy, 20 minutes outside of Cuzco. There are three service categories: Expedition (from S232 one way), Vistadome (from S347 one way) and the luxurious Hiram Bingham (from S1736 one way).

Inca Rail (www.incarail.com) has three buses daily from Ollantaytambo and four service levels.

 GETTING AROUND

TO & FROM THE AIRPORT

The airport is about 6km south of the city center. The *combi* lines Imperial and C4M (S0.80, 20 minutes) run from Av El Sol to just outside the airport. A taxi to or from the city center to the airport costs S30. An official radio taxi from within the airport costs S40. With advance reservations, many hotels offer free pickup.

BUS

Local rides on public transportation cost only S1, though it's easier to walk or just take a taxi than to figure out where any given *combi* is headed.

TAXI

There are no meters in taxis, but there are set rates. At the time of research, trips within the city center cost S8 and destinations further afield, such as El Molino, cost S12. Check with your hotel whether this is still correct, and rather than negotiate, simply hand the correct amount to your driver at the end of your ride; he is unlikely to argue if you seem to know what you're doing.

Official taxis, identified by a lit company telephone number on the roof, are more expensive than taxis flagged down on the street, but they are safer.

TATEYAMA/SHUTTERSTOCK ©

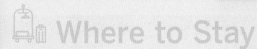
Where to Stay

Cuzco has hundreds of lodgings of all types and prices. Book ahead in peak season, between June and August, especially the 10 days before Inti Raymi on June 24 and Fiestas Patrias (Independence Days) on July 28 and 29.

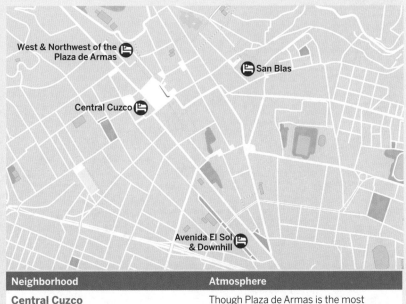

Neighborhood	Atmosphere
Central Cuzco	Though Plaza de Armas is the most central area, premium rates are charged for the location.
West & Northwest of the Plaza de Armas	Many of the side streets that climb northwest away from the plaza towards Sacsaywamán (especially Tigre, Tecsecocha, Suecia, Kiskapata, Resbalosa and 7 Culebras) are bursting with cheap crash pads. There are also many options west of the Plaza de Armas around Plaza Regocijo, in the commercial area towards the Mercado Central, and downhill from the center in the streets northeast of Av El Sol.
San Blas	Hilly San Blas has the best views and is deservedly popular.
Avenida El Sol & Downhill	Similar to Central Cuzco, accommodations along Av El Sol tend to be bland, expensive and set up for tour groups.

THE SACRED VALLEY

The Sacred Valley at a Glance...

Tucked under the tawny skirts of formidable foothills, the beautiful Río Urubamba valley, known as El Valle Sagrado (The Sacred Valley), is about 15km north of Cuzco as the condor flies, via a narrow road of hairpin turns. Long the home of attractive colonial towns and isolated weaving villages, in recent years it has become a destination in its own right. Star attractions are the markets and the lofty Inca citadels of Pisac and Ollantaytambo, but the valley is also packed with other Inca sites. Trekking routes are deservedly gaining in popularity. Adrenaline activities range from rafting to rock climbing.

The Sacred Valley in Two Days

Head to the stunning **Pisac Ruins** (p107) with lofty views of plunging gorges. Follow a series of hiking trails around the area, allowing several hours to go at your own pace. Polish your pre-Columbian history knowledge at the new **Museo Inkariy** (p191) afterwards. On day two, visit **rural communities** and learn to cook local Andean dishes, trek to highland lakes, and hear about local natural medicine and artisan traditions.

The Sacred Valley in Four Days

On day three, visit **Chinchero** (p188) for a typical Andean village experience, combining Inca ruins with a colonial church. On day four, see what was left behind by the Inca at the lofty fortress and temple of the **Ollantaytambo Ruins** (p187) before enjoying the cobblestone streets of this historic Inca town.

Abra Málaga
Pass (45km)

Ollantaytambo Ruins

Ollantaytambo

▲
Nevado
Verónica

Lares

Río Urubamba

Aguas
Calientes
(30km);
Machu Picchu
(40km)

Urubamba

Huarán

Yucay

Calca

Tarabamba

Wayllabamba

Amaru

Chinchero

Maras

Patabamba

Pisac

Pisac Ruins

Huarocondo

Paucartambo
(40km)

Anta

Cuzco

Huambutiyo

Oropesa

Andahuayillas (7km)

Ⓝ 0   10 km
    0   5 miles

Arriving in the Sacred Valley

Bus Urubamba is the valley's principal transportation hub. The bus terminal is about 1km west of town.

Minivan or Taxi The most comfortable option to Pisac, the entry point to the valley.

Train Two companies run between Ollantaytambo and Aguas Calientes. The station is less than 1km southwest of the village center.

Where to Stay

Foreign-run mystical and spiritual retreats on the outskirts of Pisac offer packages with shamanic ceremonies; some are vastly more commercial than others.

Ollantaytambo hosts lots of budget and midrange accommodations in the streets east of the Plaza de Armas.

VADIM NEFEDOFF/SHUTTERSTOCK ©

Pisac Ruins

A truly awesome site with relatively few tourists, this hilltop Inca citadel lies high above the village on a triangular plateau with a plunging gorge on either side.

Great For...

☑ Don't Miss

Taking a taxi up to the ruins and walking the 4km back to town.

Terracing

The ruins' most impressive feature is the agricultural terracing, which sweeps around the south and east flanks of the mountain in huge and graceful curves, almost entirely unbroken by steps (which require greater maintenance and promote erosion). Instead, the terracing is joined by diagonal flights of stairs made of flagstones set into the terrace walls. Above the terraces are cliff-hugging footpaths, watched over by caracara falcons and well defended by massive stone doorways, steep stairs and a short tunnel carved out of the rock.

❶ Need to Know

Boleto turístico adult/student S130/70; ⏲7am-6pm

✕ Take a Break

Vendors sell drinks and snacks at the top.

★ Top Tip

Note that organized tours, while often informative, are more rushed than private tours.

Ceremonial Center

This dominating site guards not only the Urubamba Valley below, but also a pass leading into the jungle to the northeast. Topping the terraces is the site's ceremonial center, with an *intihuatana* (literally 'hitching post of the sun'; an Inca astronomical tool), several working water channels, and some painstakingly neat masonry in the well-preserved temples.

A path leads up the hillside to a series of ceremonial baths and around to the military area. Looking across the Kitamayo Gorge from the back of the site, you'll also see hundreds of holes honeycombing the cliff wall. These are Inca tombs that were plundered by *huaqueros* (grave robbers),

and are now completely off-limits to tourists.

Hiking to the Ruins

At the time of writing, the trail starting above the west side of the church in town was closed. Check for updates in Pisac. When it's open, it's a two-hour climb up and takes 1½ hours to return. Worthwhile but grueling, the hike is good training for the Inca Trail! The footpath has many crisscrossing trails, but if you aim toward the terracing, you won't get lost. To the west, or the left of the hill as you climb up on the footpath, is the Río Kitamayo gorge; to the east, or right, is the Río Chongo valley.

Alternatively, you can hire a taxi (S60 round-trip) from near the bridge into town to drive you up the 7.5km paved road to the ruins.

Either way, you should allow several hours to explore the site.

Pinkulluna

Ollantaytambo Ruins

Both fortress and temple, these spectacular Inca ruins rise above Ollantaytambo, making a splendid half-day trip.

Great For...

☑ **Don't Miss**

Hiring a local guide is worthwhile to demonstrate how to turn on the faucet of the royal baths.

Inca Victory

The huge, steep terraces that guard Ollantaytambo's spectacular Inca ruins mark one of the few places where the Spanish conquistadors lost a major battle.

The rebellious Manco Inca had retreated to this fortress after his defeat at Sacsaywamán. In 1536, Hernando Pizarro, Francisco's younger half-brother, led a force of 70 cavalrymen to Ollantaytambo, supported by large numbers of indigenous and Spanish foot soldiers, in an attempt to capture Manco Inca.

The conquistadors, showered with arrows, spears and boulders from atop the steep terracing, were unable to climb to the fortress. In a brilliant move, Manco Inca flooded the plain below the fortress through previously prepared channels. With Spaniards' horses bogged down in the water, Pizarro ordered a

Ollantaytambo ruins

ⓘ Need to Know

Boleto turístico adult/student S130/70;
⊙7am-5pm

✕ Take a Break

There are bars and local restaurants just around the corner from the ruins.

★ Top Tip

The *boleto turístico* tourist card, used for admission, is valid for 10 days and for 16 other sites across the region.

hasty retreat, chased down by thousands of Manco Inca's victorious soldiers.

Yet the Inca victory would be short lived. Spanish forces soon returned with a quadrupled cavalry force and Manco fled to his jungle stronghold in Vilcabamba.

Construction

Though Ollantaytambo was a highly effective fortress, it also served as a temple. A finely worked ceremonial center is at the top of the terracing. Some extremely well-built walls were under construction at the time of the conquest and have never been completed. The stone was quarried from a mountainside 6km away. Transporting the huge stone blocks to the site was a stupendous feat. The Inca used a crafty technique to move massive blocks across the Río Urubamba, carting the blocks to the riverside then diverting the entire river channel around them.

Hiking & Views

The 6km hike to the Inca quarry on the opposite side of the river is a good walk from Ollantaytambo. The trail starts from the Inca bridge by the entrance to the village. It takes a few hours to reach the site, passing several abandoned blocks known as *piedras cansadas* (tired stones).

Looking back towards Ollantaytambo, you can see the enigmatic optical illusion of a pyramid in the fields and walls in front of the fortress. A few scholars believe this marks the legendary place where the original Incas first emerged from the earth.

Pinkulluna

It's a very steep climb from town up the hillside to these **ruins** (Lari s/n; admission S10; ⊙ dawn-dusk), but the views are magnificent. You will see the Ollantaytambo ruins from the best vantage point, and it's nice to wander around an Inca site that isn't swamped with tour groups. There are terraces and a handful of constructions in decent shape. Wear sturdy shoes.

Ruinas Inca

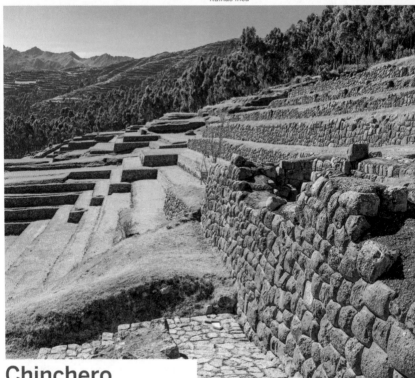

SL_PHOTOGRAPHY/GETTY IMAGES ©

Chinchero

Known to the Inca as the birthplace of the rainbow, this typical Andean village combines Inca ruins with a colonial church, some wonderful mountain views and a colorful Sunday market.

Great For...

☑ **Don't Miss**

Centro de Textiles Tradicionales (www. textilescusco.org/index.php/chinchero; ⊙9am-4pm) on Manzares is the best artisan workshop in town.

On a high plain with sweeping views to snow-laden peaks, Chinchero's setting is starkly beautiful. As it is very high, it's unwise to spend the night until you're somewhat acclimated. Entry to the historic precinct, where the ruins, the church and the museum are all found, is by the *boleto turístico*, valid for 10 days.

Ruinas Inca

The most extensive **ruins** (boleto turístico adult/student S130/70; ⊙9am-6pm) here consist of terracing. If you start walking away from the village through the terraces on the right-hand side of the valley, you'll also find various rocks carved into seats and staircases.

🛈 Need to Know

Combis (minibuses) and *colectivos* (shared transportation) traveling between Cuzco and Urubamba stop on the corner of the highway and Calle Manco Capac II.

✕ Take a Break

Other than the restaurants attached to accommodations (open to non-guests), there are few eating options in town.

★ Top Tip

Chinchero is the best value, most authentic place to buy woven goods in the region. Each weaving cooperative has its own specialty design.

Iglesia Colonial de Chinchero

Among the most beautiful churches in the valley, this colonial **church** (boleto turístico adult/student S130/70; ⊗8am-5:30pm) is built on Inca foundations. The interior, decked out in merry floral and religious designs, is well worth seeing.

Mercado de Chinchero

The Chinchero **market** (⊗7am-4pm), held on Tuesday, Thursday and especially Sunday, is less touristy than its counterpart in Pisac and well worth a special trip. On Sunday, traditionally dressed locals descend from the hills for the produce market, where the ancient practice of *trueco* (bartering) still takes place; this is a rare opportunity to observe genuine bartering.

What's Nearby?

On the far side of the valley, a clear trail climbs upward before heading north and down to the Río Urubamba Valley (about four hours). At the river, the trail turns left and continues to a bridge at Wayllabamba. Cross it for the Sacred Valley road to Calca (turn right, about 13km) or Urubamba (turn left, about 9km). You can flag down any passing bus until mid-afternoon or continue walking to Yucay, where the trail officially ends.

Pisac

Welcome to the international airport for the cosmic traveler, according to one seasoned local. It's not hard to succumb to the charms of sunny Pisac, a bustling and fast-growing colonial village at the base of a spectacular Inca fortress perched on a mountain spur. Its pull is universal and recent years have seen an influx of expats and New Age followers in search of an Andean Shangri-la.

⊙ SIGHTS

Iglesia de San Pedro Apostol   Church
(Plaza Constitución) Traditionally dressed locals descend from the hills to attend mass in Quechua, including men in highland dress blowing horns, and *varayocs* (local officials) with silver staffs of office. It's held at 11am on Sundays. Travelers can attend but shouldn't take photos. The church recently reopened after its controversial demolition and rebuild in colonial style.

Jardín Botanico   Gardens
(☎084-63-5563; Grau, cuadra 4; admission S8; ☺8am-4:30pm) A private enterprise with a huge courtyard full of beautiful specimens and a resident cat.

Mercado de Artesania   Market
(Plaza Constitución; ☺8am-4pm) Pisac is known far and wide for its market, by far the biggest and most touristy in the region. While there are still some local arts and crafts of note, watch out for mass-produced goods invading from as far as Colombia. Its massive success has it filling the Plaza Constitución and surrounding streets every day.

⊕ TOURS

Parque de la Papa   Ecotour
(☎084-24-5021; www.ipcca.info/about-parque-de-la-papa; Pisac) Day treks and cooking workshops are some of the offerings of this wonderful nonprofit, which promotes potato diversity and communal farming.

Quechua elders in traditional dress

WOLLERTZ/SHUTTERSTOCK ©

EATING

Doña Clorinda Peruvian $$

(📞084-20-3051; Urb San Luis, La Rinconada; mains S18-35; ⊘9am-5pm) In a lovely colonial home, this longtime Pisac mainstay serves up hearty Andean fare. Order some home-made *chicha morada* (blue corn juice) to go with heaping plates of *arroz chaufa* (Peruvian fried rice), trout, beef and *rocoto relleno* (stuffed peppers) with kapchi. A classic.

Mullu Fusion $$

(📞084-20-3073; www.mullu.pe; San Francisco s/n, 2nd fl, Plaza Constitución; mains S30-56; ⊘9am-9pm) The balcony of this chill and welcoming place may be the best spot to watch market-day interactions in the plaza below. The menu is fusion (think Thai meets Amazonian while flirting with highland Peruvian). Traditional lamb is tender to falling-off-the-bone; soups, alpaca burgers and blended juices also satisfy.

Ulrike's Café Cafe $$

(📞084-20-3195; Manuel Prado s/s; mains S15-33; ⊘9am-9pm; 🛜🚐) This sunny cafe is consistently tasty, serving up a great vegetarian *menú* (set meal), plus homemade pasta, house-made bagels and melt-in-the-mouth cheesecake. The fluffy carrot cake is legendary. There's a book exchange and special events. English, French and German are spoken.

ℹ️ GETTING THERE & AWAY

Buses to Urubamba (S5 to S7, one hour) leave frequently from the downtown bridge between 6am and 8pm. **Minibuses to Cuzco** (Amazonas s/n; S5, one hour) leave from Calle Amazonas when full. Many travel agencies in Cuzco also operate tour buses to Pisac, especially on market days.

Urubamba

A busy and unadorned urban center, Urubamba is a transport hub surrounded by bucolic foothills and snowy peaks. The advantages of its lower altitude and relative

Museo Inkariy

This wonderful new **museum** (📞984-666-698, 084-79-2819; www.museoinkariy.com; Carr Pisac-Ollantaytambo Km 53; adult/child 6-17 S35/20; ⊘9am-5pm) takes visitors into the world of the fascinating pre-Columbian civilizations that came before the Inca. It acknowledges the reality that the Inca built on knowledge developed over millennia of habitation in Peru. Each culture, including the Inca, has its own building with two rooms. One is dedicated to history, with key artifacts and succinct overviews in Spanish and English. The other features a compelling scenario of life-sized figures rendered expertly in action, á la *National Geographic*.

It's also entertaining for children. Reserve ahead for a guided tour in English. There's also an on-site cafe and gift shops.

Golden mask
PABLOPICASSO/SHUTTERSTOCK ©

proximity to Machu Picchu make it popular with both high-end hotels and package tours. While there is little of historical interest, nice countryside and great weather make Urubamba a convenient base from which to explore the extraordinary salt flats of Salineras and the terracing of Moray.

⊙ SIGHTS

Salineras de Maras Natural Feature

(Salt Pans; admission S10; ⊘9am-4:30pm) Salineras is among the most spectacular sights

 Community Tourism in the Sacred Valley

In recent times, rural communities of the valley have become far more accessible to visitors. While usually hospitable to passersby, they feature little infrastructure for visitors, so it's best to organize a visit in advance.

La Tierra de los Yachaqs (🗗971-502-223; www.yachaqs.com) is a rural tourism network. Guests visit Andean communities, trek to highland lakes and learn about natural medicine and artisan traditions.

Parque de la Papa (p190) is a non-profit that works to promote community farming. It offers activities including day hikes and cooking classes.

For a guided trip to visit traditional communities, check out these recommended operators: **Journey Experience** (www.thejoex.com) **Chaski Ventura** (www.chaskiventura.com) and **Respons** (www.respons.org).

Peruvian corn
A35MMPORHORA/5HUTTERSTOCK ©

in the whole Cuzco area, with thousands of salt pans that have been used for salt extraction since Inca times.

A hot spring at the top of the valley discharges a small stream of heavily salt-laden water, which is diverted into salt pans and evaporated to produce a salt used for cattle licks. It all sounds very pedestrian but the overall effect is beautiful and surreal.

🏃 ACTIVITIES

Many outdoor activities that are organized from Cuzco take place near here, including horseback riding, rock climbing, mountain biking, paragliding and hot-air balloon trips.

Cusco for You   Horse Riding
(🗗987-417-250, 987-841-000; www.cuscoforyou.com; Carr a Salineras de Maras, Pichingoto; 1hr ride S238) Highly recommended for horseback-riding and trekking trips from one to eight days long. Horseback-riding day trips go to Moray and Salineras and other regional destinations. Ask about special rates for families and groups. With an optional transportation service to the ranch, which also has accommodations and dining.

Sacred Wheels   Cycling
(🗗984-626-811, 954-700-844; 3hr tour from S264) Even the casual rider can enjoy these mountain-bike tours that visit the valley and urban Urubamba, with both gentle and challenging routes.

🛍 SHOPPING
Seminario Cerámicas   Ceramics
(🗗084-20-1002; www.ceramicaseminario.com; Berriozabal 405; ⊙8am-7pm) The internationally known local potter Pablo Seminario creates original work with a preconquest influence. His workshop – actually a small factory – is open to the public and offers a well-organized tour through the entire ceramics process.

🍴 EATING & DRINKING
**Tierra Cocina
Artesanal**   Peruvian $$
(🗗980-728-604; Av Berriozabal 84; mains S35-42; ⊙noon-8pm Thu-Tue; 🖋) 🍃 The gorgeous smells wafting in from the kitchen will lure you into this unassuming restaurant serving hearty country-style Andean dishes in the warm ambience of a small Spanish-tile home. There's slow-cooked beef simmering

Salineras de Maras (p191)

in the kitchen, homemade alpaca sausage, trout ceviche and corn *pepian* (stew). With organic meats and good vegetarian options.

Huacatay   Peruvian $$
(☑084-20-1790; Arica 620; mains S32-50; ⊗1-9:30pm Mon-Sat) In a little house tucked down a narrow side street, Huacatay makes a lovely night out. Though not every dish is a hit, the tender alpaca steak, served in a port reduction sauce with creamy quinoa risotto and topped with a spiral potato chip, is the very stuff memories are made of. Staff aim to please and there's a warm ambience.

Cervecería Valle Sagrado   Brewery
(Sacred Valley Brewery; ☑984-553-892; www. facebook.com/cerveceriadelvalle; Carr Urumbamba a Ollantaytambo, paradero Puente Pachar; mains S5-26; ⊗noon-8pm Wed-Sun) Located 7km outside of town toward Urubamba, this affable American-style brewery serves its own award-winning brews, including the highly quaffable Inti Punku IPA. You can try a flight of five different beers for S10. It's filled with chilled-out locals and expats.

Good pub grub includes deep-fried pickles and cheeseburgers. Check out its Facebook page for news on monthly barbecues.

ℹ INFORMATION

Banco de la Nación (☑084-20-1291; cnr Ugarte & Jiron Sagrario; ⊗8am-5:30pm Mon-Fri, 9am-1pm Sat) Changes US dollars and has an ATM.

ℹ GETTING THERE & AWAY

The bus terminal is about 1km west of town on the highway. Buses leave every 15 minutes for Cuzco (S7, two hours) via Pisac (S5, one hour) or Chinchero (S5, 50 minutes). Buses (S1.50, 30 minutes) and *colectivos* (S3, 25 minutes) to Ollantaytambo leave often.

A standard *mototaxi* (three-wheeled motorcycle rickshaw taxi) ride around town costs S2.

> *Outdoor activities in the area include horseback riding and rock climbing*

Things to Do in Ollantaytambo

Charmed by this small town? There's plenty to do if you want to extend your stay:

o Occurring during Pentecost in late May or early June, Señor de Choquechilca is the town's most important annual event. It commemorates the local miracle of the Christ of Choquechilca, when a wooden cross appeared by the Inca bridge, and is celebrated with music, dancing and colorful processions.

o Day hike to Intipunku (p204), an old Inca lookout.

o Hike or mountain bike to **Pumamarka**, a nearly forgotten Inca ruin, a half-day trip. Local hotels can give you directions.

Llama, Pumamarka
BCHYLA/SHUTTERSTOCK ©

Ollantaytambo

Dominated by two massive Inca ruins, the quaint village of Ollantaytambo, also called Ollanta, is the best surviving example of Inca city planning, with narrow cobblestone streets that have been continuously inhabited since the 13th century. After the hordes passing through on their way to Machu Picchu die down around late morning, Ollanta is a lovely place to be. It's perfect for wandering the mazy, narrow byways, past stone buildings and babbling irrigation channels, pretending you've stepped back in time. It also offers access to excellent hiking and biking.

TOURS

Coffee & distillery tours   Food
(☏084-20-4014; www.elalbergue.com; Estación de Tren, El Albergue; tours S50) Led by El Albergue B&B, these tours offer a fascinating behind-the-scenes look at a small-scale coffee roaster and distiller of *cañazo*, a sugarcane alcohol that's the oldest spirit in the Americas. Brought by the Spanish colony, the rustic Andean digestif is now taking on new dimensions as a high-end spirit. Participants get a free coffee or cocktail.

EATING

Chuncho   Peruvian $$
(☏084-20-4014; www.chuncho.pe; Ventidierio; mains S27-47; ⊘noon-11pm) This concept restaurant connects visitors to the bounty of ancestral Andean foods, admittedly, most of them tubers. It's a great idea, with traditional soups, rehydrated potato dishes, tarwi bean salads, tasty alpaca and *cuy* (guinea pig). Sample all with a banquet, the half-portion (S65) easily feeds two. But the real standout is the craft cocktails made with Caña Alta, a locally produced sugarcane spirit.

El Albergue Restaurante   International $$
(☏084-20-4014; Estación de Tren; mains S29-45; ⊘5:30-10am, noon-3pm & 6-9pm; 🖉) 🌿 This whistle-stop cafe serves elegant and well-priced Peruvian fare. It's inviting, with an open kitchen bordered by heaping fruit bowls and candles adorning linen-topped tables. Start with the *causas* (potato dish) or organic greens from the garden. Lamb medallions with *chimichurri* (herb sauce) is a standout, as is the molle-pepper steak spiced from the tree outside. Access via the train platform.

Hearts Café   Cafe $$
(☏084-20-4078; cnr Ventiderio & Av Ferrocarril; mains S11-28; ⊘7am-9pm; 🖉) Serving healthy and hearty food, beer and wine and good coffee, Hearts is a longtime local presence, with some organic produce and box lunches

AGUSTINA CAMILION/SHUTTERSTOCK ©

Ollantaytambo village

for excursions. Breakfasts like *huevos rancheros* (fried eggs with beans served on a tortilla) target the gringo palette, and the corner spot with outdoor tables was made for people-watching.

ℹ️ GETTING THERE & AWAY

BUS

Frequent *combis* and taxi *colectivos* shuttle between Urubamba and Ollantaytambo (S2 and S3 respectively, 30 minutes) from 6am to 5pm. **Buses** are located outside the fruit and vegetable market.

To Cuzco, it's easiest to change in Urubamba.

TRAIN

Ollantaytambo is a transport hub between Cuzco and Machu Picchu.

Inca Rail (📞084-43-6732; www.incarail.com; Av Ferrocarril s/n; ⏱6am-7:45pm Mon-Sat) 🖋 Three departures daily from Ollantaytambo and four classes of service (one way S231 to S330). Children get significant discounts.

Peru Rail (www.perurail.com; Av Ferrocarril s/n; ⏱5am-9pm) Service to Aguas Calientes with multiple departures daily. Offers three classes of service, though some trips feature extras. One-way fares: Expedition (from S232), Vistadome (from S315) and the luxurious Sacred Valley (from S581).

MACHU PICCHU

Machu Picchu at a Glance...

For many visitors to Peru and even South America, a visit to the Inca city of Machu Picchu is the long-anticipated highpoint of their trip. In a spectacular location, it's the best-known archaeological site on the continent. This awe-inspiring ancient city was never revealed to the conquering Spaniards and was virtually forgotten until the early part of the 20th century. Now, in the high season from late May until early September, 2500 people arrive daily. Despite this great tourist influx, the site manages to retain an air of grandeur and mystery, and is a must for all visitors to Peru.

Machu Picchu in Two Days

Machu Picchu is huge, so it's best to spend at least two days, using Aguas Calientes as a base camp to allow ample time to explore the **ruins**. Staying in town also allows you to get up early and beat the midday crowds at Machu Picchu. If you are also climbing **Wayna Picchu** (p206) or **Cerro Machu Picchu** (p207), you may need even more time.

Machu Picchu in Four Days

Put aside at least four days to hike the **Inca Trail**, with time to return and recover from the strenuous trek. The ancient trail was laid by the Inca, from the Sacred Valley to Machu Picchu. You will push yourself up and down and across mountains, past rivers and lakes and feel proud to reach Machu Picchu on day four.

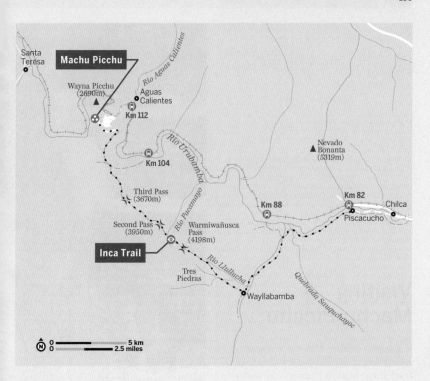

Santa Teresa

Machu Picchu

Wayna Picchu (2690m)

Aguas Calientes

Km 112

Km 104

Río Aguas Calientes

Río Urubamba

Nevado ▲ Bonanta (5319m)

Third Pass (3670m)

Second Pass (3950m)

Inca Trail

Warmiwañusca Pass (4198m)

Río Pacamayo

Km 88

Km 82

Chilca

Piscacucho

Río Llulucha

Tres Piedras

Wayllabamba

Quebrada Sauquchayoc

0 — 5 km
0 — 2.5 miles

Arriving in Machu Picchu

Unless trekking the Inca Trail, Aguas Calientes is the entry point to Machu Picchu. Cuzco is the launching point for Aguas Calientes.

Bus From Aguas Calientes, the only option up to Machu Picchu is a 20-minute bus ride.

Air The nearest airport is in Cuzco, which only serves Bolivia or domestic flights. Entry to Peru is always via Lima.

Where to Stay

Lodgings in Aguas Calientes are consistently overpriced – probably costing two-thirds more than counterparts in less-exclusive locations. There's a range of midrange accommodations, alongside some luxury offerings and budget options. Book well ahead for the best selection.

Visiting Machu Picchu

A sublime stone citadel. A staggering cloud-forest perch. And a movie-like backstory. Machu Picchu is an extraordinary Inca settlement and Unesco World Heritage Site.

Great For...

ℹ Need to Know

www.machupicchu.gob.pe; adult/student S152/77; ⏱6am-6pm

★ **Top Tip**

Try to visit outside peak times (between 10am and 2pm); June through August are the busiest months.

Unless you arrive via the Inca Trail, you'll officially enter the ruins through a ticket gate on the south side of Machu Picchu. About 100m of footpath brings you to the mazelike main entrance of Machu Picchu proper, where the ruins lie stretched out before you, roughly divided into two areas separated by a series of plazas.

Entrance tickets often sell out: buy them in advance in Cuzco. The site is limited to 5940 visitors daily, with 400 paid spots for hiking Wayna Picchu and Cerro Machu Picchu. Visitation is limited to a morning or afternoon ticket: morning tickets are valid between 6am and noon while afternoon tickets are valid between noon and 5:30pm.

Local guides (per person S150, in groups of six to 10 S30) are readily available for hire at the entrance. Their expertise varies,

look for one wearing an official guide ID from DIRCETUR.

Buying Machu Picchu Tickets

You would think accessing the continent's number one destination might be easier. Get ready. Currently, Machu Picchu tickets can be purchased online (www.machupic-chu.gob.pe), though not all foreign credit cards go through. If you reserve online, can't get your card to work and happen to be in Cuzco, you can deposit the amount due at a Banco de la Nación outlet within a three-hour window; later check in via the website to print your ticket.

In Cuzco, you can also purchase tickets from the **DIRCETUR outlet** (Map p158; ☎084-58-2030 ext 2000; www.dirceturcusco. gob.pe; Garcilaso s/n, Museo Historico Regional; ☉7am-7:30pm Mon-Sat) in the Museo

Funerary Rock

Histórico or the **Dirección Regional de Cultura Cusco** (DIRCETUR; Map p158; ☏084-58-2030; www.dirceturcusco.gob.pe; Maruri 340; ⊘7:15am-6:30pm Mon-Sat). Both outlets accept Peruvian soles, Visa or Mastercard. If you want to risk waiting, you can also purchase them from the Centro Cultural (p218) in Aguas Calientes, but only in Peruvian soles. Note that Aguas Calientes ATMs frequently run out of cash. Student tickets must be purchased in person with valid photo ID from the institution.

For a reasonable fee, travel agencies can also obtain tickets, which some readers recommend.

> ☑ **Don't Miss**
>
> Museo de Sitio Manuel Chávez Ballón (p216) near Puente Ruinas at the base of the climb to Machu Picchu.

FABIOM/GETTY IMAGES ©

Entry to Machu Picchu requires a valid photo ID.

Lastly, ticketing procedures can change, but iPeru (p177) can offer the latest updates. Good luck.

Inside the Machu Picchu Complex

Hut of the Caretaker of the Funerary Rock   Ruins

An excellent viewpoint to take in the whole site. It's one of a few buildings that has been restored with a thatched roof, making it a good shelter in the case of rain. The Inca Trail enters the city just below this hut. The carved rock behind the hut may have been used to mummify the nobility, hence the hut's name.

Ceremonial Baths   Ruins

If you head straight into the ruins from the main entry gate, you pass through extensive terracing to a beautiful series of 16 connected ceremonial baths that cascade across the ruins, accompanied by a flight of stairs.

Temple of the Sun   Ruins

Just above and to the left of the ceremonial baths is Machu Picchu's only round building, a curved and tapering tower of exceptional stonework. This structure is off-limits and best viewed from above.

Royal Tomb   Ruins

Below the Temple of the Sun, this almost hidden, natural rock cave was carefully carved by Inca stonemasons. Its use is highly debated; though known as the Royal Tomb, no mummies were actually ever found here.

Sacred Plaza   Plaza

Climbing the stairs above the ceremonial baths, there is a flat area of jumbled rocks, once used as a quarry. Turn right at the top of the stairs and walk across the quarry

> ✕ **Take a Break**
>
> Bring drinking water. Bringing food is not officially allowed.

on a short path leading to the four-sided Sacred Plaza. The far side contains a small viewing platform with a curved wall, which offers a view of the snowy Cordillera Vilcabamba in the far distance and the Río Urubamba below.

Temple of the Three Windows   Ruins
Important buildings flank the remaining three sides of the Sacred Plaza. The Temple of the Three Windows features huge trapezoidal windows that give the building its name.

Principal Temple   Ruins
The 'temple' derives its name from the massive solidity and perfection of its construction. The damage to the rear right corner is the result of the ground settling below this corner rather than any inherent weakness in the masonry itself.

House of the High Priest   Ruins
Little is known about these mysterious ruins, located opposite the Principal Temple.

Sacristy   Ruins
Behind and connected to the Principal Temple lies this famous small building. It has many well-carved niches, perhaps used for the storage of ceremonial objects, as well as a carved stone bench. The Sacristy is especially known for the two rocks flanking its entrance; each is said to contain 32 angles, but it's easy to come up with a different number whenever you count them.

Intihuatana   Ruins
This Quechua word loosely translates as the 'Hitching Post of the Sun' and refers to the carved rock pillar, often mistakenly called a sundial, at the top of the Intihuatana hill. The Inca astronomers were able to predict the solstices using the angles of this pillar. Thus, they were able to claim control over the return of the lengthening summer days. Its exact use remains unclear, but its elegant simplicity and high craftwork make it a highlight.

Central Plaza   Plaza
The plaza separates the ceremonial sector from the residential and industrial areas.

Prison Group   Ruins
At the lower end of this area is the Prison Group, a labyrinthine complex of cells, niches and passageways, positioned both under and above the ground.

Temple of the Condor   Ruins
This 'temple' is named for a carving of the head of a condor with rock outcrops as outstretched wings. It is considered the centerpiece of the Prison Group.

Ruins Outskirts

The Inca Trail ends after its final descent from the notch in the horizon called **Intipunku** (Sun Gate; ⊘checkpoint closes around

Temple of the Condor

3pm) Looking at the hill behind you as you enter the ruins, you can see both the trail and Intipunku. This hill, called Machu Picchu (old peak), gives the site its name.

Access from the Machu Picchu ruins may be restricted. It takes about an hour to reach Intipunku. If you can spare at least a half-day for the round-trip, it may be possible to continue as far as **Wiñay Wayna** (Huiñay Huayna). Expect to pay S15 or more as an unofficial reduced-charge admission fee to the Inca Trail, and be sure to return before 3pm, which is when the checkpoint typically closes.

Inca Drawbridge

A scenic but level walk from the Hut of the Caretaker of the Funerary Rock takes you right past the top of the terraces and out along a narrow, cliff-clinging trail to the Inca drawbridge. In under a half-hour's walk, the trail gives you a good look at cloud-forest vegetation and an entirely different view of Machu Picchu. This walk is recommended, though you'll have to be content with photographing the bridge from a distance, as someone crossed the bridge some years ago and tragically fell to their death.

☑ Don't Miss

Hike an hour to Intipunku (Sun Gate) for a different angle overlooking Machu Picchu.

★ Top Tip

There are no signposts here – it's not a museum – so read up or hire a guide.

IONUT DAVID/ALAMY STOCK PHOTO ©

Wayna Picchu

Wayna Picchu is the small, steep mountain at the back of the ruins. Wayna Picchu is normally translated as 'Young Peak,' but the word *picchu,* with the correct glottal pronunciation, refers to the wad in the cheek of a coca-leaf chewer. Access to Wayna Picchu is limited to 400 people per day – the first 200 in line are let in at 7am, and another 200 at 10am. A **ticket** (S48), which includes a visit to the Moon Temple, may only be obtained when you purchase your Macchu Picchu entrance ticket. These spots sell out a week in advance in low season and a month in advance in high season, so plan accordingly.

At first glance, it would appear that Wayna Picchu is a challenging climb but, although the ascent is steep, it's not technically difficult. However, it is not recommended if you suffer from vertigo. Hikers must sign in and out at a registration booth located beyond the central plaza between two thatched buildings. The 45- to 90-minute scramble up a steep footpath takes you through a short section of Inca tunnel.

Take care in wet weather as the steps get dangerously slippery. The trail is easy to follow, but involves steep sections, a ladder and an overhanging cave, where you have to bend over to get by. Part way up Wayna Picchu, a marked path plunges down to your left, continuing down the rear of Wayna Picchu to the small **Temple of the Moon**. From the temple, another cleared path leads up behind the ruin and steeply onward up the back side of Wayna Picchu.

Hut of the Caretaker of the Funerary Rock (p203)

The descent takes about an hour, and the ascent back to the main Wayna Picchu trail longer. The spectacular trail drops and climbs steeply as it hugs the sides of Wayna Picchu before plunging into the cloud forest. Suddenly, you reach a cleared area where the small, well-made ruins are found.

Cerro Machu Picchu (admission S48) is a very good alternative if you miss out on Wayna Picchu tickets.

The Mystery of Machu Picchu

Machu Picchu is not mentioned in any of the chronicles of the Spanish conquistadors. Nobody apart from local Quechua people knew of Machu Picchu's existence until American historian Hiram Bingham was guided to it by locals in 1911.

Despite scores of more recent studies, knowledge of Machu Picchu remains sketchy. Even today archaeologists are forced to rely heavily on speculation and educated guesswork as to its function. Some believe the citadel was founded in the waning years of the last Inca as an attempt to preserve Inca culture or rekindle their predominance, while others think that it may have already become an uninhabited, forgotten city at the time of the conquest.

A more recent theory suggests that the site was a royal retreat or the country palace of Pachacutec, abandoned at the time of the Spanish invasion. The site's director believes that it was a city, and a political, religious and administrative center. Its location, and the fact that at least eight access routes have been discovered, suggests that it was a trade nexus between Amazonia and the highlands.

It seems clear from the exceptionally high quality of the stonework and the abundance of ornamental work that Machu Picchu was once vitally important as a ceremonial center. Indeed, to some extent, it still is: Alejandro Toledo, the country's first indigenous Andean president, impressively staged his inauguration here in 2001.

❶ Need to Know

Drones, tripods and backpacks over 20L are not allowed into the ruins. Walking sticks are allowed.

ANNA GORIN/GETTY IMAGES ©

★ Top Tip

For really in-depth explorations, take along a copy of *Exploring Cusco* by Peter Frost.

Machu Picchu

CITADEL HIGHLIGHTS

This great 15th-century Inca citadel sits at 2430m on a narrow ridgetop above the Río Urubamba. Traditionally considered a political, religious and administrative center, but new theories suggest that it was a royal estate designed by Pachacutec, the Inca ruler whose military conquests transformed the empire. Trails linked it to the Inca capital of Cuzco and important sites in the jungle. As invading Spaniards never discovered it, experts still dispute when the site was abandoned and why.

At its peak, Machu Picchu was thought to have some 500 inhabitants. An engineering marvel, its famous Inca walls have polished stone fitted to stone, with no mortar in between. The citadel took thousands of laborers 50 years to build – today its cost of construction would exceed a billion US dollars.

Making it habitable required leveling the site, channeling water from high mountain streams through stone canals and building vertical retaining walls that became agricultural terraces for corn, potatoes and coca. The drainage system also helped combat heavy rains (diverting them for irrigation), while east-facing rooftops and farming terraces took advantage of maximum sun exposure.

The site is a magnet to mystics, adventurers and students of history alike. While its function remains hotly debated, the essential grandeur of Machu Picchu is indisputable.

TOP TIPS

- ➡ Visit before midmorning crowds.
- ➡ Allow at least three hours to visit.
- ➡ Wear walking shoes and a hat.
- ➡ Bring drinking water.
- ➡ Gain perspective walking the lead-in trails.

ADAMK92/GETTY IMAGES ©

Intihuatana
'Hitching Post of the Sun', this exquisitely carved rock was likely used by Inca astronomers to predict solstices. It's a rare survivor since invading Spaniards destroyed *intihuatanas* throughout the kingdom to eradicate what they considered to be pagan blasphemy.

Western Agricultural Terraces

Sacred Plaza

To Hut of the Caretaker of the Funerary Rock

Temple of the Three Windows
Enjoy the commanding views of the plaza below through the huge trapezoidal windows framed by 3-ton lintels. Rare in Inca architecture, the presence of three windows may indicate special significance.

MARKUS DANIEL/GETTY IMAGES ©

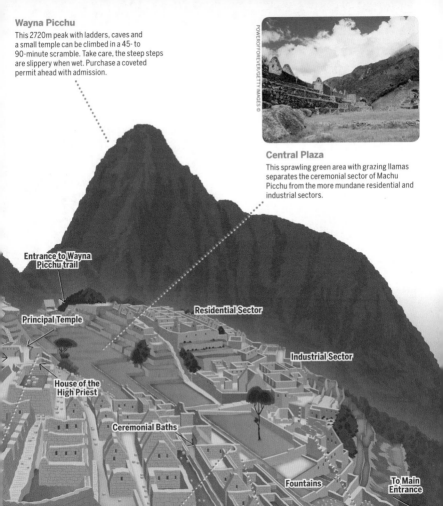

Wayna Picchu

This 2720m peak with ladders, caves and a small temple can be climbed in a 45- to 90-minute scramble. Take care, the steep steps are slippery when wet. Purchase a coveted permit ahead with admission.

Central Plaza

This sprawling green area with grazing llamas separates the ceremonial sector of Machu Picchu from the more mundane residential and industrial sectors.

Entrance to Wayna Picchu trail

Principal Temple

Residential Sector

Industrial Sector

House of the High Priest

Ceremonial Baths

Fountains

To Main Entrance

To Agricultural Terraces

Temple of the Sun

This off-limits rounded tower is best viewed from above. Featuring the site's finest stone-work, an altar and trapezoidal windows, it may have been used for astronomical purposes.

Royal Tomb

Speculated to have special ceremonial significance, this natural rock cave sits below the Temple of the Sun. Though it is off-limits, visitors can view its steplike altar and sacred niches from the entrance.

Temple of the Condor

Check out the condor-head carving with rock outcrops that resemble outstretched wings. Behind, an off-limits cavity reaches a tiny underground cell that may only be entered by bending double.

Phuyupatamarka (p214)

The Inca Trail

The views of snowy mountain peaks, distant rivers and cloud forests are stupendous – and walking from one cliff-hugging pre-Columbian ruin to the next is a mystical and unforgettable experience.

The most famous hike in South America, the four-day Inca Trail is walked by thousands every year. Although the total distance is only about 24 miles, the ancient trail laid by the Inca from the Sacred Valley to Machu Picchu winds its way up and down and around the mountains, snaking over three high Andean passes en route, which have collectively led to the route being dubbed 'the Inca Trail'.

Great For...

☑ Don't Miss

Hot springs in the towns along the way will help weary hiking legs to recover.

Booking Your Trip

It is important to book your trip at least six months in advance for dates between May and August. Outside these months, you may get a permit with a few weeks' notice, but it's very hard to predict. Only licensed operators can get permits, but you can check general availability at www. camino-inca.com.

MATTHEW WILLIAMS-ELLIS/GETTY IMAGES ©

Alpaca

ℹ Need to Know

Most trekking agencies run buses to the start of the trail, also known as Piscacucho or Km 82.

✖ Take a Break

Most tours include meals and snacks. Bring a refillable water bottle.

★ Top Tip

The Inca Trail is best visited in the dry season, April to October, and is closed in February.

Consider booking a five-day trip to lessen the pace and enjoy more wildlife and ruins. Other positives include less-crowded campsites and being able to stay at the most scenic one – Phuyupatamarka (3600m) – on the third evening.

Regulations & Fees

The Inca Trail is the only trek in the Cuzco area that cannot be walked independently – you must go with a licensed operator. Prices cost US$595 to US$6000 and above.

Only 500 people each day (including guides and porters) are allowed to start the trail. You must go through an approved Inca Trail operator. Permits are issued to them on a first-come, first-served basis. You will need to provide your passport number to get a permit, and carry the passport with

you to show at checkpoints along the trail. Be aware that if you get a new passport but had applied with your old, it may present a problem.

Permits are nontransferable: name changes are not allowed.

Choosing an Operator

While it may be tempting to quickly book your trek and move onto the next item on your to-do list, it's a good idea to examine the options carefully before sending that deposit. If price is your bottom line, keep in mind that the cheapest agencies may cut corners by paying their guides and porters lower wages. Other issues are substandard gear (eg leaky tents) and dull or lackadaisical guiding.

Yet paying more may not mean getting more, especially since international operators take their cut and hire local Peruvian agencies. Talk with a few agencies to get a sense of their quality of service. You might ask if the guide speaks English (fluently or just a little), request a list of what is included and inquire about group size and the kind of transportation used. Ensure that your tour includes a tent, food, a cook, one-day admission to the ruins and the return train fare.

Porters who carry group gear – tents, food etc – are also included. You'll be expected to carry your own personal gear, including sleeping bag. If you are not an experienced backpacker, it may be a good idea to hire a porter to carry your personal gear; this usually costs around US$50 per day for about 10kg.

If you prefer more exclusive services, it's possible to organize private trips with an independent licensed guide (US$1250 to US$2000 per person).

For a list of agencies and guides based in Cuzco, see p164.

The Two-Day Inca Trail

This 10km version of the Inca Trail gives a fairly good indication of what the longer trail is like. It's a real workout, and passes through some of the best scenery and most impressive ruins and terracing of the longer trail.

It's a steep three- or four-hour climb from Km 104 to Wiñay Wayna, then another two hours or so on fairly flat terrain to Machu Picchu. You may be on the trail a couple of hours longer, just to enjoy the views and explore. We advise taking the earliest train possible from Cuzco or Ollantaytambo.

The two-day trail means overnighting in Aguas Calientes, and visiting Machu Picchu the next day, so it's really only one day of walking. The average price is US$400 to US$535.

Llactapata

What to Expect

Even if you are not carrying a full backpack, this trek requires a good level of fitness. In addition to regularly exercising, you can get ready with hikes and long walks in the weeks before your trip (also a good time to test out your gear). Boots should be already worn in by the time you go. On the trail, you may have to deal with issues such as heat and altitude. Just don't rush it; keep a reasonable pace and you should do fine.

Day One

After crossing the Río Urubamba (2600m) and taking care of registration formalities, you'll climb gently alongside the river to the trail's first archaeological site, **Llactapata** (Town on Top of the Terraces), before heading south down a side valley of the Río Cusichaca. (If you start from Km 88, turn west after crossing the river to see the little-visited site of **Q'ente**, about 1km away, then return east to Llactapata on the main trail.)

The trail leads 7km south to the hamlet of **Wayllabamba** (Grassy Plain; 3000m), near which many tour groups will camp for the first night. You can buy bottled drinks and high-calorie snacks here, and take a breather to look over your shoulder for views of the snow-capped **Nevado Verónica** (5750m).

Day Two

Wayllabamba is situated near the fork of Ríos Llullucha and Cusichaca. The trail crosses the Río Llullucha, then climbs steeply up along the river. This area is known as **Tres Piedras** (Three White Stones; 3300m), though these boulders are no longer visible. From here it is a long, very steep 3km climb through humid woodlands.

The trail eventually emerges on the high, bare mountainside of **Llulluchupampa** (3750m), where water is available and the flats are dotted with campsites, which get very cold at night. This is as far as you can reasonably expect to get on your first day, though many groups will actually spend their second night here.

From Llulluchupampa, a good path up the left-hand side of the valley climbs for a two- to three-hour ascent to the pass of **Warmiwañusca**, also colorfully known as 'Dead Woman's Pass.' At 4200m above sea

NIARKRAD/SHUTTERSTOCK ©

ℹ Need to Know

Take cash (in Peruvian soles) for tipping; an adequate amount is S100 for a porter and S200 for a cook.

level, this is the highest point of the trek, and leaves many a seasoned hiker gasping. From Warmiwañusca, you can see the Río Pacamayo (Río Escondido) far below, as well as the ruin of Runkurakay halfway up the next hill, above the river.

The trail continues down a long and knee-jarringly steep descent to the river, where there are large campsites at **Paq'amayo**. At an altitude of about 3600m, the trail crosses the river over a small footbridge and climbs toward **Runkurakay**; at 3750m this round ruin has superb views. It's about an hour's walk away.

Day Three

Above Runkurakay, the trail climbs to a false summit before continuing past two small lakes to the top of the second pass at 3950m, which has views of the snow-laden Cordillera Vilcabamba. You'll notice a change in ecology as you descend from this pass – you're now on the eastern, Amazon slope of the Andes and things immediately get greener. The trail descends to the ruin of **Sayaqmarka**, a tightly constructed complex perched on a small mountain spur, which offers incredible views. The trail continues downward and crosses an upper tributary of the Río Aobamba (Wavy Plain).

The trail then leads on across an Inca causeway and up a gentle climb through some beautiful cloud forest and an **Inca tunnel** carved from the rock. This is a relatively flat section and you'll soon arrive at the third pass at almost 3600m, which has grand views of the Río Urubamba valley, and campsites where some groups spend their final night, with the advantage of watching the sun set over a truly spectacular view, but with the disadvantage of having to leave at 3am in the race to reach the Sun Gate in time for sunrise. If you are camping here, be careful in the early morning as the steep incline makes the following steps slippery.

Just below the pass is the beautiful and well-restored ruin of **Phuyupatamarka**

(City Above the Clouds), about 3570m above sea level. The site contains six beautiful ceremonial baths with water running through them. From Phuyupatamarka, the trail makes a dizzying dive into the cloud forest below, following an incredibly well-engineered flight of many hundreds of Inca steps (it's nerve-racking in the early hours, use a headlamp). After two or three hours, the trail eventually zigzags its way down to a collapsed red-roofed white building that marks the final night's campsite.

A 500m trail behind the old, out of use, pub leads to the exquisite little Inca site of **Wiñay Wayna**, which is variously translated as 'Forever Young,' 'To Plant the Earth Young' and 'Growing Young' (as opposed to 'growing old'). Peter Frost writes that the Quechua name refers to an orchid

(*Epidendrum secundum*) that blooms here year-round. The semitropical campsite at Wiñay Wayna boasts one of the most stunning views on the whole trail, especially at sunrise. For better or worse, the famous pub located here is now deteriorated and no longer functioning. A rough trail leads from this site to another spectacular terraced ruin, called **Intipata**, best visited on the day you arrive to Wiñay Wayna (consider coordinating it with your guide if you are interested).

Day Four

From the Wiñay Wayna guard post, the trail winds without much change in elevation through the cliff-hanging cloud forest for about two hours to reach **Intipunku** (Sun Gate) – the penultimate site on the trail, where it's tradition to enjoy your first

glimpse of majestic Machu Picchu while waiting for the sun to rise over the surrounding mountains.

The final triumphant descent takes almost an hour. Trekkers generally arrive long before the morning trainloads of tourists, and can enjoy the exhausted exhilaration of reaching their goal without having to push past enormous groups of visitors.

★ Top Tip

As a courtesy, don't occupy the dining tent until late if it's where the porters sleep.

❶ Need to Know

Make sure you have international travel insurance that covers adventure activities.

Aguas Calientes

Also known as Machu Picchu Pueblo, this town lies in a deep gorge below the ruins. A virtual island, it's cut off from all roads and enclosed by stone cliffs, towering cloud forest and two rushing rivers.

Despite its gorgeous location, Aguas Calientes has the feel of a gold-rush town, with a large itinerant population, slack services that count on one-time customers and an architectural tradition of rebar and unfinished cement. With merchants pushing the hard sell, it's hard not to feel overwhelmed. Your best bet is to go without expectations.

Yet spending the night offers one distinct advantage: early access to Machu Picchu, which turns out to be a pretty good reason to stay.

Note that the footpath from the train station to the Machu Picchu bus stop is stepped. Wheelchair access to the bus stop is via the small bridge to Sinchi Roca and through the center of town.

◉ SIGHTS

Museo de Sitio Manuel Chávez Ballón   Museum

(admission S22; ⊘9am-5pm) This museum has superb information in Spanish and English on the archaeological excavations of Machu Picchu and Inca building methods. Stop here before or after the ruins to get a sense of context (and to enjoy the air-conditioning and soothing music if you're walking back from the ruins after hours in the sun).

There's a small botanical garden with orchids outside, down a cool if nerve-testing set of Inca stairs. It's by Puente Ruinas, at the base of the footpath to Machu Picchu.

Las Termas   Hot Springs

(admission S20; ⊘5am-8:30pm) Weary trekkers soak away their aches and pains in the town's hot springs, 10 minutes' walk up Pachacutec from the train tracks. These tiny, natural thermal springs, from which Aguas Calientes derives its name, are nice enough but far from the best in the area, and get scummy by late morning.

Aguas Calientes

Towels can be rented cheaply outside the entrance to the hot springs.

ACTIVITIES

Putucusi   Hiking
This jagged minimountain sits directly opposite Machu Picchu. Parts of the walk are up ladders, which get slippery in the wet season. The view across to Machu Picchu is worth the trek. Allow three hours. Follow the railway tracks about 250m west of town and you'll see a set of stairs, the start of a well-marked trail.

EATING

Restaurants range from basic eateries to fine dining. Touts standing in the street will try to herd you into their restaurant, but take your time making a selection. Standards are not very high in most restaurants – if you go to one that hasn't been recommended, snoop around to check the hygiene first. Since refrigeration can be a problem, it's best to order vegetarian if you're eating in low-end establishments.

Indio Feliz   French $$
(☎084-21-1090; Lloque Yupanqui 4; mains S34-48; ⏱11am-10pm) Hospitality is the strong suit of French cook Patrik at this multi-award-winning restaurant, but the food does not disappoint. Start with *sopa a la criolla* (mildly spiced, creamy noodle soup with beef and peppers). There are also nods to traditional French cooking – like Provençal tomatoes, crispy-perfect garlic potatoes and a melt-in-your-mouth apple tart.

The candlelit decor shows the imagination of a long-lost castaway with imitation Gauguin panels, carved figurehead damsels, colonial benches and vintage objects. The *menú* (set meal; S78) is extremely good value for a decadent dinner. Indio Feliz has good wheelchair access, a fireplace lit on cold days and may eventually add an upstairs bar and terrace, another reason not to leave.

 Porter Welfare on the Inca Trail

In the past, Inca Trail porters have faced excessively low pay, enormous carrying loads and poor working conditions. Relatively recent laws now stipulate a minimum payment of S170 to porters, adequate sleeping gear and food, and treatment for on-the-job injuries. At checkpoints on the trail, porter loads are weighed (each is allowed 20kg of group gear and 5kg of their own gear).

Yet there is still room for improvement and the best way to help is to choose your outfitter wisely. A quality trip will set you back at least US$500. The cheaper trips cut costs and often affect porter welfare.

BOB POOL/SHUTTERSTOCK ©

Tree House   Fusion $$
(☎084-21-1101; www.thetreehouse-peru.com; Huanacaure s/n; mains S38-60; ⏱4:30am-10pm) The rustic ambience of Tree House provides a cozy setting to enjoy its inviting fusion menu, which is served alongside South American wines, craft beers and cocktails.

Dishes like stuffed wontons with tamarind sauce, alpaca tenderloin and crisp quinoa-crusted trout are lovingly prepared. For dessert, lip-smacking chocolate mousse. With raw and vegan options. Reserve ahead. It's part of the Rupa Wasi hotel.

Hiram Bingham's Explorations

When the local Quechua people led American historian Hiram Bingham to Machu Picchu in 1911, the site was completely unknown to the outside world. In the 1860s a couple of German adventurers had looted the site, apparently with the Peruvian government's permission, but it was then forgotten.

You can read Bingham's own account of his 'discovery' in the classic book *Inca Land: Explorations in the Highlands of Peru*, first published in 1922 and now available as a free download from Project Gutenberg (www.gutenberg.org).

Bingham was searching for the lost city of Vilcabamba, the last stronghold of the Inca, and thought he had found it at Machu Picchu. We now know that the remote ruins at Espíritu Pampa, much deeper in the jungle, are actually the remains of Vilcabamba. The Machu Picchu site was initially overgrown with thick vegetation, forcing Bingham's team to be content with roughly mapping the site. Bingham returned in 1912 and 1915 to carry out the difficult task of clearing the thick forest, when he also discovered some of the ruins on the so-called Inca Trail. Peruvian archaeologist Luis E Valcárcel undertook further studies in 1934, as did a Peruvian-American expedition under Paul Fejos in 1940 and 1941.

Machu Picchu (p200)
GFED/GETTY IMAGES ©

Mapacho   Cafe $$

(📱984-759-634; Av Imperio de los Incas 614; mains S20-48; ⊙10am-10pm) This friendly streetside cafe is popular with the backpacking set. Perhaps it's all the craft beer and burgers on offer. It's worth checking out the *arroz chaufa* (fried rice) and *lomo saltado (*strips of beef stir-fried with onions, tomatoes, potatoes and chili).

Chullpi   Peruvian $$$

(📱914-169-687; Av Imperio de los Incas 140; mains S49-69; ⊙11:30am-11pm) Touting *'cocina de autor,'* this stylish shoebox of a restaurant serves beautifully plated food, but in its mass production it might not quite live up to gourmet standards. The fare is classic Andean – including grilled trout, shredded pork and *wallpa chupe* (a chicken-tomato stew).

There are also soups and *causas* (creamy potato dishes). Tour groups have a tendency to take over – reserve ahead.

Café Inkaterra   Peruvian $$$

(📱084-21-1122; Machu Picchu Pueblo Hotel; menú lunch/dinner S93/122; ⊙11:30am-4pm & 6-10pm; 🚶♿) Upstream from the train station, this tucked-away riverside restaurant is housed in elongated thatched rooms with views of water tumbling over the boulders. There's a set menu (starter, main dish and dessert), with gluten-free and vegetarian options, and a decent kids menu to entice the young ones. The *lomo saltado* bursts with flavor.

ℹ INFORMATION

BCP (Av Imperio de los Incas s/n) ATM.

Centro Cultural (Machu Picchu Tickets; 📱084-21-1196; Av Pachacutec s/n; ⊙5:30am-8:30pm) This is the only spot in town selling Machu Picchu entrance tickets. It's cash only and never a sure thing last minute.

iPerú (📱084-21-1104; Av Pachacutec, cuadra 1; ⊙9am-6pm Mon-Sun) A helpful information center for everything Machu Picchu.

GALYNA ANDRUSHKO/SHUTTERSTOCK ©

ℹ️ GETTING THERE & AWAY

TRAIN

All train companies have ticket offices in the train station.

To Cuzco (three hours), **Peru Rail** (www.peru rail.com) has service to Poroy and taxis connect to the city, another 20 minutes away.

To Ollantaytambo (two hours), both Peru Rail and Inca Rail (p311) provide service. Inca Rail offers a ticket with connecting bus service to Cuzco.

To **Santa Teresa** (via Hidroelectrica Station, 45 minutes), Peru Rail travels at 6:45am, 1:30pm and 3:40pm daily.

BUS

There is no road access to Aguas Calientes. The only buses go from the **bus stop** (where you can purchase tickets) up the hill to Machu Picchu (round-trip S80, 25 minutes) from 5:30am to 4pm; buses return until 6pm.

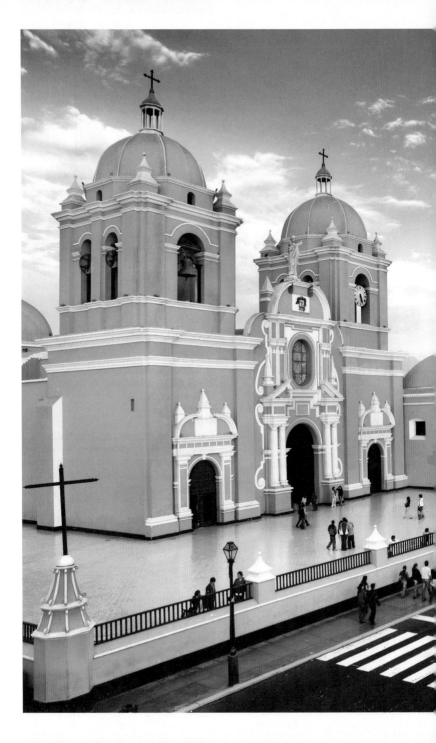

TRUJILLO

Trujillo at a Glance...

Stand in the right spot and the glamorously colonial streets of old Trujillo look like they've barely changed in hundreds of years. Well, there are more honking taxis now – but the city, with its polychrome buildings and profusion of colonial-era churches, still manages to put on a dashing show. Most people come here to visit the remarkable pre-Inca archaeological sites nearby, spending just a short time wandering the compact city center. The behemoth Chimú capital of Chan Chan, on the outskirts of town, was the largest pre-Columbian city in the Americas, making it the top attraction in the region.

Trujillo in Two Days

Spend the first morning exploring **Chan Chan** (p224), the Chimú capital, including the **Museo de Sitio Chan Chan** (p225). Grab a late lunch at one of the trendy cafes on Calle Pizarro. On the second morning, visit the colonial mansion **Casa Ganoza Chopitea** (p228) and Plaza de Armas. Then head to the fascinating **Huacas del Sol y de la Luna** (p232).

Trujillo in Three Days

A third day gets you more time with the *casonas* (large houses) in Trujillo, its Plaza de Armas, elegant colonial streets and the ancient Moche artifacts at **Museo de Arqueología** (p229).

The rest of the day can be spent in the nearby beach town of **Huanchaco** riding the epic Pacific breakers or admiring the narrow reed boats on the *malecón* (boardwalk). Seal the evening with a seafood dinner.

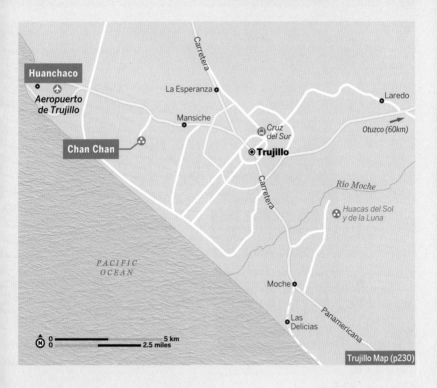

Trujillo Map (p230)

Arriving in Trujillo

Aeropuerto de Trujillo The airport is 10km northwest of town.

Bus Most buses arrive at the north end of town at España and Amazonas or, if coming from the south, at terminals on the Panamericana Sur.

Where to Stay

In Trujillo, the most comfortable and convenient location is anywhere within two blocks of Plaza de Armas, especially north near Calle Pizarro. Note that many budget and midrange hotels can be noisy if you get the street-side rooms.

Beachbums may consider staying in the laidback surfer village of Huanchaco, just 20 minutes up the road.

TBRADFORD/GETTY IMAGES ©

Chan Chan

Built around AD 1300 and covering 36 sq km, Chan Chan is the largest pre-Columbian city in the Americas and the largest adobe city in the world.

At the height of the Chimú empire, Chan Chan housed some 60,000 inhabitants and contained a vast wealth of gold, silver and ceramics (which the Spanish quickly looted).

The capital consisted of 10 walled citadels, also called royal compounds. Each contained a royal burial mound filled with funerary offerings, including dozens of sacrificed young women and chambers full of ceramics, weavings and jewelry. Over time, devastating El Niño floods and heavy rainfall have severely eroded the mud walls of the city – you'll need an active imagination to fill in the details. Today the most impressive aspect of the site is its sheer size.

Note that Chan Chan is best visited with a guide from Trujillo or on-site, as signage is extremely limited. Much of the site is covered with tent-like structures to protect it from erosion.

Great For...

☑ **Don't Miss**

The sea-related friezes in the Audience Rooms.

❶ Need to Know

www.chanchan.gob.pe; admission S10, guide for groups of 1-5 S40; ☉9am-4pm, museum closed Mon

✕ Take a Break

The only food sold nearby is the snacks near the ticket booth.

★ Top Tip

Chan Chan is on the road between Trujillo and Huanchaco, making it easy to visit the ruins and beach in one day.

Palacio Nik An

The area known as the Palacio Nik An (also called the Tschudi Complex) is the only section of Chan Chan that's partially restored. The complex's centerpiece is a massive restored **Ceremonial Courtyard**, with 4m-thick interior walls that are decorated with recreated geometric designs. Ground-level designs closest to the door, representing three or four sea otters, are the only originals left. Nearby, an outside wall – one of the best restored in the complex – displays friezes of fish and seabirds.

Other elements in the complex include the set of labyrinthine **Audience Rooms**, filled with friezes of birds, fish and waves, as well as the **Gran Hachaque Ceremonial**, a freshwater pool surrounded by a verdant border of reeds and grasses. Also on view is a **Mausoleum**, where a king was buried with human sacrifices, as well as the fascinating **Assembly Room**, a large rectangular room with 24 seats set into niches in the walls. Its acoustic properties are such that speakers sitting in any one of the niches can be clearly heard all over the room.

Museo de Sitio Chan Chan

The site **museum** (www.chanchan.gob.pe; admission free with Chan Chan ticket; ☉9am-4pm Tue-Sun) contains exhibits explaining Chan Chan and the Chimú culture. It is a short walk away on the main road, about 500m before the Chan Chan turnoff. The museum has a few signs in Spanish and English, but a guide is still useful. A sound-and-light show plays in Spanish every 30 minutes. The aerial photos and maps showing the huge extension of Chan Chan are fascinating, as tourists can only visit a tiny portion of the site.

GERAINT ROWLAND PHOTOGRAPHY/GETTY IMAGES ©

Huanchaco

This once-tranquil fishing hamlet, 12km outside Trujillo, woke up one morning to find itself a brightly high-lighted paragraph on Peru's Gringo Trail. Huanchaco's fame comes from its excellent surf breaks and the long, narrow reed boats you'll see lining the malecón.

Great For...

☑ Don't Miss

Huanchaco's wide selection of seafood restaurants.

Beach & Surf

Though you can almost picture Huanchaco on postcards of days gone by, the beach is distinctly average. Nevertheless, the slow pace of life attracts a certain type of beach bum and the town has managed to retain much of its villagey appeal.

The curving, gray-sand beach here is fine for swimming during the December to April summer, but expect serious teeth chatter during the rest of the year. The good surf, perfect for beginners, draws its fair share of followers and you'll see armies of bleached-blond surfer types ambling the streets with boards under their arms. Expect decent waves year-round. The beach break starts about 800m south of the pier – with a rock and sand bottom. It rarely connects for longer rides, but you can get plenty of fun

Traditional reed boats

MATYAS REHAK/SHUTTERSTOCK ©

ℹ Need to Know

Combis (minivans) and yellow and red *micros* (small buses) to Huanchaco frequently leave from Trujillo (S2).

✕ Take a Break

Restaurante Mococho (www.facebook. com/restaurantemococho; Bolognesi 535; mains S36, whole fish per 1kg S110; ⊙1-3pm, closed Mon) – the specialty is steamed whole fish in sauce.

★ Top Tip

Tour operators on the main road organize direct trips to regional archaeological sites from Huanchaco.

lefts and shortish rights anywhere on the beach.

You can rent surfing gear (S35 per day for a wet suit and surfboard) from several places along the main drag. Lessons cost about S70 for a 1½-hour to two-hour session. Check at **Otra Cosa** (📞044-46-1302; www.otracosa.org; Las Camelias 431) for local volunteering opportunities.

Caballitos de Totora

Huanchaco's defining characteristic is that a small number of local fishers are still using the very same narrow reed boats depicted on 2000-year-old Moche pottery. The fishers paddle and surf these neatly crafted boats like seafaring gauchos, with their legs dangling on either side – which explains the nickname given to these

elegantly curving steeds: *caballitos de tortora* (little horses). The inhabitants of Huanchaco are among the few remaining people on the coast who remember how to construct and use the boats, each one only lasting a few months before becoming waterlogged. The fishers paddle out as far as a mile, but can only bring in limited catches because of the size of their vessels (which now also integrate styrofoam for buoyancy).

The days of Huanchaco's reed-boat fishers are likely numbered. Recent reports say that erosion and other environmental factors are affecting the beds where the fishers plant and harvest the reeds, and many youngsters are opting to become surf instructors, professionals or commercial fishers rather than following in their parents' hard-paddled wakes.

⊙ SIGHTS

Trujillo's spacious and spit-shined main square, surely the cleanest in the Americas and definitely one of the prettiest, hosts a colorful assembly of preserved colonial buildings and an impressive statue dedicated to work, the arts and liberty. Elegant mansions abound, including **Hotel Libertador.**

Casa Ganoza
Chopitea   Historic Building
(Independencia 630; ⊙5:30-11:30pm Mon-Sat) Northeast of the cathedral, this c 1735 mansion, also known as Casa de los Léones, is considered to be the best-preserved mansion of the colonial period in Trujillo. The details are stunning, from the elaborate gateway at the entrance to 300-year-old frescoes and Oregon-pine pillars.

Take note of the 'JHS' insignia above the entrance, between the male and female lions (from which the Casa de los Léones name derives). It stands for 'Jesus,' 'Hombre' (Man), 'Salvador' (Savior) and stems

from the building's time as a convent. Best of all, perhaps, is that it now houses the wonderful Casona Deza cafe (p231).

Casa de Urquiaga   Historic Building
(Pizarro 446; ⊙9:15am-3:15pm Mon-Fri, 10am-1pm Sat) **FREE** Owned and maintained by Banco Central de la Reserva del Perú since 1972, this beautiful colonial mansion's history dates to 1604, though the original house was completely destroyed in the earthquake of 1619. Rebuilt and preserved since, it now houses exquisite period furniture, including a striking writer's desk once used by Simón Bolívar, who organized much of his final campaign to liberate Peru from the Spanish empire from Trujillo in 1824.

Palacio Iturregui   Historic Building
(Pizarro 688; admission S5; ⊙8-10am) This imposing gray early-19th-century mansion is impossible to ignore. Built in neoclassical style, it has beautiful window gratings, 36 slender interior columns and gold moldings on the ceilings. General Juan Manuel

Colonial building

Iturregui lived here after he famously proclaimed independence.

Museo de Arqueología Museum

(Junín 682; admission S5; ☺9am-2:30pm Mon, to 4:30pm Tue-Sat) This well-curated museum features a rundown of Peruvian history from 12,000 BC to the present day, with an emphasis on Moche, Chimú and Inca civilizations as well as the lesser-known Cupisnique and Salinar cultures. It's also worth popping in for the house itself: a restored 17th-century mansion known as La Casa Risco, which features striking cedar pillars and gorgeous painted courtyard walls.

Casa de la
Emancipación Notable Building

(Pizarro 610; ☺9am-1pm & 4-8pm) Now the Banco BBVA Continental, this building features a mishmash of colonial and Republican styles and is best known as the site where Trujillo's independence from colonial rule was formally declared on December 29, 1820. Check out the unique cubic Cajabamba marble stone flooring; there are also galleries dedicated to revolving art exhibitions, Peruvian poet César Vallejo and period furniture. It hosts live-music events as well – look for posters around town.

Basilica Menor
Catedral Church

(Plaza de Armas s/n; admission to museum S4; ☺church 7am-1pm & 4-8pm daily, museum 9am-1pm & 4-7pm Mon-Fri, 9am-1pm Sat) Known simply as 'La Catedral,' this bright, canary-yellow church fronting the plaza was begun in 1647, destroyed in 1759, and rebuilt soon afterward. The cathedral has a famous basilica, which is generally open to visitors, and a museum of religious and colonial art, though there are intriguing frescoes in the basement (along with a few bats).

☺ TOURS

There are dozens of tour agencies in Trujillo. Some supply guides who speak English

📖 Trujillo's
Bloody History

The Trujillo area has been inhabited for millennia, with several prominent pre-Incan civilizations popping up in the fertile oasis.

Francisco Pizarro founded Trujillo in 1534, and he thought so highly of this patch of desert he named it after his birthplace in Spain's Estremadura. Spoiled by the fruits of the fertile Moche valley, Trujillo never had to worry about money – wealth came easily. With life's essentials taken care of, thoughts turned to politics and life's grander schemes, and so the city's reputation for being a hotbed of revolt began. The town was besieged during the Inca rebellion of 1536, and in 1820 was the first Peruvian city to declare independence from Spain.

The tradition continued into the 20th century, as bohemians flocked, poets put pen to paper (including Peru's best poet, César Vallejo) and rebels raised their fists defiantly in the air. It was here that the Alianza Popular Revolution Americana (APRA) workers' party was formed – and where many of its members were later massacred.

Trujillo's colonial mansions and churches, most of which are near the Plaza de Armas, are worth seeing, though they don't keep very regular opening hours. The creamy pastel shades and beautiful wrought-iron grillwork fronting almost every colonial building are unique Trujillo touches.

Liberation Monument, Plaza de Armas

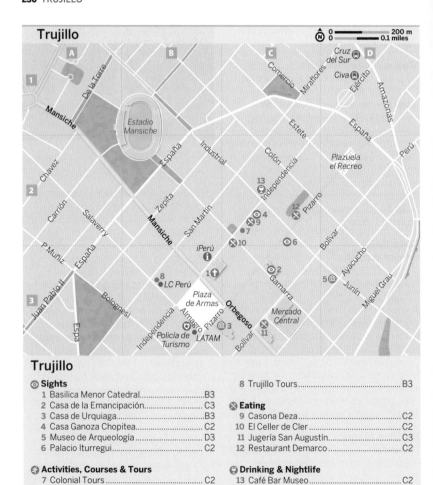

Trujillo

⊙ **Sights**
1 Basilica Menor Catedral..............................B3
2 Casa de la Emancipación..........................C3
3 Casa de Urquiaga......................................B3
4 Casa Ganoza Chopitea..............................C2
5 Museo de Arqueología D3
6 Palacio Iturregui.......................................C2

⊕ **Activities, Courses & Tours**
7 Colonial Tours C2

8 Trujillo Tours..B3

⊗ **Eating**
9 Casona Deza..C2
10 El Celler de Cler C2
11 Jugería San Augustín.................................C3
12 Restaurant Demarco C2

⊙ **Drinking & Nightlife**
13 Café Bar Museo..C2

but don't know much about the area; some supply guides who are well informed but don't speak English. Entrance fees are not included in the listed tour prices. Most full-day tours cost around S35 to S60, including transport and guide.

Trujillo Tours   Cultural
(☑044-23-3091; www.trujillotours.com; Almagro 301; ⊙7:30am-1pm & 4-8pm) This friendly operation has three- to four-hour tours to

Chan Chan, Huanchaco and Huacas del Sol y de la Luna, as well as city tours. Tours are available in English, French, Portuguese and German.

Colonial Tours   Tour
(☑044-29-1034; www.colonialtoursnorteperu. com; Independencia 616) Full-day guided tours to all the major archaeological sites. Tends to offer big discounts when things are slow.

EATING

The 700 *cuadra* (block) of Pizarro is where Trujillo's power brokers hang out and families converge, and they're kept well fed by a row of trendy yet reasonably priced cafes and restaurants. Some of the best eateries in Trujillo are found a short taxi ride outside the town center.

Jugería
San Augustín Sandwiches $

(Bolívar 526; sandwiches S3.50-7.50; ⊗8:30am-1pm & 4-8pm Mon-Sat, 9am-1pm Sun) You can spot this place by the near-constant lines snaking around the corner in summer as locals queue for the drool-inducing juices. But don't leave it at that. The chicken and *lechón* (suckling pig) sandwiches, slathered with all the fixings, are what you'll be telling friends back home about on a postcard.

El Celler de Cler Peruvian $$

(✎044-31-7191; cnr Gamarra & Independencia; mains S38-58; ⊗6pm-1am) This atmospheric spot is the only place in Trujillo to enjoy dinner (coupled with an amazing cocktail) on a 2nd-floor balcony – the wraparound number dates to the early 19th century. The food is upscale, featuring pasta and grills, and delicious. Antiques fuel the decor, from a 1950s-era American cash register to an extraordinary industrial-revolution pulley lamp from the UK.

Mar Picante Peruvian $$

(www.marpicante.com; Húsares de Junín 412; mains S20-40; ⊗10am-5pm) This hugely popular place has recently undergone an overhaul and is now all polished concrete and industrial metal beams, but the food remains outrageously good. If you come to Trujillo without sampling its *ceviche mixto* ordered with a side of something spicy, you haven't lived life on the edge.

Restaurant Demarco Peruvian $$

(✎044-23-4251; Pizarro 725; mains S15-47; ⊗7:30am-11pm; ☎) An elegant choice, with veteran cummerbund-bound waiters who fawn over you like in the 1940s, this table-clothed classic offers a long list of sophisticated meat and seafood dishes, along with good-value lunch specials (S13.50 to S18.50) and pizzas.

Casona Deza Peruvian $$

(Independencia 630; mains S23-46; ⊗5:30-11:30pm Mon-Sat; ☎) ✐ Expect excellent espresso, house-made desserts and tasty pizzas and pasta, often sourced organically, at this spacious, atmospheric cafe that occupies one of the city's most fiercely preserved colonial homes.

DRINKING & NIGHTLIFE

Trujillo has the best nightlife in the region, with loads of interesting bars in and around the center and some happening clubs a bit further afield.

El Tragsu Bar

(Las Hortencias 588; ⊗9pm-4am Mon-Sat) This popular place south of the center is one of the best pubs in Peru, with a classic themed front room complete with elf decorations and an elegant wooden bar for those who want to converse. There's also a steamy split-level band room where the dial is stuck on 'full party' mode.

Café Bar Museo Bar

(cnr Junín & Independencia; ⊗5pm-late Mon-Sat) This locals' favorite shouldn't be a secret. The tall, wood-paneled walls covered in artsy posters and the classic marble-top bar feel like a cross between an English pub and a Left Bank cafe. Hands down the most interesting place to drink in Trujillo. There's a limited menu of bar snacks if you want to make a night of it.

ENTERTAINMENT

Wachaque Live Music

(✎943-779-327; Los Algarrobos 574; ⊗7pm-3am Thu-Sat) Overlooking pleasant Parque California, this welcoming modern place is billed as a gastrobar, but while the food is pretty good, it's more of an upmarket bar/

 **Huacas del Sol
y de la Luna**

If there's one must-see archaeological site in the region, this is it. The **Temples of the Sun and the Moon** (www.huacasdemoche.pe; site admission S10, museum S5; ⊕9am-4pm), attributed to the Moche period, are more than 700 years older than Chan Chan, yet parts of the complex are remarkably well preserved. Located on the south bank of the Río Moche, the main attraction here is the **Huaca de la Luna** with its phenomenal multicolored friezes. The entrance price includes an English-speaking guide; individual travelers need to wait for a group to fill. The larger **Huaca del Sol** is closed to visitors.

Archaeologists believe the Huaca de la Luna was the religious and ceremonial center of the Moche capital, while the Huaca del Sol was the administrative center. The two edifices are separated by 500m of open desert that once contained the dwellings and other buildings of the common residents.

Enthusiastic local guides will walk you through different parts of the complex and explain the richly colored motifs depicting Moche gods and zoomorphic figures, before leading you to the spectacular finale: the magnificent, richly decorated external wall. Many of the guides are volunteers, so tips are appreciated.

Combis (S1.50) for the Huacas del Sol y de la Luna leave from Av Los Incas in Trujillo every 15 minutes or so.

Bas relief, Huaca de la Luna
SL-PHOTOGRAPHY/SHUTTERSTOCK ©

disco hybrid. Get there early to grab one of the tables on the mezzanine, overlooking the stage where live bands belt out varied Latin music.

INFORMATION

iPerú (☎044-29-4561; www.peru.travel; Independencia 467, oficina 106; ⊕9am-6pm Mon-Sat, to 1pm Sun) Provides tourist information, maps and a list of certified guides and travel agencies.

Policía de Turismo (☎044-29-1705; Almagro 442; ⊕8am-11pm) Shockingly helpful, the tourist police wear white shirts around town and some deputies speak English, Italian and/or French. This is its information office, but if you need to make a report you'll have to go to the headquarters on Federico Gerdes 105.

GETTING THERE & AWAY

AIR

The **airport** (TRU) is 10km northwest of town. **LATAM** (☎044-22-1469; www.latam.com; Almagro 480) has three daily flights between Lima and Trujillo. **Avianca** (☎080-01-8222; www.avianca.com; Real Plaza, César Vallejo Oeste 1345; ⊕10am-9pm) flies the same route twice a day, while **LC Perú** (☎044-29-0299; www.lcperu.com; Almagro 305; ⊕9am-8pm) has one evening flight.

BUS

Buses often leave Trujillo full, so booking a little earlier is advised. Several companies that go to southern destinations have terminals on the Panamericana Sur, the southern extension of Moche, and Ejército; check where your bus actually leaves from when buying a ticket.

Línea has services to most destinations of interest to travelers and is one of the more comfortable bus lines.

There's an enclave of bus companies around España and Amazonas offering Lima-bound night buses (eight hours).

Civa (☎044-25-1402; www.civa.com.pe; Ejército 285) Offers 8:30pm and 9:30pm buses to Lima.

Cruz del Sur (080-11-1111; www.cruzdelsur.
com.pe; Amazonas 437) One of the biggest and
priciest bus companies in Peru. It goes to Lima
six times a day and has evening buses to Guayaquil from Monday to Saturday.

Móvil Tours (017-16-8000; www.moviltours.
com.pe; Panamerica Sur 3955) Specializes in very
comfortable long-haul tourist services. It has a

10pm service to Lima, and 9:40pm and 10:10pm
departures to Huaraz.

ⓘ GETTING AROUND

A short taxi ride around town costs about S4. For
sightseeing, taxis charge about S30 (in town) to
S40 (out of town) per hour.

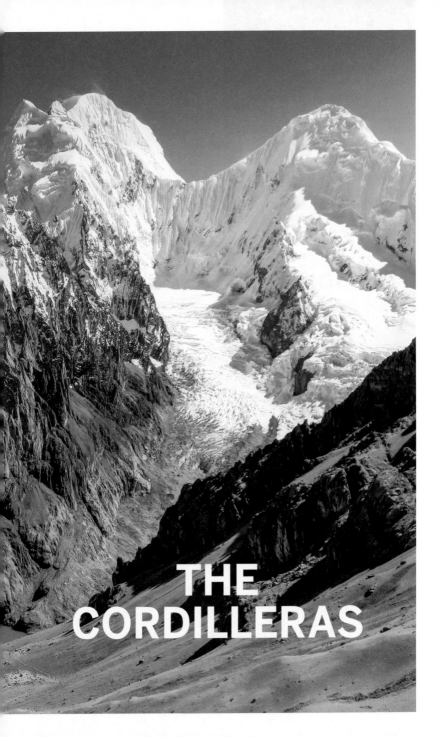

THE
CORDILLERAS

The Cordilleras at a Glance...

Ground zero for outdoor-adventure worship in Peru, the Cordilleras are one of the preeminent hiking, trekking and backpacking spots in South America. It offers some of Peru's most majestic vistas, from glaciated white peaks razoring their way through expansive lime-green valleys to scores of pristine jade lakes, ice caves and torrid springs. Huaraz is a hotbed of hiking inspiration. New adventurers mix it up with experienced climbers to share their recent thrills and show off their snaps. Land here first to fill up on good food and plan your next adventure in the Cordilleras.

The Cordilleras in Three Days

On day one, hang in Huaraz to plan your trek and acclimatize. Get your bearings in town and then make your way out to the **Monumento Nacional Wilkahuaín** (p246), a replica of the Chavín temple. On day two take a tour to the ruins of **Chavín de Huántar** (p242). Devote day three to further acclimatization with perhaps a hike part-way up to **Laguna Churup** (p241).

The Cordilleras in Five Days

A fourth day allows you time to tackle a hike to **Laguna 69** (p241), which is doable in a day, leaving day five for a trip to equally spectacular **Laguna Parón** (p240). For those with **Santa Cruz Trek** (p244) ambitions, you'll need three days acclimatizing and at least three more on the trail. Carb-up at **Mi Comedia** (p249) on your last night.

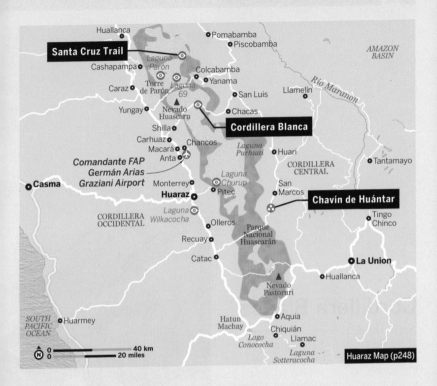

Huallanca
●Pomabamba
●Piscobamba

Santa Cruz Trail

AMAZON BASIN

Cashapampa● *Laguna Parón* Colcabamba
Caraz● Torre ●Yanama
de Parón *Laguna 69* ●San Luis Llamelín
Yungay● Nevado ●Chacas
Huascorn

Cordillera Blanca

Shilla●
Carhuaz● Chancos
Macará● *Laguna Purhuai* ●Huari ●Tantamayo
Anta●

Comandante FAP Germán Arias Graziani Airport Monterrey● *Laguna Churup* San **CORDILLERA CENTRAL**
●Pitec ●Marcos

Huaraz

Chavín de Huántar

Casma **CORDILLERA OCCIDENTAL** *Laguna Wilkacocha* ●Olleros ●Tingo Chinco

Recuay● *Parque Nacional Huascarán*
Catac● ●**La Union**

Nevado Pastoruri ●Huallanca

SOUTH PACIFIC OCEAN ●Huarmey Hatun ●Aquia
Machay Chiquián
Lago Conococha ●Llamac
40 km
20 miles *Laguna Sotteracocha* Huaraz Map (p248)

Arriving in the Cordilleras

Comandante FAP Germán Arias Graziani Airport The Huaraz airport is actually at Anta, 23km north of town. A taxi will cost about S40.

Bus Buses from Lima and most other destinations arrive in central Huaraz.

Where to Stay

Hotel prices can double during holiday periods and rooms become very scarce. Better hotels, at the southeast fringe of central Huaraz, are often perched higher, making for better views of Huascarán.

Cordillera Blanca

One of the most breathtaking parts of the continent (both figuratively and literally), the Cordillera Blanca is the world's highest tropical mountain range and encompasses some of South America's highest mountains.

Great For...

ⓘ **Need to Know**

Even experienced mountaineers would do well to add a local guide to their trekking group.

🍴 Take a Break

Ask in Huaraz what amount of food and water is required for your trek, or bring a cook.

ALEKSAVA/GETTY IMAGES ©

Parque Nacional Huascarán

This 3400-sq-km park encompasses practically the entire area of the Cordillera Blanca above 4000m, including more than 600 glaciers and nearly 300 lakes, and protects such extraordinary and endangered species as the giant *Puya raimondii* plant, the spectacled bear and the Andean condor.

Visitors to the park can register (bring your passport) and pay the park fee at the **park office** (✆043-42-2086; www.sernanp.gob.pe; Sal y Rosas 555; ✆8:30am-1pm & 2:30-6pm Mon-Fri) in Huaraz, although most of the main entrances to the park also sell tickets. Fees are S30 per person for a day visit, S60 for a three-day visit and S150 for a month.

Laguna Parón

Silent awe enters people's expressions when they talk of **Laguna Parón** (admission S5). Nestled at 4185m above sea level, along a bumpy road 25km east of Caraz, and surrounded by spectacular snow-covered peaks, many claim this to be the most beautiful lake in the Cordillera Blanca. It is certainly the largest, despite its water levels being lowered from 75m to 15m in the mid-1980s to prevent a collapse of Huandoy's moraine.

Ringed by formidable peaks, Parón offers close-up views of Pirámide de Garcilaso (5885m), Huandoy (6395m), Chacraraju (6112m) and several 1000m granite rock walls. The challenging rock-climbing wall of Torre de Parón, known as the Sphinx, is also found here.

Laguna Parón

Most people visit the lake as part of an organized tour out of Huaraz or Caraz (from S50). Going solo, you can organize a taxi in Caraz for around S150 round-trip with waiting time. The journey from Caraz takes 1½ hours on an unpaved road.

Hiking

Laguna Churup   Hiking

If overnight trekking isn't your bag, but you'd like to experience the sight of some of the area's extravagant high-altitude lakes, this one-day hike is for you. It begins at the hamlet of Pitec (3850m), just above Huaraz, and takes you to the emerald green Laguna Churup (4450m), at the base of

Nevado Churup. Note the altitudes and the ascent (it's a steep 600m straight up). The walk takes roughly six hours and is a good acclimatization hike.

Laguna 69   Hiking

This vivid blue lake surrounded by snow-covered peaks is the jewel of the Cordilleras. Set at 4600m, it's a challenging second acclimatization hike. 'Sixty-nine' is most commonly visited as a day trip from Huaraz and has become increasingly popular in recent years. Don't expect to have the place to yourself. Swimming in the lake is prohibited.

Acclimatize!

It is important that trekkers freshly arrived in the Cordilleras spend several days in Huaraz acclimatizing before sallying forth into the mountains. Huaraz is located at an altitude of 3091m – a sharp jump in elevation if you're arriving from sea level – but most Cordillera hikes go much higher, climbing to altitudes between 3500m and 5000m.

Rush into the high country and it's possible you'll end up suffering from dizziness, nausea or worse, putting a premature end to your trekking trip or, at best, turning the whole thing into one long miserable pain-fest.

On your first day, take it easy by pursuing some gentle, flat walks around town. On day two, depending on how you feel (everyone is different), you might want to try the **Laguna Wilkacocha hike**, one of the few trails around Huaraz that doesn't climb above 4000m. On day three, well-trained hikers may feel strong enough to break the 4000m barrier by shinning it up to Laguna Churup.

> ★ **Top Tip**
> The dry season, May to September, offers the best trekking conditions.

AGUSTAVO/GETTY IMAGES ©

> ☑ **Don't Miss**
> Lakes, ruins and hot springs en route – it's not just about seeing the (spectacular) mountains.

KLUBLU/SHUTTERSTOCK ©

Chavín de Huántar

Chavín de Huántar is the most intriguing of the many relatively independent, competitive ceremonial centers constructed throughout the central Andes.

The quintessential site of Peru's Mid–Late Formative Period (c 1200–500 BC), Chavín de Huántar is a phenomenal achievement of ancient construction, with large temple-like structures above ground and labyrinthine (now electronically lit) underground passageways. Although not as initially impressive as sites like Machu Picchu and Kuélap, Chavín tells an engrossing story when combined with its excellent affiliated museum.

Edificio A

The largest and most important building, called Edificio A, has withstood some mighty earthquakes over the years. Built on three different levels of stone-and-mortar masonry, the walls here were at one time embellished with tenon heads (blocks carved to resemble human heads with

Great For...

☑ **Don't Miss**

The carved tenon heads at the Museo Nacional de Chavín.

Tello Obelisk

San Marcos
Huaraz
Chavín de Huántar
Recuay
Parque Nacional Huascarán
Catac
La Union
Huallanca

ℹ Need to Know

Admission S15; ⊘9am-4pm Tue-Sun

🍽 Take a Break

Buongiorno (Calle 17 de Enero Sur s/n; mains S20-35; ⊘7am-7pm Tue-Sun) is a sophisticated Peruvian-Italian restaurant in a pleasant garden setting right next to the ruins.

★ Top Tip

Stay overnight in under-appreciated Chavín town and have the ruins to yourself in the morning.

its prominent, central placement in this ceremonial center, is sometimes referred to as the Smiling God – although its appearance seems anything but friendly.

Museo Nacional de Chavín

This outstanding **museum** (☎043-45-4011; 17 de Enero s/n; ⊘9am-5pm Tue-Sun) **FREE**, funded jointly by the Peruvian and Japanese governments, houses most of the intricate tenon heads carved with horror-stricken expressions from Chavín de Huántar, as well as the magnificent Tello Obelisk, another stone object of worship with low relief carvings of a caiman and other fierce animals.

The museum is located around 2km from the ruins on the north side of town – it's an easy 25-minute walk.

animal or perhaps hallucinogen-induced characteristics backed by stone spikes for insertion into a wall). Only one of these remains in its original place, although around 30 others may be seen in the local museum.

Lanzón de Chavín

A series of tunnels underneath the Castillo are an exceptional feat of engineering, comprising a maze of complex corridors, ducts and chambers. In the heart of this complex is an exquisitely carved, 4.5m monolith of white granite known as the Lanzón de Chavín. In typical terrifying Chavín fashion, the low-relief carvings on the Lanzón represent a person with snakes radiating from his head and a ferocious set of fangs, most likely feline. The Lanzón, almost certainly an object of worship given

Santa Cruz Trail

The Santa Cruz is one of South America's classic multiday treks: lightly trodden, spectacular from start to finish, and achievable by anyone of decent fitness who's had adequate time to acclimatize.

Running for 45km through the Cordillera Blanca between the villages of Vaqueria and Cashapampa, the trek takes hikers along the verdant Quebrada Huarípampa, over the (literally) dizzying Punta Union Pass (4760m) and down through the deeply gouged Quebrada Santa Cruz Valley.

Unlike the Inca trail, no permit system exists for the Santa Cruz, and you can undertake it solo without a guide (although many Huaraz agencies offer the trip). The trail can be hiked in either direction but the easiest and recommended route is to head east–west from Vaqueria to Cashapampa. By starting in Vaqueria, you avoid a grueling, hot and dusty ascent at the very beginning of the hike. Finishing in Cashapampa leaves you with more transportation options at the end.

Great For...

☑ Don't Miss

The side trip to Alpamayo Base Camp underneath the magnificent Nevado Alpamayo (5947m).

❶ Need to Know

You'll need to buy a S60 pass at the Park Office (p240) in Huaraz.

✗ Take a Break

This is wilderness terrain. Pack in all your own supplies.

★ Top Tip

Allow at least three to four days acclimatizing in and around Huaraz.

The Basics

Head-turning sights along the way include emerald lakes, views of many of the Cordillera's peaks, beds of brightly colored alpine wildflowers and stands of red qeñua trees.

The Santa Cruz is one of the most popular routes for international trekkers. Most days of the year there are enough other people around to keep you on track. Signposting is sporadic, but sufficient. Take care on your approach to Punta Union if it's misty (small piles of stones act as markers) and stay alert around the dried-up lakes in the Santa Cruz Valley, where the path has been redirected.

It's not difficult to complete the trail in three days. However, four days offer more opportunities for side trips, the most popular being the short punt up to Alpamayo Base Camp. Water is available from rivers en route, though you'll need to treat it as

grazing livestock is everywhere. There are no dangerous animals or tricky climbing sections to worry about. Instead, the main challenge is altitude, particularly as you approach Punta Union.

Punta Union

The second day of the hike is the toughest as the path starts to gain height, pushing up past Laguna Morococha and through a spiraling rocky buttress over the Punta Union Pass, which appears from below as an angular notch in a seemingly unbroken rocky wall. The panoramas from both sides of the pass are captivating should the weather cooperate, but beware: it can be cold on top year-round with occasional snow.

Sierra Andina Mountain Trail

First run in 2016, this 45km-long high-altitude **'marathon'** (www.sierraandina marathon.com; ⊘ mid-Aug) follows the standard Santa Cruz trail route between Vaqueria (where it starts) and Cashapampa. It's 3km longer and a lot harder than a traditional 42km marathon; there are six aid stations en route — and, by jove, you'll need them.

Huaraz

Huaraz is the restless capital of this Andean adventure kingdom and its rooftops command exhaustive panoramas of the city's dominion: one of the most impressive mountain ranges in the world. Nearly wiped out by the earthquake of 1970, Huaraz isn't going to win any Andean-village beauty contests anytime soon, but it does have personality – and personality goes a long way.

This is first and foremost a trekking metropolis. Dozens of outfits help plan trips, rent equipment and organize a list of adventure sports as long as your arm. An endless lineup of quality restaurants and hopping bars keep the belly full and the place lively till long after the tents have been put away.

SIGHTS

Monumento Nacional Wilkahuaín
Ruins

(adult/student S5/2; ⊘9am-5pm Tue-Sun) This small Wari ruin about 8km north of Huaraz is remarkably well preserved, dating from about AD 600 to 900. It's an imitation of the temple at Chavín done in the Tiwanaku style (square temples on raised platforms). Wilkahuaín means 'grandson's house' in Quechua. The three-story temple has seven rooms on each floor, each originally filled with bundles of mummies. The bodies were kept dry using a sophisticated system of ventilation ducts. A one-room museum gives some basic background information in English and Spanish.

✪ ACTIVITIES

Whether you're arranging a mountain expedition or going for a day hike, Huaraz is the place to start – it is the epicenter for planning and organizing local Andean adventures. Numerous outfits can pre-arrange entire trips so that all you need to do is show up at the right place at the right time. Many visitors go camping, hiking and climbing in the mountains without any local help and you can too if you have the experience. Just remember, though, that carrying

Huaraz

GALYNA ANDRUSHKO/SHUTTERSTOCK ©

a backpack full of gear over a 4800m pass requires much more effort than hiking at low altitudes.

Quechuandes   Trekking

(📞943-386-147; www.quechandes.com; Santa Gadea 995; ⊗9am-8pm Mon-Sat, from 11am Sun) A very well organized agency that gets rave reviews for its quality guides and ethical approach to treks. Management will assess your level before sending you out into the mountains or renting gear, to ensure you are up to the task. In addition to offering treks, summit expeditions and mountaineering courses, its staff are experts in rock climbing and bouldering.

Mountain Bike
Adventures   Mountain Biking

(📞972-616-008; www.chakinaniperu.com; Lúcar y Torre 530, 2nd fl; 2-day tours from US$380; ⊗9am-1pm & 3-8pm) Mountain Bike Adventures has been in business for well over a decade and receives repeated visits from mountain bikers for its decent selection of bikes, knowledgeable and friendly service, and good safety record. It offers guided tours, ranging from an easy five-hour cruise to 12-day circuits around the Cordillera Blanca.

Eco Ice Peru   Trekking

(www.ecoice-peru.com; Figueroa 1185; 3- to 4-day treks from US$240; ⊗8am-6pm) Run by a gregarious and passionate young guide, this agency gets top reviews from travelers for its customer service, guides, *arrieros* (mule drives) and food. Treks often end with a dinner at the owner's pad in Huaraz.

Andean Kingdom   Adventure

(📞944-913-011; www.andeankingdomhuaraz. com; Parque Ginebra; climbing trips from S120; ⊗9am-9pm Mon-Sat) A laid-back but enthusiastic agency offering day courses for aspiring climbers, logistical support for experts and the usual day excursions, with an obvious bias toward climbing trips (Los Olivos and Hatun Machay feature highly).

 Rock Climbing

Rock climbing is one of the Cordillera Blanca's biggest pastimes and its popularity is growing. Huaraz is an ideal place to plan excursions, rent gear and set off from on day trips. There are good climbs for beginners at Chancos, while the Los Olivos area has the most varied routes and is located conveniently close to Huaraz. Avid climbers will find some gnarly bolted sport climbs at Recuay and Hatun Machay, located 30km and 70km south of Huaraz respectively. For some big-wall action that will keep you chalked up for days, head to the famous Torre de Parón, known locally as the Sphinx. Most trekking tour agencies offer climbing trips, for both beginners and advanced climbers, as part of their repertoire. Many also rent gear. No serious climber should leave base camp without a copy of *Huaraz: The Climbing Guide* (2014) by David Lazo and Marie Timmermans, with detailed descriptions of over 1000 climbing routes backed up with photos and color-coded maps.

Cordillera Blanca
COREY RICH/GETTY IMAGES ©

TOURS

All activity within Parque Nacional Huascarán – whether mountaineering or hiking – technically requires that you are accompanied by a certified guide, although in practice this is not enforced at most park entrances. Even so, it is well worth taking a guide even for nontechnical activities as conditions change rapidly in the mountains

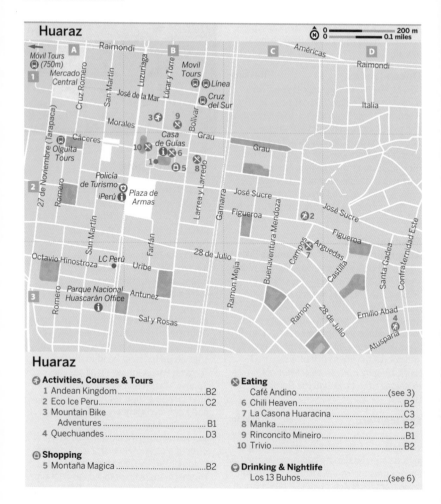

Huaraz

⊕ Activities, Courses & Tours
1 Andean Kingdom B2
2 Eco Ice Peru............................... C2
3 Mountain Bike
   Adventures B1
4 Quechuandes D3

🛍 Shopping
5 Montaña Magica B2

🍴 Eating
  Café Andino ....(see 3)
6 Chili Heaven B2
7 La Casona Huaracina C3
8 Manka B2
9 Rinconcito Mineiro....................... B1
10 Trivio B2

🍺 Drinking & Nightlife
  Los 13 Buhos............................(see 6)

and altitude sickness can seriously debilitate even experienced hikers. Furthermore, a good guide will ensure you see things you otherwise may have missed.

All guides must be licensed by the Peruvian authorities and registered with the national-parks office. Mountaineers and trekkers should check out Casa de Guías (p250), the headquarters of the **Mountain Guide Association of Peru**. It maintains a list of its internationally certified guides, all of whom are graduates of a rigorous training program. Bear in mind that international certification is not necessary to work in the park and there are also some excellent independent guides from other associations certified to work in the region.

Many agencies arrange full trekking and climbing expeditions that include guides, equipment, food, cooks, porters and transportation. Depending on the number of people, the length of your trip and what's included, expect to pay from under S100 for an easy day out to up to S750 for more technical mountains per person per day. Try not to base your selection solely on price, as you often get what you pay for. Do your research; things change, good places go bad and bad places get good.

One of the best resources for guides in Huaraz is other travelers who have just come back from a trek and can recommend (or not recommend) their guides based on recent experience.

The South American Explorers Club in Lima is also an excellent source of information and maps.

🏷 SHOPPING

Montaña Magica Sports & Outdoors

(☑949-680-107; Parque Ginebra 25; ☺10am-2pm & 4-8pm Mon-Sat) Forget your kit? Head to Mountain Magic where you can stock up on a full gamut of decent trekking and mountaineering gear from rain jackets to camping stoves.

❌ EATING

Manka Peruvian, Italian **$**

(☑043-23-4306; Bautista 840; menú S10; ☺8:30am-11pm) If you were curious about what happens when Peruvian *cocina* (cuisine) collides with Italian *cucina* then, let us tell you, it's a taste worth savoring. For proof, head straight to this simply decorated restaurant whose mix-and-match menu can deliver bruschetta for starters, *lomo saltado* (strips of beef stir-fried with onions, tomatoes, potatoes and chili) for a main and a delectable chocolate mousse for desert.

Mi Comedia Italian **$$**

(☑043-58-7954; Centenario 351; mains S22-38; ☺5-11pm Mon-Sat) Many restaurants claim great pizzas with some even uttering the word 'Naples' blasphemously in the description. But at Mi Comedia the Italian boasts are no exaggeration. This is about as Neapolitan as a pizza can get in Peru without the DOC Campania ingredients.

Café Andino Cafe **$$**

(www.cafeandino.com; Lúcar y Torre 530, 3rd fl; breakfast S8-24, mains S18-35; ☺9am-10pm; 📶🍴) This modern top-floor cafe has space and light in spades, comfy lounges, art, photos, crackling fireplace, books and groovy tunes – it's the ultimate South American traveler hangout and meeting spot. You can get breakfast anytime (Belgian waffles, *huevos rancheros*), and snacks you miss (nachos). It's also the best place in town for information about trekking in the area.

Chili Heaven Indian, Thai **$$**

(Parque Ginebra; mains S17-35; ☺noon-11pm) Whether you send your appetite to India or Thailand, the fiery curries at this hot spot will seize your taste buds upon arrival, mercilessly shake them up and then spit them back out the other side as if you've died and gone to chili heaven (hence the name).

Trivio International **$$**

(☑043-22-0416; Parque del Periodista; mains S21-37; ☺8am-midnight) 🍃 Cementing a three-way marriage of craft beer, micro-roasted coffee and food made with local ingredients, Trivio joins a few Huaraz restaurants that wouldn't be alien in Lima. The decor is North America hip, the clientele predominantly gringo, and the food clever enough to excite the taste buds but filling enough to cover the hole left by your recent four-day trek.

Treat it as a bar, coffee shop or casual restaurant. Hiking boots, fleeces and backpacks are de rigueur.

Rinconcito Mineiro Peruvian **$$**

(Morales 757; menú S8-16, mains S12-35; ☺7am-11pm; 📶) This popular place is *the* spot to tuck into homey and cheap Peruvian daily *menús* (set meals). The daily blackboard of 10 or so options includes an excellent *lomo saltado*, plus grilled trout, *tacu-tacu* (a Peruvian fusion dish of rice, beans and a protein) and the like.

 Swapping Hiking Tales in Huaraz

Huaraz is the urban decompression chamber through which practically all hikers, trekkers and mountaineers pass and swap stories. Plans of daring ice climbs, mountain-biking exploits and rock-climbing expeditions are hatched over ice-cold beers in fireplace-warmed hostels and bars.

Lurking quietly on the sidelines, and worth a day of quiet contemplation, are the enigmatic 3000-year-old ruins of Chavín de Huántar (p242).

SVITLANA BELINSKA/ALAMY STOCK PHOTO ©

It's all served in a welcoming and clean space, tastefully decorated with regional crafts.

La Casona Huaracina   Peruvian $$

(📞43-39-6420; Campos 735; mains S22-42; ⊙11am-10pm) The colonial architectural style is noticeably absent in Huaraz until you step into the sparkling Huaracina whose clever designers have drawn inspiration from the graceful buildings of Arequipa. The business is split into three interconnecting spaces: a smart lounge bar, a *pasteleria* (pastry shop) and the restaurant, all decked out with astute attention to detail (glass lampshades, elaborate balustrades, bookshelves).

🍸 DRINKING & NIGHTLIFE

Los 13 Buhos   Bar

(Parque Ginebra; ⊙11am-2am) Halfway up some monstrous Andean pass with a 15kg pack on your back, it's not uncommon to start dreaming of 13 Buhos with its Luchos craft beer, pool table and delectable afternoon 'snacks' (waffles anyone?).

If you needed an incentive to finish your trek, this could be it – the chance to flop down at an alfresco table outside Huaraz' finest craft beer bar with a plate of Thai curry and a *blondie ale* exaggerating (but only slightly) about your rugged adventures in the Cordillera Blanca.

ℹ️ INFORMATION

Casa de Guías (📞043-42-1811; www.agmp. pe; Parque Ginebra 28G; ⊙9am-1pm & 4-8pm Mon-Fri, 8am-noon Sat) Runs mountain safety and rescue courses and maintains a list of internationally certified guides. Also mounts rescue operations to assist climbers in emergencies. If you are heading out on a risky ascent, it's worth consulting with them first.

Clínica San Pablo (📞043-42-8811; Huaylas 172; ⊙24hr) North of town, this is the best medical care in Huaraz. Some doctors speak English.

iPerú (📞043-42-8812; iperuhuaraz@promperu. gob.pe; Pasaje Atusparia, Oficina 1, Plaza de Armas; ⊙9am-6pm Mon-Sat, to 1pm Sun) Has general tourist information but little in the way of trekking info.

Policía de Turismo (📞043-42-1341; Luzuriaga 724; ⊙24hr) On the west side of the Plaza de Armas.

ℹ️ GETTING THERE & AWAY

AIR

The Huaraz **airport** (ATA) is actually at Anta, 23km north of town. A taxi will cost about S40.

LC Perú (📞043-42-4734; www.lcperu.pe; Luzuriaga 904; ⊙9am-7pm Mon-Fri, to 6pm Sat) is currently the only company offering service, with flights to/from Lima (US$120, one hour) on Tuesdays, Thursdays and Saturdays. Flights leave in the morning, but they are often cancelled at short notice.

Huaraz

BUS

Huaraz has no central bus station. Rather buses leave from different company offices, most of which are located in and around Raimondi and Bolívar streets a couple of blocks north of the Plaza de Armas.

Cruz del Sur (☎043-42-8726; Bolívar 491) Has 11am and 10pm luxury nonstop services to Lima (S35 to S75, eight hours). Arguably, the most comfortable and reliable buses.

Línea (☎043-42-6666; Bolívar 450) Has excellent buses to Lima (S35 to S80, eight hours, twice daily) and Trujillo (S30 to S55, seven hours, once daily).

Movil Tours (www.moviltours.com.pe; Bolívar 452) Buses to Lima (S35 to S135, eight hours, 10 daily), Chimbote (S40 to S60, five hours, one daily) and Trujillo (S45 to S75, seven hours, two daily). They leave from a **terminal** (☎043-42-2555; www.moviltours.com.pe; Confraternidad Internacional Oeste 451) 1.5km northwest of the Plaza de Armas.

Olguita Tours (☎043-39-6309, 943-644-051; Mariscal Caceres 338) Runs half-a-dozen daily buses to Chavín de Huántar (S12, 2½ hours) and Huari (S15, 4½ hours).

THE AMAZON BASIN

The Amazon Basin at a Glance...

The best-protected tract of the world's most biodiverse forest is a strange, sweltering, seductive country-within-a-country. Tribes still exist here that have never had contact with outside civilization. More plant types flourish in one rainforest hectare than in any European country, and fauna is so fantastic it defies the most imaginative sci-fi comic. As the 21st century encroaches on this enticing expanse of wilderness, exploitation of the rainforest's abundant natural resources threatens to irreversibly damage it. For now, however, the Peruvian Amazon offers phenomenal wildlife-spotting, forays into untamed forest from the jungle's best selection of lodges, and raucous city life.

The Amazon Basin in Four Days

Visits to **Parque Nacional Manu** (p256) are usually one week, but three-night stays are possible and still allow you to spot a wide range of tropical wildlife. Trips to Manu often go overtime, so allow an extra day, which can be used to visit a 1906 Amazon riverboat housing the **Historical Ships Museum** (p263), if you have time.

The Amazon Basin in Six Days

With an extra two days, see more of Manu or get deep into the largest of Peru's parks, **Reserva Nacional Pacaya-Samiria** (p258). Camp and spot manatees, pink dolphins, giant turtles and hundreds of bird species. Hire a guide from Lagunas and go by dugout canoe, or take a comfortable ship from Iquitos.

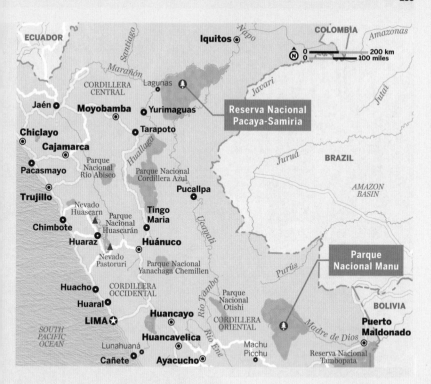

Arriving in the Amazon Basin

Coronel FAP Francisco Secada Vignetta International Airport Iquitos' airport is 7km from the center. A taxi into town costs about S15.

Ferry Ports are situated between 2km and 3km north of the center of Iquitos.

Where to Stay

If you are after the total jungle-immersion experience, there is no shortage of lodges. Find your base, then explore the jungle to your heart's content. (Features to look out for include pools and jungle or plaza views.)

The best hotels tend to be booked up on Friday and Saturday nights, and during major festivals such as San Juan. The busiest season is from May to September, when prices may rise slightly.

RPBAIAO/SHUTTERSTOCK ©

Parque Nacional Manu

Covering almost 20,000 sq km (about the size of Wales), this park is one of the best places in South America to scout out a whole shebang of tropical wildlife.

This national park starts in the eastern slopes of the Andes and plunges down into the lowlands, hosting great diversity over a wide range of cloud-forest and rainforest habitats. The most progressive aspect of the park is the fact that so much of it is very carefully protected – a rarity anywhere in the world. Unesco declared Manu a Biosphere Reserve in 1977 and a World Natural Heritage site in 1987.

Virgin jungle lies up the Río Manu northwest of Boca Manu (the entrance point for the park). Two hours upstream is the oxbow lake of **Cocha Juárez**, where giant river otters are often encountered. About four hours further, **Cocha Salvador**, one of the park's largest and most beautiful lakes, has guided camping and hiking possibilities.

Great For...

☑ **Don't Miss**

Cocha Otorongo, an oxbow lake with a wildlife-viewing observation tower, six hours into the jungle.

Capybara family

❶ Need to Know

Entry per 1/2-3/4+ days S30/60/150); ✐

✕ Take a Break

Food is included in tour packages, along with transportation, accommodations and guides.

★ Top Tip

Best in the dry season (June to November); the park may be closed during rainy months (January to April).

Wildlife Spotting

These are not wide-open habitats like the African plains. Thick vegetation will obscure many animals, and a skilled guide is very useful in helping you to see them.

During a one-week trip, you can reasonably expect to see scores of different bird species, several monkey species and possibly a few other mammals.

Jaguars (sightings are on the increase in the zona reservada), tapirs, giant anteaters, tamanduas, capybaras, peccaries and giant river otters are among the common large Manu mammals. But they are elusive, and you can consider a trip very successful if you see two or three of these creatures during a week's visit.

Smaller mammals you might see include kinkajous, pacas, agoutis, squirrels, brocket deer, ocelots and armadillos. Other animals include river turtles and caiman (which are frequently seen), snakes (which are less often spotted) and a variety of other reptiles and amphibians. Colorful butterflies and less pleasing insects also abound.

Visiting & Staying

There are two lodges within the park, plus a tented camp: you can't stay at any of these accommodations independently, but all are included on tours. Note that it is illegal to enter the park without a guide. Going with an organized group can be arranged in Cuzco or with international tour operators.

Permits, which are necessary to enter the park, are arranged by tour agencies. Most visits are for a week, although three-night stays at a lodge can be arranged.

Travelers often report returning from Manu several days late. Don't plan an international airline connection the day after a Manu trip!

Sloth

Reserva Nacional Pacaya-Samiria

This huge national reserve is home to Amazon manatees, pink and gray river dolphins, two species of caiman and giant South American river turtles, alongside around 450 bird species.

Great For...

Reserva Nacional Pacaya-Samiria

Iquitos

Lagunas

Moyobamba

Yurimaguas

Tarapoto

Ucayali

Javari

ℹ️ Need to Know

Per person per day S30, incl entrance fee, guide, food & accommodations S150

★ **Top Tip**

Bring plenty of insect repellent and plastic bags (to cover luggage), and be prepared to camp out.

At 20,800 sq km Pacaya-Samiria provides local people with food and a home, and protects ecologically important habitats. An estimated 42,000 people live on and around the reserve; juggling the needs of human inhabitants while protecting wildlife is the responsibility of some 30 rangers. Staff also teach inhabitants how to best harvest the natural renewable resources to benefit the local people and to maintain thriving populations of plants and animals.

The area close to Lagunas has suffered from depletion: allow several days to get deep into the least-disturbed areas. Noteworthy points in the reserve include **Lago Pantean**, where you can check out caimans and go medicinal-plant collecting; and **Tipischa de Huana**, where you can see the giant *Victoria regia* waterlilies, big enough for a small child to sleep upon without sinking.

When to Go

The best time to go is during the dry season, when you are more likely to see animals along the riverbanks. Rains ease off in late May; it then takes a month for water levels to drop, making July and August the best months to visit (with excellent fishing). September to November isn't too bad, and the heaviest rains begin in January. The months of February to May are the worst times to go. February to June tend to be the hottest months, with animal viewing best in the early morning and late afternoon.

Pink dolphins

Visiting

Official information is available at the agencies offering Pacaya-Samiria tours in Iquitos and Lagunas.

The best way to visit the reserve is to go by dugout canoe with a guide from Lagunas and spend several days camping and exploring. Alternatively, comfortable ships visit from Iquitos.

If coming from Lagunas, Santa Rosa is the main entry point, where you pay the park entrance fee (often included in tour prices).

Guided Tours from Lagunas

Spanish-speaking guides are available in Lagunas. It is illegal to hunt within the reserve (though fishing for the pot is OK). The going rate is S150 per person per day for a guide, a boat and accommodations in huts, tents and ranger stations (for short trips prices could be slightly higher). Food and park fees are extra, although the guides can cook for you.

In the past, there was such a plethora of guides in Lagunas that to avoid harassment and price cutting, an official guides association was formed. This then split into separate organizations. Good options include **Acatupel** (☑948-976-610; www.acatupel. com; Padre Lucero 1324) and **Huayruro Tours** (☑965-662-555, 065-40-1186; www.peruselva. com; Alfonso Aiscorbe 424), an increasingly prominent association that is great for helping plan tours (agency staff speak English; its guides are Spanish-speaking but know the reserve extremely well). It offers tours of up to 22 days and is involved in programs like turtle reintroduction within the reserve.

River Cruises from Iquitos

Cruising the Amazon is an expensive business: the shortest trips can cost over US$1000. It's a popular pastime, too, and advance reservations are often necessary (and often mean discounts). Cruises naturally focus on the Río Amazonas, both downriver (northeast) toward the Brazil–Colombia border and upriver to Nauta, where the Ríos Marañón and Ucayali converge. Beyond Nauta, trips continue up these two rivers to the Pacaya-Samiria reserve.

☑ **Don't Miss**

Quebrada Yanayacu, where the river water is black from dissolved plants.

CHRISTIAN VINCES/SHUTTERSTOCK ©

✕ **Take a Break**

Ask your guide what food is provided as part of the tour.

Iquitos

Linked to the outside world by air and by river, Iquitos is the world's largest city that cannot be reached by road. It's a prosperous, vibrant jungle metropolis and the northern Amazon Basin's chief city, teeming with the usual, inexplicably addictive Amazonian anomalies. You may well arrive in Iquitos for the greater adventure of a boat trip down the Amazon but whether it's sampling rainforest cuisine, the buzzing nightlife or one of Peru's most fascinating markets in the floating shantytown of Belén, this thriving city will entice you to stay awhile.

◉ SIGHTS

Iquitos' cultural attractions, while limited, dwarf those of other Amazon cities: especially boosted by the arrival of two museums in the period between 2013 and 2014. The cheery Malecón (riverside walk) runs between Nauta and Ricardo Palma: perhaps the most diverting sight of all!

Remnants of the rubber-boom days include *azulejos,* tiles imported from Portugal to decorate the rubber barons' mansions. Many buildings along Raimondi and Malecón Tarapaca are decorated with these tiles.

Belén Mercado   Market
`FREE` At the southeast end of town is the floating shantytown of Belén, consisting of scores of huts, built on rafts, which rise and fall with the river. During the low-water months, these rafts sit on the river mud, but for most of the year they float on the river – a colorful and chaotic sight. Seven thousand people live here, and canoes float from hut to hut selling and trading jungle produce.

The best time to visit the area is at 7am, when people from the jungle villages arrive to sell their produce. To get here, take a cab to 'Los Chinos,' walk to the port and rent a canoe to take you around.

The market here, located within the city blocks in front of Belén, is the raucous, crowded affair common to most Peruvian towns. In fact, because of the fluctuating water levels that make this market so muddy and mosquito-plagued, Belén is

Iquitos

MATYAS REHAK/SHUTTERSTOCK ©

a level more squalid again. All kinds of strange and exotic products, from bottled *ayahuasca* (derivative of a halucinogenic jungle vine) to insect grubs, are sold among the more mundane bags of rice, sugar, flour and cheap household goods. Look for the bark of the *chuchuhuasi* tree, which is soaked in rum for weeks and used as a tonic (it's served in many of the local bars). *Chuchuhuasi* and other Amazon plants are common ingredients in herbal pain-reducing and arthritis formulas manufactured in Europe and the USA.

The market makes for exciting shopping and sightseeing, but do remember to watch your wallet.

Historical Ships Museum   Museum
(Plaza Castilla; admission S10; ⊗8am-8pm)
Moored below Plaza Castilla is the diverting Historical Ships Museum, on a 1906 Amazon riverboat, the gorgeously restored three-deck *Ayapua*. The exhibitions reflect the Amazon River's hodgepodge past: explorers, tribes, rubber barons and the filming of the 1982 Werner Herzog movie *Fitzcarraldo*. Included in the entrance price is a half-hour historic-boat ride on the river (Río Itaya out to the Río Amazonas proper).

Malecón   Viewpoint
(Malecóns Maldonado & Tarapaca) The sight of Iquitos' sophisticated riverside walkway, edged by swanky bars and restaurants and yet cut off from the rest of the world by hundreds of kilometers of jungle river, is as spectacular as it is surreal. Tours are touted and jungle food is served from stalls, while below are decaying old riverboats, and the lower town's huts on stilts are at the mercy of rapidly changing river levels.

Casa de Fierro   Historic Building
(Iron House; cnr Putumayo & Raymondi) `FREE`
Every guidebook mentions the 'majestic' Casa de Fierro (Iron House), designed by Gustave Eiffel (of Eiffel Tower fame). It was made in Paris in 1860 and imported piece by piece into Iquitos around 1890, during the rubber-boom days, to beautify the city. It's the only survivor of three different iron

 Herzog's Amazon

Eccentric German director Werner Herzog, often seen as obsessive and bent on filming 'reality itself,' shot two movies in Peru's jungle: *Aguirre, the Wrath of God* (1972) and *Fitzcarraldo* (1982). Herzog's accomplishments in getting these movies made at all – during havoc-filled filming conditions – are in some ways more remarkable than the finished products.

Klaus Kinski, the lead actor in *Aguirre*, was a volatile man prone to extreme fits of rage. Herzog's documentary *My Best Fiend* details such incidents, as when Kinski, after altercations with a cameraman on the Río Nanay, prepared to desert the film crew on a speedboat. Herzog had to threaten to shoot him with a rifle to make him stay.

When filming *Fitzcarraldo,* the first choice for the lead fell ill and the second, Mick Jagger, abandoned the set to do a Rolling Stones tour. Herzog called upon Kinski once more, who soon antagonized the Matsiguenka tribespeople being used as extras: one even offered to murder him for Herzog. Then there was the weather: droughts so dire that the rivers dried and stranded the film's steamship for weeks, followed by flash floods that wrecked the boat entirely.

The director once said he saw filming in the Amazon as 'challenging nature itself.'

On the set of *Fitzcarraldo*

Uprooting Belén

The order has come from on high: Belén – perhaps the character-defining district of Iquitos – needs to be moved. The main reason cited is sanitation. When water levels are high, this shantytown-market on the river floats, but it sits on the stinking mud when the water drops. But how do you relocate an entire district, and to where? It's proving a headache. At the time of writing, a few families of the hundreds living here have signed up for the scheme. The rest have strongly opposed it and, as you will see if you visit the market here, staying put. Without residents' consent, and with a relocation threatening the only livelihood most of them know (fishing and river trade), any uprooting of Belén will be a struggle taking many years.

JESS KRAFT/SHUTTERSTOCK ©

houses originally imported here. It resembles a bunch of scrap-metal sheets bolted together, was once the location of the Iquitos Club and is now, in humbler times, a general store.

Museum of Indigenous
Amazon Cultures   Museum
(Malecón Tarapaca 332; admission S15; ⊗8am-7:30pm) This intuitively presented museum takes you through the traits, traditions and beliefs of the tribes of the Amazon Basin, with a focus on the Peruvian Amazon. Some 40 Amazonian cultures are represented.

🟢 ACTIVITIES
Dawn on the Amazon
Tours & Cruises   Cruise
(☑065-22-3730; www.dawnontheamazon.com; Malecón Maldonado 185; day-trips incl lunch per person from US$85, multiday cruises per day from US$225) This small outfit offers a great deal for independent travelers. The *Amazon I* is a beautiful 11m wooden craft with modern furnishings, available for either day trips or river cruises up to two weeks. Included are a bilingual guide, all meals and transfers.

You can travel along the Amazon, or along its quieter tributaries. While many cruise operators have fixed departures and itineraries, Dawn on the Amazon's can be adapted to accommodate individual needs. The tri-river cruise is a favorite local trip: while on board, fishing and bird-watching are the most popular activities.

R & F Expeditions   Cruise
(☑999-954-004; www.rfexpeditions.com; 4 days & 3 nights per person from US$3150) The RF *Amazonas* (new in 2016) is a wood-built four-deck vessel offering cruises along the Río Amazonas from Iquitos, sporting an observation deck, spa, lovely bar-restaurant and 13 stunning cedar-paneled suites varying between 33 and 48 sq meters. This, then, is your ticket to enjoy cruise activities like community visits, wildlife-watching forays and even a visit to a rum distillery.

🔵 SHOPPING
Mercado de
Artesanía San Juan   Arts & Crafts
(Av José Abelardo Quiñones) Craft market: out of town on the road to the airport.

EATING
The city has excellent restaurants. However, many regional specialties feature endangered animals, such as *chicharrón de lagarto* (fried alligator) and *sopa de tortuga* (turtle soup). More environmentally friendly dishes include ceviche made with river fish, *chupín de pollo* (a tasty soup of chicken,

egg and rice) and *juanes* (banana leaves stuffed with chicken or pork and rice).

Belén Mercado
Market $

(cnr Próspero & Jirón 9 de Diciembre; menús from S5) There are great eats at Iquitos' markets, particularly the Belén *mercado* where a *menú* (set menu), including *jugo especial* (jungle juice) costs S5. Look out for specialties including meaty Amazon worms, *ishpa* (simmered sabalo fish intestines and fat) and *sikisapa* (fried leafcutter ants; abdomens are supposedly tastiest) and watch your valuables. Another good market for cheap eats is **Mercado Central** (Lores cuadra 5; snacks from S1).

Dawn on the Amazon Cafe
International $$

(http://dawnontheamazoncafe.com; Malecón Maldonado 185; mains S10-30; ⏰7:30am-10pm Mon-Sat; 🛜) This traveler magnet on the Malecón, with its tempting row of street-front tables, sports a menu divided up into North American, Peruvian, Spanish and Chinese. Travel wherever your taste buds desire but bear in mind that the steamed

fresh fish is very good. Ingredients are all non-MSG and those on gluten-free diets are catered for.

Le Bateau Ivre
International $$

(Malecón Tarapaca 268; mains S20-40; ⏰6am-midnight; 🛜) This is laid out with TLC by the Belgian owner with a New York–style breakfast bar (OK, Amazon version thereof) and upper-level mezzanine seating looking down on the main eating area. The cuisine refuses to be pigeon-holed: there's Argentine steaks, not to mention the Belgian influence, creeping across in the crepes, the escargot and the range of Belgian beers.

ChillOut Carnes y Pescados
Ceviche $$

(Napo 834; mains S20-32; ⏰10am-5pm Sun-Tue, 7-10pm Thu-Sat; ❄️) This gets our nod for first prize in the keenly contested battle for number one in the city's *cevichería* (ceviche restaurant) contest. An air-conditioned interior, a little street-front courtyard and, most crucially of all, delicious, huge platters of ceviche.

Belén Mercado

☞ Road to Nowhere?

Talk of a road connecting Iquitos to the rest of Peru, through the jungle to the current terminus of the Peruvian road network at Saramiriza, has long been the goal of developers. Those in favor were particularly buoyed by the construction of the Carr Interocéanica, which now connects Puerto Maldonado with Cuzco in Peru and with Brazil, and has been cited as a major contributor to that city's recent prosperity. Backers of the Iquitos–Saramiriza road included Pedro Pablo Kuczynski, 66th President of Peru. He vowed to complete the road link by the end of his term in 2021: but Kuczynski resigned from office in March 2018. For now at least, Iquitos will have to rely on air and river for its links to the outside world.

Buses, Iquitos
MATYAS REHAK/SHUTTERSTOCK ©

Espresso Cafe-Bar   Cafe $$

(www.facebook.com/espressocafeiquitos; cnr Próspero & Morona; mains S21-32; ⊘noon-midnight) Elegant rubber boom-style refurbishments are all the rage in Iquitos and this 2nd-floor people-watching spot has nailed the vibe. Airy, high-ceilinged and stylishly furnished, the service here is also gracious. Cue, then, the partaking of a delightful range of coffees, infusions, cocktails and cakes as well as sandwiches, barbecue wings, bruschetta and the like.

Al Frio y al Fuego   Fusion $$

(☎965-607-474; www.facebook.com/alfrio yalfuegorestaurante; Embarcadero Av La Marina 138; mains S40-50; ⊘noon-11pm Mon-Sat, to 6pm Sun; 👪) Take a boat out to this floating foodie paradise in the middle of the mouth of the Río Itaya to sample some of the city's best food. The emphasis is on river fish (such as the delectable *doncella*), but the *parrillas* (grills) are inviting, too. The address given is the boat embarkation point.

🍷 DRINKING & NIGHTLIFE

Arandú Bar   Bar

(Malecón Maldonado 113; ⊘till late) The liveliest of several thumping Malecón bars, full of funky art, great for people-watching and always churning out loud rock-and-roll.

Musmuqui   Bar

(Raimondi 382; ⊘5pm-midnight Sun-Thu, to 3am Fri & Sat) Locally popular lively bar with two floors and an extensive range of aphrodisiac cocktails concocted from wondrous Amazon plants.

ℹ️ INFORMATION

MONEY

Several banks provide an ATM, including **BCP** (Próspero & Putamayo), which has secure ATMs.

TOURIST INFORMATION

Various jungle guides and jungle lodges also give tourist information, obviously promoting their services, which is fine if you are looking for them but otherwise rarely helpful.

iPerú (☎065-26-0251; Main Hall, Francisco Secada Vignetta Airport; ⊘when flights are arriving/departing)

iPerú (☎065-23-6144; Napo 161; ⊘9am-6pm Mon-Sat, to 1pm Sun)

ℹ️ GETTING THERE & AWAY

AIR

Iquitos' small but busy **airport**, 7km from the center, receives flights from Lima, Pucallpa and Tarapoto. Charter companies at the airport have five-seat passenger planes to almost anywhere in the Amazon, if you have a few hundred US bucks going spare.

LATAM (LAN; ☎065-23-2421; Próspero 232; ⊘9am-6:30pm Mon-Fri, to 1pm Sat) Direct daily

Al Frio y al Fuego

runs to Lima, plus flights to Cuzco on Mondays, Wednesdays and Saturdays.

Star Perú (☎065-23-6208; Napo 260; ⊗8:30am-6:30pm Mon-Fri, to 5:30pm Sat) Star Perú operates two daily flights to and from Lima: the morning flight stops at Pucallpa and the afternoon flight at Tarapoto. Fares are about US$70 to Lima and US$60 to Pucallpa or Tarapoto.

BOAT

Iquitos is Peru's largest, best-organized river port. You can theoretically travel all the way from Iquitos to the Atlantic Ocean, but most boats out of Iquitos ply only Peruvian waters, and voyagers necessarily change boats at the tri-border with Colombia and Brazil. If you choose to arrive or depart by river, you'll end up at one of six ports, which are between 2km and 3km north of the city center.

ℹ GETTING AROUND

Squadrons of *mototaxis* are the bona fide transport round town. They are fun to ride, though they don't provide much protection in an accident. Always enter *mototaxis* from the sidewalk side – passing traffic pays scant heed to embarking passengers – and keep your limbs inside at all times.

Scrapes and fender benders are common. Most rides around Iquitos cost a standard S1.50 to S3; to the airport it's about S8 for a *mototaxi* and S15 for the harder-to-spot cabs. Your accommodation will always order you a taxi on request.

Lagunas

Travelers come to muddy, mosquito-rich Lagunas because it is the best embarkation point for a trip to the western portion of the Reserva Nacional Pacaya-Samiria. The town is a spread-out, remote place; there are stores, but stock is limited (and slightly pricier than elsewhere in Peru), so it's wise to bring your own supplies as back-up. There are no money-changing facilities and hardly any public phones or restaurants.

Regular boats downriver from Yurimaguas to Lagunas take about 10 to 12 hours and leave Yurimaguas' **La Boca** port between 7am and 8am most days. Times are posted on boards at the port in both Yurimaguas and Lagunas for a day in advance. Fast boats from Yurimaguas usually head off around 2:30am (from La Boca): they take 4½ to 5½ hours to arrive in Lagunas.

Salineras de Maras (p191), Sacred Valley

In Focus

Lima (p35)

CHRISTIAN VINCES/SHUTTERSTOCK ©

Peru Today

The past decade has seen Peru emerge as one of the region's fastest growing economies. Though the pace of progress has slowed, there are many positives. That doesn't mean there are no tangles to be worked out – environmental woes, a growing drug trade and political uncertainty – but by and large, Peru is finding its way.

A Culture of Payoffs

Want to test your Spanish? See how well you can follow Peruvian politics as analyzed by your disgruntled Lima taxi driver. It isn't easy. In the past few years, national events have taken more twists and turns than an Andean highway. It goes something like this. In 2017 President Pedro Pablo Kuczynski was found to have taken payoffs from a scandal-ridden construction company. His impeachment stalled for a lack of votes – votes that were later shown to be bought by his supporters. Kuczynski eventually resigned and was replaced by Vice President Martín Vizcarra in 2018.

Just several months afterward, tapes emerged showing judges negotiating fees for favorable court decisions. Since the executive branch has the power to name judges, it revealed a potentially infinite cycle of political corruption. A spate of judges, including the

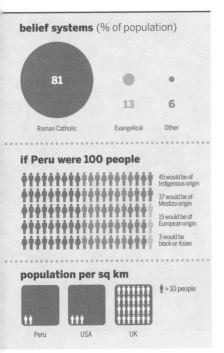

belief systems (% of population)

81

13

6

Roman Catholic   Evangelical   Other

if Peru were 100 people

45 would be of Indigenous origin

37 would be of Mestizo origin

15 would be of European origin

3 would be black or Asian

population per sq km

🚹 ≈ 10 people

Peru   USA   UK

president of the judiciary, resigned after the scandal. Yet the public still clamors for reforms with public protests in cities throughout the country. One could say the roots of corruption run deep.

Precarious Growth

Over the past decade, Peru has had one of the region's fastest growing economies, averaging at a rate of 5.9%, according to World Bank data. No small feat, the national poverty rate has been halved in the space of a mere decade. However, the good times haven't trickled down to everyone: rural areas account for 44% of the population below the poverty line, with indigenous populations and the Andean highlands hit the hardest.

Between 2014 and 2017, Peru's growth slowed, largely in response to the drop in the price of its main export, copper, in the international market. Many think the economy is poised to rebound, both with industry, including growing mining profits, and investments in infrastructure. Tourism is also big: the number of foreign travelers going to Peru almost tripled between 2003 and 2014 from 1.3 to 3.2 million.

Growth has its own painful costs. Mining has caused serious environmental concerns, with heavy metal pollution a huge issue in mining communities. And then there's fast population growth: the influx of 400,000 Venezuelan refugees in one year, with more on the way, is straining infrastructure and social services.

The Machu Picchu Gold Rush

When two tourist trains collided in the middle of the 2018 high season, injuring 15 people, the fever pitch of Machu Picchu visitation was finally seeing hard consequences. With 1.3 million visitors in 2016, the site visitation increased 38% over five years. It seems becoming one of the New Seven Wonders of the World has its price.

Unesco has long been pressuring for better control of the visitation at the site. In response, Machu Picchu introduced timed entry tickets in July, 2017, with morning and afternoon sessions. While visitation is now more evenly distributed throughout the day, even more tourists are allowed in on a daily basis, with administrators even considering adding a third time slot, which would put even greater demands on local transportation and infrastructure.

Some responsible Cuzco tour operators have already responded to the Machu Picchu quandary by offering a more diverse portfolio of tours to disperse the overflow. Many in the tourism industry fear the eventual consequences of overexploitation.

Mural, Huaca de la Luna (232), Trujillo

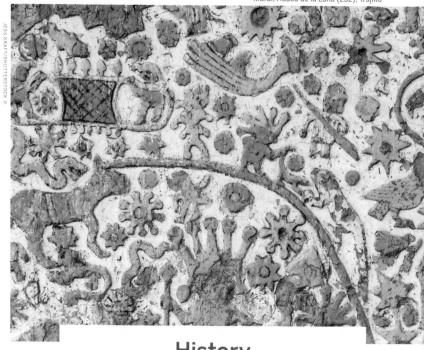

History

In 1532, when Francisco Pizarro landed to conquer Peru in the name of God and the Spanish crown, the region had already seen the epic rise and fall of civilizations. Yet the conquest changed everything: from that seismic clash between Inca and Spaniard came new cultures, new races, new voices, new cuisines – ultimately, a new civilization.

8000 BC	c 3000 BC	200 BC
Hunting scenes are painted in caves by hunter-gatherers near Huánuco in the central highlands and in Toquepala in the south.	Settlement of Peru's coastal oases begins; some of the first structures are built north of present-day Lima.	The Nazca culture on the coast starts construction of a series of giant glyphs that adorn the desert to this day.

Nazca pottery (p274)

CHRISTIAN VINCES/SHUTTERSTOCK ©

Earliest Settlers

There is some debate about how long, exactly, there has been a human presence in Peru. Some scholars have suggested that humans occupied the Andes as far back as 14,000 BC (with at least one academic reporting that it could precede even that early date). The most definitive archaeological evidence, however, puts humans in the region at around 8000 BC. Caves in Lauricocha (near Huánuco) and Toquepala (outside Tacna) bear paintings that record hunting scenes from that era. The latter shows a group of hunters cornering and killing what appears to be a group of camelid animals.

In 4000 BC, taming of llamas and guinea pigs began in the highlands – followed by the domestication of potatoes, gourds, cotton, *lúcuma* (an earthy Andean fruit), quinoa, corn and beans. By 2500 BC, once-nomadic hunters and gatherers clustered into settlements along the Pacific, surviving on fishing and agriculture.

Along with Egypt, India and China, Peru is considered one of the six cradles of civilization (a site where urbanization accompanied agricultural innovation) – the only one

AD 1
The southern coast sees the rise of the Paracas Necropolis culture, known for intricate textiles depicting warriors, animals and gods.

200
The Tiwanaku begin their 400-year domination of the area around Lake Titicaca, into what is today Bolivia and northern Chile.

500
The Moche culture begins construction on the Huacas del Sol y de la Luna, adobe temples situated outside present-day Trujillo.

located in the southern hemisphere. Ongoing excavations at Caral, on the coast about 200km north of Lima, continue to uncover evidence of what is the oldest civilization in the Americas.

Chavín Horizon

Lasting roughly from 1000 BC to 300 BC, and named after the site of Chavín de Huántar, this was a rich period of development for Andean culture – when artistic and religious phenomena appeared, perhaps independently, over a broad swath of the central and northern highlands, as well as the coast. The salient feature of this era is the repeated representation of a stylized feline deity, perhaps symbolizing spiritual transformations experienced under the influence of hallucinogenic plants.

Birth of Local Cultures

After 300 BC, numerous local settlements achieved importance at a regional level. South of Lima, in the area surrounding the Península de Paracas, lived a coastal community whose most significant phase is referred to as Paracas Necropolis (AD 1–400), after a large burial site. It is here that some of the finest pre-Columbian textiles in the Americas have been unearthed: colorful, intricate fabrics that depict oceanic creatures, feline warriors and stylized anthropomorphic figures.

To the south, the people of the Nazca culture (200 BC–AD 600) carved giant, enigmatic designs into the desert landscape that can only be seen from the air. Known as the Nazca Lines, these were mapped early in the 20th century – though their exact purpose remains up for debate. The culture is also known for its fine textile and pottery works, the latter of which used – for the first time in Peruvian history – a polychrome (multicolored) paint technique.

During this time, the Moche culture settled the area around Trujillo between AD 100 and 800. This was an especially artistic group (they produced some of the most remarkable portrait art in history), leaving behind important temple mounds, such as the Huacas del Sol y de la Luna (Temples of the Sun and Moon), near Trujillo, and the burial site of Sipán, outside Chiclayo. The latter contains a series of tombs that have been under excavation since 1987 – one of the most important archaeological discoveries in South America since Machu Picchu. A catastrophic drought in the latter half of the 6th century may have contributed to the demise of the Moche as a culture.

Wari Expansion

As the influence of regional states waned, the Wari, an ethnic group from the Ayacucho Basin, emerged as a force to be reckoned with for 500 years beginning in AD 600. They were vigorous military conquerors who built and maintained important outposts throughout a

c 800	c 850	1100–1200
The fiercely independent Chachapoyas build Kuélap, a citadel in the northern highlands.	The Chimú begin development of Chan Chan, outside present-day Trujillo, a sprawling adobe urban center.	The Inca emerge as a presence in Cuzco; according to legend, they were led to the area by a divine figure known as Manco Cápac.

vast territory that covered an area from Chiclayo to Cuzco. Though their ancient capital lay outside present-day Ayacucho – the ruins of which can still be visited – they also operated the major lowland ceremonial center of Pachacamac, just outside Lima, where people from all over the region came to pay tribute.

As with many conquering cultures, the Wari attempted to suppress other groups by emphasizing their own traditions over local belief. Thus from about AD 700 to 1100, Wari influence is noted in the art, technology and architecture of most areas in Peru. These include elaborate, tie-dyed tunics, and finely woven textiles featuring stylized human figures and geometric patterns, some of which contained a record-breaking 398 threads per linear inch. The Wari are most significant, however, for developing an extensive network of roadways and for greatly expanding the terrace agriculture system – an infrastructure that would serve the Inca well when they came into power just a few centuries later.

Regional Kingdoms

The Wari were eventually replaced by a gaggle of small nation-states that thrived from about 1000 until the Inca conquest of the early 15th century. One of the biggest and best studied of these are the Chimú of the Trujillo area, whose capital was the famed Chan Chan, the largest adobe city in the world. Their economy was based on agriculture and they had a heavily stratified society with a healthy craftsman class, which produced painted textiles and beautifully fashioned pottery that is distinctive for its black stain.

Closely connected to the Chimú are the Sicán from the Lambayeque area, renowned metallurgists who produced the *tumi* – a ceremonial knife with a rounded blade used in sacrifices. (The knife has since become a national symbol in Peru and replicas can be found in crafts markets everywhere.)

To the south, in the environs of Lima, the Chancay people (1000–1500) produced fine, geometrically patterned lace and crudely humorous pottery, in which just about every figure seems to be drinking.

In the highlands, several other cultures were significant during this time. In a relatively isolated and inaccessible patch of the Utcubamba Valley in the northern Andes, the cloud-forest-dwelling Chachapoyas people built the expansive mountain settlement of Kuélap, one of the most intriguing and significant highland ruins in the country. To the south, several small altiplano (Andean plateau) kingdoms near Lake Titicaca left impressive *chullpas* (funerary towers). The best remaining examples are at Sillustani and Cutimbo.

Enter the Inca

According to Inca lore, their civilization was born when Manco Cápac and his sister Mama Ocllo, children of the sun, emerged from Lake Titicaca to establish a civilization in the Cuzco Valley. Whether Manco Cápac was a historical figure is up for debate, but what is

1438–71	1532	1717
The reign of Inca Yupanqui – also known as Pachacutec – represents a period of aggressive empire-building for the Inca.	Atahualpa wins control over Inca territories and the Spanish land in Peru – in less than a year, Atahualpa is dead.	The Spanish crown establishes the Viceroyalty of New Granada, covering modern-day Ecuador, Colombia and Panama.

certain is that the Inca civilization was established in the area of Cuzco at some point in the 12th century. The reign of the first several *incas* (kings) is largely unremarkable – and for a couple of centuries it remained a small, regional state.

Expansion took off in the early 15th century, when the ninth king, Inca Yupanqui, defended Cuzco – against incredible odds – from the invading Chanka people to the north. After the victory, he took on the boastful new name of 'Pachacutec' ('Transformer of the Earth') and spent the next 25 years bringing much of the Andes under his control. Under his reign, the Inca grew from a regional fiefdom in the Cuzco Valley into a broad empire of about 10 million people known as Tawantinsuyo (Land of Four Quarters). The kingdom covered most of modern Peru, plus pieces of Ecuador, Bolivia and Chile. This was made more remarkable by the fact that the Inca, as an ethnicity, never numbered more than about 100,000.

Pachacutec allegedly gave Cuzco its layout in the form of a puma and built fabulous stone monuments in honor of Inca victories, including Sacsaywamán, the temple-fortress at Ollantaytambo and possibly Machu Picchu. He also improved the network of roads that connected the empire, further developed terrace agricultural systems and made Quechua the lingua franca.

Atahualpa's Brief Reign

Inca kings continued the expansions of the empire, first started by Pachacutec. Pachacutec's grandson, Huayna Cápac, who began his rule in 1493, took over much of modern-day Ecuador all the way into Colombia. Consequently, he spent much of his life living, governing and commanding his armies from the north, rather than Cuzco.

By this time, the Spanish presence was already being felt in the Andes. Smallpox and other epidemics transmitted by European soldiers were sweeping through the entire American continent. These were so swift, in fact, that they arrived in Peru before the Spanish themselves, claiming thousands of indigenous lives – including, in all likelihood, that of Huayna Cápac, who succumbed to some sort of plague in 1525.

Without a clear plan of succession, the emperor's untimely death left a power vacuum. The contest turned into a face-off between two of his many children: the Quito-born Atahualpa, who commanded his father's army in the north, and Huáscar, who was based in Cuzco. The ensuing struggle plunged the empire into a bloody civil war, reducing entire cities to rubble. Atahualpa emerged as the victor in April 1532. But the vicious nature of the conflict left the Inca with a lot of enemies throughout the Andes – which is why some tribes were so willing to cooperate with the Spanish when they arrived five months later.

The Spanish Invade

In 1528, explorer Francisco Pizarro and his right-hand-man Diego de Almagro landed in Tumbes in September 1532, with a shipload of arms, horses and slaves, as well as a battalion of 168 men. Atahualpa, in the meantime, was in the process of making his way down

1781	1821	1826
Inca noble Túpac Amaru II is brutally executed by the Spanish in Cuzco after leading an unsuccessful indigenous rebellion.	José de San Martín declares Peru independence but true sovereignty comes when Simón Bolívar's forces vanquish the Spanish in 1824.	The last of the Spanish military forces depart from Callao, after which the country descends into a period of anarchy.

from Quito to Cuzco to claim his hard-won throne. When the Spanish arrived, he was in the highland settlement of Cajamarca, enjoying the area's mineral baths.

Pizarro quickly deduced that the empire was in a fractious state. He and his men charted a course to Cajamarca and approached Atahualpa with royal greetings and promises of brotherhood. But the well-mannered overtures quickly devolved into a surprise attack that left thousands of Inca dead and Atahualpa a prisoner of war. (Between their horses, their armor and the steel of their blades, the Spanish were practically invincible against fighters armed only with clubs, slings and wicker helmets.)

In an attempt to regain his freedom, Atahualpa offered the Spanish a bounty of gold and silver. Thus began one of the most famous ransoms in history – with the Inca attempting to fill an entire room with the precious stuff in order to placate the unrelenting appetites of the Spanish. But it was never enough. The Spanish held Atahualpa for eight months before executing him with a garrote at the age of 31.

The Inca empire never recovered from this fateful encounter. The arrival of the Spanish brought on a cataclysmic collapse of indigenous society. One scholar estimates that the native population – around 10 million when Pizarro arrived – was reduced to 600,000 within a century.

Tumultuous Colony

Following Atahualpa's death, the Spanish got to work consolidating their power. On January 6, 1535, Pizarro sketched out his new administrative center in the sands that bordered the Río Rímac on the central coast. This would be Lima, the so-called 'City of Kings' (named in honor of Three Kings' Day), the new capital of the viceroyalty of Peru, an empire that for more than 200 years would cover much of South America.

It was a period of great turmoil and the Spanish ruled by terror. Rebellions erupted regularly. Atahualpa's half-brother Manco Inca (who had originally sided with the Spanish and served as a puppet emperor under Pizarro) tried to regain control of the highlands in 1536 but was ultimately forced to retreat. He was stabbed to death by a contingent of Spanish soldiers in 1544.

The Spanish were also doing plenty of fighting among themselves, splitting into a complicated series of rival factions, each wanting control of the new empire. In 1538 De Almagro was sentenced to death by strangulation for attempting to take over Cuzco. Three years later, Pizarro was assassinated in Lima by a band of disgruntled De Almagro supporters. Other conquistadors met equally violent fates. Things grew relatively more stable after the arrival of Francisco de Toledo as viceroy, an efficient administrator who brought some order to the emergent colony.

Until independence, Peru was ruled by a series of Spanish-born viceroys appointed by the Crown. Immigrants from Spain held the most prestigious positions, while *criollos* (Spaniards born in Peru) were confined to middle management. *Mestizos* (people of mixed descent) were placed even further down the social scale. Full-blooded *indígenas* resided at

1879–83	**1911**	**1924**
Chile wages war against Peru and Bolivia over nitrate-rich lands in the Atacama; Peru loses the conflict and the Tarapacá region.	US historian Hiram Bingham arrives at the ruins of Machu Picchu; his 'discovery' of the ancient city is chronicled in *National Geographic*.	Víctor Raúl Haya de la Torre founds APRA, a populist, anti-imperialist political party that is immediately declared illegal.

Monasterio de Santa Catalina (p94), Arequipa

COLACAT/SHUTTERSTOCK ©

the bottom, exploited as *peones* (expendable laborers) in a feudal system that granted colonists land titles that included the property of all the indigenous people living in that area.

Tensions between *indígenas* and Spaniards reached boiling point in the late 18th century, when the Spanish Crown levied a series of new taxes that hit indigenous people the hardest. In 1780 José Gabriel Condorcanqui – a descendant of the Inca monarch Túpac Amaru – arrested and executed a Spanish administrator on charges of cruelty. His act unleashed an indigenous rebellion that spread into Bolivia and Argentina. Condorcanqui adopted the name Túpac Amaru II and traveled the region fomenting revolution.

The Spanish reprisal was swift and brutal. In 1781 the captured indigenous leader was dragged to the main plaza in Cuzco, where he would watch his followers, his wife and his sons killed in a day-long bout of violence, before being drawn and quartered himself. Pieces of his remains were displayed in towns around the Andes as a way of discouraging further insurrection.

Independence

By the early 19th century, *criollos* in many Spanish colonies had grown increasingly dissatisfied with their lack of administrative power and the Crown's heavy taxes, leading to revolutions all over the continent. In Peru, the winds of change arrived from two directions. Argentine revolutionary José de San Martín led independence campaigns in Argentina and Chile, before entering Peru by sea at the port of Pisco in 1820. With San Martín's arrival, royalist forces retreated into the highlands, allowing him to ride into Lima unobstructed. On July 28, 1821, independence was declared. But real independence wouldn't materialize for another three years. With Spanish forces still at large in the interior, San Martín would need more troops to fully defeat the Spanish.

Then came Simón Bolívar, the Venezuelan revolutionary who had been leading independence fights in Venezuela, Colombia and Ecuador. In 1823 the Peruvians gave Bolívar dictatorial powers (an honor that had been bestowed on him in other countries). By the latter half of 1824, he and his lieutenant, Antonio José de Sucre, had routed the Spanish in

1932	**1948**	**1968**
More than a thousand APRA party followers are executed by the military at the ancient ruins of Chan Chan, following an uprising.	General Manuel Odría assumes power for eight years, encouraging foreign investment and cracking down on APRA.	General Juan Velasco Alvarado takes power in a coup d'état.

decisive battles at Junín and Ayacucho. The revolutionaries had faced staggering odds, but nonetheless managed to capture the viceroy and negotiate a surrender. As part of the deal, the Spanish would withdraw all of their forces from Peru and Bolivia.

New Republic

The lofty idealism of the revolution was soon followed by the harsh reality of having to govern. Peru, the young nation, proved to be just as anarchic as Peru, the viceroyalty. Between 1825 and 1841, there was a revolving door of regime changes (two dozen) as regional *caudillos* (chieftains) scrambled for power. The situation improved in the 1840s with the mining of vast deposits of guano off the Peruvian coast; the nitrate-rich bird droppings reaped unheard-of profits as fertilizer on the international market.

The country would find some measure of stability under the governance of Ramón Castilla (a *mestizo*), who would be elected to his first term in 1845. The income from the guano boom – which he had been key in exploiting – helped Castilla make needed economic improvements. He abolished slavery, paid off some of Peru's debt and established a public school system. Castilla served as president three more times over the course of two decades – at times, by force; at others, in an interim capacity; at one point, for less than a week. Following his final term, he was exiled by competitors who wanted to neutralize him politically. He died in 1867, in northern Chile, attempting to make his way back to Peru. (Visitors can see his impressive crypt at the Panteón de los Proceres in Central Lima.)

War of the Pacific

With Castilla's passing, the country once again descended into chaos. A succession of *caudillos* squandered the enormous profits of the guano boom and, in general, managed the economy in a deplorable fashion. Moreover, military skirmishes would ensue with Ecuador (over border issues) and Spain (which was trying to dominate its former South American colonies). The conflicts left the nation's coffers empty. By 1874 Peru was bankrupt.

This left the country in a weak position to deal with the expanding clash between Chile and Bolivia over nitrate-rich lands in the Atacama Desert. Borders in this area had never been clearly defined and escalating tensions eventually led to military engagement. To make matters worse for the Peruvians, President Mariano Prado abandoned the country for Europe on the eve of the conflict. The war was a disaster for Peru at every level (not to mention Bolivia, which lost its entire coastline).

Despite the brave actions of military figures such as Admiral Miguel Grau, the Chileans were simply better organized and had more resources, including the support of the British. In 1881 they led a land campaign deep into Peru, occupying the capital of Lima, during which time they ransacked the city, making off with the priceless contents of the National Library. By the time the conflict ended in 1883, Peru had permanently lost its southernmost region of Tarapacá; and it wouldn't regain the area around Tacna until 1929.

1970	**1980**	**1985**
A 7.7-magnitude earthquake in northern Peru kills almost 80,000 people, leaves 140,000 injured and another 500,000 homeless.	Guerrilla group Sendero Luminoso (Shining Path) takes its first violent action – burning ballot boxes – in the Ayacucho region.	Alan García becomes president, but his term is marked by hyperinflation and increased attacks by terrorist groups.

A New Intellectual Era

As one century gave way to the next, intellectual circles saw the rise of *indigenismo,* a continent-wide movement that advocated for a dominant social and political role for indigenous people. In Peru, this translated into a wide-ranging (if fragmented) cultural movement. Historian Luis Valcárcel attacked his society's degradation of the indigenous class. Poet César Vallejo wrote critically acclaimed works that took on indigenous oppression as themes. And José Sabogal led a generation of visual artists who explored indigenous themes in their paintings. In 1928, journalist and thinker José Carlos Mariátegui penned a seminal Marxist work – *Seven Interpretive Essays on Peruvian Reality* – in which he criticized the feudal nature of Peruvian society and celebrated the communal aspects of the Inca social order. (It remains vital reading for the Latin American left to this day.)

In this climate, in 1924, Trujillo-born political leader Victor Raúl Haya de la Torre founded the Alianza Popular Revolucionaria Americana (American Popular Revolutionary Alliance; APRA). The party espoused populist values, celebrated 'Indo-America' and rallied against US imperialism. It was quickly declared illegal by the autocratic regime of Augusto Leguía – and remained illegal for long stretches of the 20th century. Haya de la Torre, at various points in his life, lived in hiding and in exile and, at one point, endured 15 months as a political prisoner.

Dictatorships & Revolutionaries

After the start of the Great Depression in 1929, the country's history becomes a blur of dictatorships punctuated by periods of democracy. Leguía, a sugar baron from the north coast, ruled on a couple of occasions: for his first period in office (1908–12) he was elected; for the second (1919–30), he made it in via a coup d'état. He spent his first term dealing with border conflicts and the second, stifling press freedom and political dissidents.

Leguía was followed by Colonel Luis Sánchez Cerro, who served a couple of short terms in the 1930s. (Though his time in office was turbulent, Sánchez would be celebrated in some sectors for abolishing a conscription law that required able-bodied men to labor on road-building projects. The law affected poor indigenous men disproportionately, as they couldn't afford to pay the exemption fee.) By 1948 another dictator had taken power: the former army colonel Manuel Odría, who spent his time in office cracking down on the APRA and encouraging US foreign investment.

The most fascinating of Peru's 20th-century dictators, however, is Juan Velasco Alvarado, the former commander-in-chief of the army who took control in 1968. Though he was expected to lead a conservative regime, Velasco turned out to be an inveterate populist – so much so that some APRA members complained that he had stolen their party platform away from them. He established a nationalist agenda that included 'Peruvianizing' (securing Peruvian majority ownership) various industries. In his rhetoric he celebrated the indigenous peasantry, championed a radical program of agrarian reform and made Quechua an official language. He also severely restricted press freedom, which drew the

1990	1992	1996
Alberto Fujimori is elected president; his rule sees improvements in the economy, but he is plagued by charges of corruption.	Abimael Guzmán, the founder of Sendero Luminoso, is captured in Lima above a dance studio in well-to-do Surco.	Guerrillas from Movimiento Revolucionario Túpac Amaru (MRTA) take 72 hostages for four months in the Japanese ambassador's residence.

wrath of the power structure in Lima. Ultimately, his economic policies were failures – and in 1975, in declining health, he was replaced by another, more conservative military regime.

Internal Conflict

Peru returned to civilian rule in 1980, when President Fernando Belaúnde Terry was elected to office – the first election in which leftist parties were allowed to participate (including APRA, which was now legal). Belaúnde's term was anything but smooth. Social reforms took a back seat as the president tried desperately to jump-start the economy.

It was at this time that a radical Maoist group from the poor region of Ayacucho began its unprecedented rise. Founded by philosophy professor Abimael Guzmán, Sendero Luminoso (Shining Path) wanted nothing less than an overthrow of the social order via violent armed struggle. Over the next two decades, the situation escalated, with the group assassinating political leaders and community activists, attacking police stations and universities and, at one point, stringing up dead dogs all over downtown Lima.

The government sent in the military, a heavy-handed outfit that knew little about handling a guerrilla insurgency. There was torture and rape, plus disappearances and massacres, none of which did anything to put a stop to Sendero Luminoso. Caught in the middle were tens of thousands of poor *campesinos* (peasants), who bore the brunt of the casualties.

In the midst of this, Alan García was elected to the presidency in 1985. Initially, his ascent generated a great deal of hope. He was young, he was a gifted public speaker, he was popular – and he was the first member of the storied APRA party to win a presidential election. But his economic program was catastrophic and by the late 1980s Peru faced a staggering hyperinflation rate of 7500%. Thousands of people were plunged into poverty. There were food shortages and riots, and the government was forced to declare a state of emergency. Two years after completing his term, García fled the country after being accused of embezzling millions of dollars.

Fujishock

With the country in a state of chaos, the 1990 presidential elections took on more importance than ever. The contest was between famed novelist Mario Vargas Llosa and Alberto Fujimori, a little-known agronomist of Japanese descent. During the campaign, Vargas Llosa promoted an economic 'shock treatment' program that many feared would send more Peruvians into poverty, while Fujimori positioned himself as an alternative to the status quo. Fujimori won handily. But as soon as he got into office, he implemented an even more austere economic plan that, among other things, drove up the price of gasoline by 3000%. The measures, known as 'Fujishock,' ultimately succeeded in reducing inflation and stabilizing the economy – but not without costing the average Peruvian dearly.

In April 1992, Fujimori staged an *autogolpe* (coup from within), dissolving the legislature and stocking an entirely new congress with his allies. Peruvians, not unused to *caudillos*,

2001	**2003**	**2005**
Alejandro Toledo becomes the first indigenous person to govern an Andean country.	Truth and Reconciliation Commission releases its final report on Peru's internal conflict: estimates of the dead reach 70,000.	Construction of the Interoceanic Hwy, opening an overland trade route between Peru and Brazil, begins in the Amazon Basin.

tolerated the power grab, hoping that Fujimori might help stabilize the economic and political situation – which he did. The economy grew. And by the end of the year, leaders of both Sendero Luminoso and MRTA had been apprehended (though not before Sendero Luminoso had brutally assassinated community activist María Elena Moyano and detonated lethal truck bombs in Lima's Miraflores district).

By the end of his second term, Fujimori's administration was plagued by allegations of corruption. He ran for a third term in 2000 (which was technically unconstitutional) and remained in power despite not having the simple majority necessary to claim the election. Within the year, however, he was forced to flee the country after it was revealed that his security chief Vladimiro Montesinos had been embezzling government funds and bribing elected officials and the media. Fujimori formally resigned the presidency from abroad, but the legislature rejected the gesture, voting him out of office and declaring him 'morally unfit' to govern.

Fujimori is currently serving 25 years in prison for convictions including ordering extrajudicial killings and channeling millions of dollars in state funds to Montesinos. Montesinos is doing 20 years – for bribery and selling arms to Colombian rebels.

The 21st Century

In 2001, shoeshine-boy-turned-Stanford-economist Alejandro Toledo became the first person of Quechua ethnicity to be elected to the presidency. Unfortunately, Toledo inherited a political and economic mess. He also lacked a majority in congress, hampering his effectiveness in the midst of an economic recession.

Toledo was followed in office by – of all people – the APRA's Alan García, who was re-elected in 2006. His second term was infinitely more stable than the first but it wasn't without problems, including a corruption scandal and the touchy issue of how to manage the country's mineral wealth. In 2008 García signed a law that allowed foreign companies to exploit natural resources in the Amazon. The legislation generated a backlash among various Amazon tribes and led to a fatal standoff in the northern city of Bagua in 2009.

The Peruvian congress quickly revoked the law, but this issue remained a challenge for President Ollanta Humala, elected in 2011. He passed the Prior Consultation Law, historic new legislation to guarantee indigenous people rights to consent to projects affecting them and their lands. Though the economy functioned well under Humala's governance, civil unrest over a proposed gold mine in the north, as well as a botched raid on a Sendero Luminoso encampment, sent his approval rating into a tailspin by the middle of 2012.

While the explosive growth spurt of the early part of the millennium has slowed down, the country has become far more stable. Government corruption continues to be an issue, however. In 2017 president Pedro Pablo Kuczynski was found to have taken payoffs from a construction company. He avoided impeachment due to a lack of votes – despite later evidence which showed his supporters were buying votes. He resigned prior to a second scheduled impeachment vote and was replaced by Vice President Martín Vizcarra in 2018.

2009	2016	2018
Fujimori is convicted of embezzling in addition to prior convictions for ordering military death squads to carry out extrajudicial killings.	Economist Pedro Pablo Kuczynski wins the presidential race against Keiko Fujimori, the daughter of Alberto Fujimori.	Facing impeachment, President Pedro Pablo Kuczynski resigns from office and is succeeded by Vice President Martín Vizcarra.

Horseback riding, Cordillera Huayhuash

HADIYYAH/GETTY IMAGES ©

Outdoor Activities

Scale icy Andean peaks. Raft one of the world's deepest canyons. Surf heavenly Pacific breakers. Walk the flanks of a smoldering volcano known locally as a living deity. With its breathtaking, diverse landscapes, Peru is a natural adventure hub. So gear up – you're in for a wild ride.

Hiking & Trekking

Pack the hiking boots because the variety of trails in Peru is downright staggering. The main trekking centers are Cuzco and Arequipa in the southern Andes, and Huaraz in the north. Hikers will find many easily accessible trails around Peru's archaeological ruins, which are also the final destinations for more challenging trekking routes.

Peru's most famous trek is the Inca Trail to Machu Picchu. Limited permits mean this guided-only trek sells out months in advance. For those who haven't planned so far ahead, there are worthwhile alternative routes. In addition, other possibilities around Cuzco include the spectacular six-day trek around the venerated Ausangate (6384m), which will take you over 5000m passes, through huge herds of alpacas and past tiny hamlets

Tapir, Parque Nacional Manu (p256)

CORDIER SYLVAIN/GETTY IMAGES ©

★ **Best Wildlife-Watching Spots**

Parque Nacional Manu (p256)

Cañón del Colca (p110)

Islas Ballestas (p72)

Parque Nacional Huascarán (p240)

unchanged in centuries. Likewise, the isolated Inca site of Choquequirau is another intriguing destination for a trek.

In nearby Arequipa, you can get down in some of the world's deepest canyons – the world-famous Cañón del Colca and the Cañón del Cotahuasi. The scenery is guaranteed to knock you off your feet, and it's easier going than higher-altitude destinations. During the wet season, when some Andean trekking routes are impassable, Colca is the best place in Peru for DIY trekking between rural villages. The more remote and rugged Cañón del Cotahuasi is best visited with an experienced local guide and only during the dry season.

Cuzco and Huaraz (and, to a lesser degree, Arequipa) have outfitters that can provide equipment, guides and even *arrieros* (mule drivers). If you prefer to trek ultralight, you might want to purchase your own gear, especially a sleeping bag, as old-generation rental items tend to be heavy. Whether you'll need a guide depends on where you trek. Certain areas of Peru, such as along the Inca Trail, require guides; in other places, such as in the Cordillera Huayhuash, there have been muggings, so it's best to be with a local. Thankfully, scores of other trekking routes are wonderfully DIY. Equip yourself with topographic maps for major routes in the nearest major gateway towns or, better yet, at the Instituto Geográfico Nacional (IGN) or at the South American Explorers Club in Lima.

Whatever adventure you choose, be prepared to spend a few days acclimating to the dizzying altitudes – or face a heavy-duty bout of altitude sickness.

Trekking is most rewarding during the dry season (May to September) in the Andes. Avoid the wet season (December to March), when rain makes some areas impassable.

Mountain, Rock & Ice Climbing

Peru has the highest tropical mountains in the world, offering some absolutely inspired climbs, though acclimatization to altitude is essential. The Cordillera Blanca, with its dozens of snowy peaks exceeding 5000m, is one of South America's top destinations. The Andean town of Huaraz has tour agencies, outfitters, guides, information and climbing equipment for hire. Still, it's best to bring your own gear for serious ascents. Near Huaraz, Ishinca (5530m) and Pisco (5752m) provide two ascents easy enough for relatively inexperienced climbers. For experts, these mountains are also good warm-up climbs for bigger adventures such as Huascarán (6768m), Peru's highest peak.

In southern Peru, the snowy volcanic peaks around Arequipa can be scaled by determined novice mountaineers. The most popular climb is El Misti (5822m), a site of Inca human sacrifice. Despite its serious altitude, it is basically a very long, tough walk. Chachani (6075m) is one of the easier 6000m peaks in the world – though it still requires crampons, an ice ax and a good guide.

For beginners looking to bag their first serious mountain, Peru may not be the best place to start. Not all guides know the basics of first aid or wilderness search and rescue. Check out a prospective guide's credentials carefully and seek out those who are personally recommended. Carefully check any rental equipment before setting out.

As with trekking, high-elevation climbing is best done during the dry season (mid-June to mid-July).

Rafting & Kayaking

Rafting (river running) is growing in popularity around Peru, with trips that range from a few hours to more than two weeks.

Cuzco is the launch point for the greatest variety of rafting options. Choices range from a few hours of mild rafting on the Urubamba to adrenaline-pumping rides on the Santa Teresa to several days on the Apurímac, technically the source of the Amazon (with world-class rafting between May and November). A rafting trip on the Tambopata, available from June through October, tumbles down the eastern slopes of the Andes, culminating in a couple of days of floating in unspoiled rainforest.

Arequipa is another rafting center. Here, the Río Chili is the most frequently run, with a half-day novice trip leaving daily between March and November. Further afield, the more challenging Río Majes features class II and III rapids. On the south coast, Lunahuaná, not far from Lima, is a prime spot for beginners and experts alike. Between December and April, rapids here can reach class IV.

Note that rafting is not regulated in Peru. There are deaths every year and some rivers are so remote that rescues can take days. In addition, some companies are not environmentally responsible and leave camping beaches dirty. Book excursions only with reputable, well-recommended agencies and avoid cut-rate trips. A good operator will have insurance, provide you with a document indicating that they are registered, and have highly experienced guides with certified first-aid training who carry a properly stocked medical kit. Choose one that provides top-notch equipment, including self-bailing rafts, US Coast Guard–approved life jackets, first-class helmets and spare paddles. Many good companies raft rivers accompanied by a kayaker experienced in river rescue.

For more on rafting in Peru, visit www.peruwhitewater.com.

Surfing

With consistent, uncrowded waves and plenty of remote breaks to explore, Peru has a mixed surfing scene that attracts dedicated locals and international die-hards alike. Kite-surfing and paddleboarding are also emerging as popular sports, particularly in Máncora and Paracas.

Waves can be found from the moment you land. All along the southern part of Lima, surfers ride out popular point and beach breaks at Miraflores (known as Waikiki), Barran-quito and La Herradura. Herradura's outstanding left point break gets crowded when there is a strong swell. In-the-know surfers prefer the smaller crowds further south at Punta Hermosa. International and national championships are held at nearby Punta Rocas as well as Pico Alto, an experts-only 'kamikaze' reef break with some of the largest waves in Peru. Isla San Gallán, off the Península de Paracas, also provides experts with a world-class right-hand point break only accessible by boat; ask local fishers or at hotels.

The water is cold from April to mid-December (as low as 15°C/60°F), when wet suits are generally needed. Indeed, many surfers wear wet suits year-round (2/3mm will suffice), even though the water is a little warmer (around 20°C, or 68°F, in the Lima area) from January to March. The far north coast (north of Talara) stays above 21°C (70°F) most of the year.

Though waves are generally not crowded, surfing can be a challenge – facilities are limited and equipment rental is expensive. The scene on the north coast is the most organized, with surf shops and hostels that offer advice, rent boards and arrange surfing day trips. Huanchaco is a great base for these services. Serious surfers should bring their own board.

The best surfing websites include www.peruazul.com, www.vivamancora.com and www.wannasurf.com, with a comprehensive, highly detailed list of just about every break in Peru. Good wave and weather forecasts can be found at www.magicseaweed.com and www.windguru.com.

Sandboarding

Sandboarding down the giant desert dunes is growing in popularity at Huacachina and around Nazca, on Peru's south coast. Nazca's Cerro Blanco (2078m) is the highest known sand dune in the world. Some hotels and travel agencies offer tours in *areneros* (dune buggies), where you are hauled to the top of the dunes, then get picked up at the bottom. (Choose your driver carefully; some are notoriously reckless.)

Mountain Biking & Cycling

In recent years mountain biking has exploded in popularity. It is still a fledgling sport in Peru, but there is no shortage of incredible terrain. Single-track trails ranging from easy to expert await mountain bikers outside Huaraz, Arequipa and even Lima. If you're experienced, there are incredible mountain-biking possibilities around the Sacred Valley and downhill trips to the Amazon jungle, all accessible from Cuzco. Easier cycling routes include the wine country around Lunahuaná and in the Cañón del Colca, starting from Chivay.

Mountain-bike rental in Peru tends to be basic; if you are planning on serious biking it's best to bring your own. (Airline bicycle-carrying policies vary, so shop around.) You'll also need a repair kit and extra parts.

Swimming

Swimming conditions are ideal along Peru's desert coast from January to March, when the Pacific Ocean waters are warmest and skies are blue. Some of the best spots are just south of Lima. Far more attractive is the stretch of shore on the north coast, especially at laid-back Huanchaco, around Chiclayo and the perennially busy jet-set resorts of Máncora.

Only north of Talara does the water stay warm year-round. Watch for dangerous currents and note that beaches near major coastal cities are often polluted.

Horseback Riding

Horse rentals can be arranged in many tourist destinations, but the rental stock is not always treated well, so check your horse carefully before you saddle up. For a real splurge, take a ride on a graceful Peruvian *paso* horse. Descendants of horses with royal Spanish and Moorish lineage, like those ridden by the conquistadors, are reputed to have the world's smoothest gait. Stables around Peru advertise rides for half a day or longer, especially in the Sacred Valley at Urubamba.

Paragliding

Popular paragliding sites include the coastal cliff tops of suburban Miraflores in Lima and various points along the south coast, including Pisco and Paracas. There are few paragliding operators in Peru. Book ahead through the agencies in Lima.

Macaws, Parque Nacional Manu (p256)

MARTIN MECNAROWSKI/SHUTTERSTOCK ©

The Natural World

Few countries have topographies as rugged, forbidding and wildly diverse as Peru. Between snaking rivers, plunging canyons and zigzagging mountain roads, navigating Peru's landscape is about circumventing natural obstacles, a path of excitement and jaw-dropping beauty.

The Land

The third-largest country in South America – at 1,285,220 sq km – Peru is five times larger than the UK, almost twice the size of Texas and one-sixth the size of Australia. On the coast, a narrow strip of land, which lies below 1000m in elevation, hugs the country's 3000km-long shoreline. Consisting primarily of scrubland and desert, it eventually merges, in the south, with Chile's Atacama Desert, one of the driest places on earth. The coast includes Lima, the capital, and several major agricultural centers – oases watered by dozens of rivers that cascade down from the Andes. These settlements make for a strange sight: barren desert can give way to bursts of green fields within the course of a few meters. The coast contains some of Peru's flattest terrain, so it's no surprise that the country's best

★ **Top Protected Areas**

Cañón del Colca (p110)
Cordillera Blanca (p238)
Lake Titicaca (p123)
Parque Nacional Manu (p256)
Islas Ballestas (p72)

Llamas, alpacas and vicuñas, Cañón del Colca (p110)

ANITA MARTINGANO/SHUTTERSTOCK ©

road, the Carretera Panamericana (Pan-American Hwy), borders much of the Pacific from Ecuador to Chile.

The Andes form the spine of the country. Rising steeply from the coast, and growing sharply in height and gradient from north to south, they reach spectacular heights of more than 6000m just 100km inland. Peru's highest peak, Huascarán (6768m), located northeast of Huaraz, is the world's highest tropical summit and the sixth-tallest mountain in the Americas. Though the Peruvian Andes resides in the tropics, the mountains are laced with a web of glaciers above elevations of 5000m. Between 3000m and 4000m lie the agricultural highlands, which support more than a third of Peru's population.

The eastern Andean slopes receive much more rainfall than the dry western slopes and are draped in lush cloud forests as they descend into the lowland rainforest of the Amazon. Here, the undulating landscape rarely rises more than 500m above sea level as various tributary systems feed into the mighty Río Amazonas (Amazon River), the largest river in the world. Weather conditions are hot and humid year-round, with most precipitation falling between December and May.

Wildlife

With its folds, bends and plunging river valleys, Peru is home to countless ecosystems, each with its own unique climate, elevation, vegetation and soil type. As a result, it has a spectacular variety of plant and animal life. Colonies of sea lions occupy rocky outcroppings on the coast, while raucous flocks of brightly colored macaws descend on clay licks in the Amazon. In the Andes, rare vicuñas (endangered relatives of the alpaca) trot about in packs as condors take to the wind currents. Peru is one of only a dozen or so countries in the world considered to be 'megadiverse.'

Birds

Peru has more than 1800 bird species – that's more than the number of species found in North America and Europe together. From the tiniest hummingbirds to the majestic Andean condor, the variety is colorful and seemingly endless; new species are discovered regularly.

Along the Pacific, marine birds of all kinds are most visible, especially in the south, where they can be found clustered along the shore. Here you'll see exuberant Chilean flamingos, oversized Peruvian pelicans, plump Inca terns sporting white-feather moustaches and bright orange beaks, colonies of brown boobies engaged in elaborate mating dances, cormorants, and endangered Humboldt penguins, which can be spotted waddling around the Islas Ballestas.

In the highlands, the most famous bird of all is the Andean condor. Weighing up to 10kg, with a 3m-plus wingspan, this monarch of the air (a member of the vulture family) once ranged over the entire Andean mountain chain from Venezuela to Tierra del Fuego. Considered the largest flying bird in the world, the condor was put on the endangered species list in the 1970s, due mostly to loss of habitat and pollution. But it was also hunted to the brink of extinction because its body parts were believed to increase male virility and ward off nightmares. Condors usually nest in impossibly high mountain cliffs that prevent predators from snatching their young. Their main food source is carrion and they're most easily spotted riding thermal air currents in the canyons around Arequipa.

Other prominent high-altitude birds include the Andean gull (don't call it a seagull!), which is commonly sighted along lakes and rivers as high as 4500m. The mountains are also home to several species of ibis, such as the puna ibis, which inhabits lakeside marshes, as well as roughly a dozen types of cinclodes, a type of ovenbird (their clay nests resemble ovens) endemic to the Andes. Other species include torrent ducks, which nest in small waterside caves, Andean geese, spotted Andean flickers, black-and-yellow Andean siskins and, of course, a panoply of hummingbirds.

Swoop down toward the Amazon and you'll catch sight of the world's most iconic tropical birds, including boisterous flocks of parrots and macaws festooned in brightly plumed regalia. You'll also see clusters of aracaris, toucans, parakeets, toucanets, ibises, regal gray-winged trumpeters, umbrella birds donning gravity-defying feathered hairdos, crimson colored cocks-of-the-rock, soaring hawks and harpy eagles. The list goes on.

Mammals

The Amazon is home to a bounty of mammals. More than two dozen species of monkeys are found here, including howlers, acrobatic spider monkeys and wide-eyed marmosets. With the help of a guide, you may also see sloths, bats, piglike peccaries, anteaters, armadillos and coatis (ring-tailed members of the raccoon family). And if you're really lucky, you'll find giant river otters, capybaras (a rodent of unusual size), river dolphins, tapirs and maybe one of half a dozen elusive felines, including the fabled jaguar.

Toward the west, the cloud forests straddling the Amazon and the eastern slopes of the Andean highlands are home to the endangered spectacled bear. South America's only bear is a black, shaggy mammal that grows up to 1.8m in length, and is known for its white, masklike face markings.

The highlands are home to roving packs of camelids: llamas and alpacas are the most easily spotted since they are domesticated, and used as pack animals or for their wool; vicuñas and guanacos live exclusively in the wild. On highland talus slopes, watch out for the viscacha, which looks like the world's most cuddly rabbit. Foxes, deer and domesticated *cuy* (guinea pigs) are also highland dwellers, as is the puma (cougar or mountain lion).

On the coast, huge numbers of sea lions and seals are easily seen on the Islas Ballestas. While whales are very rarely seen offshore, dolphins are commonly seen. In the coastal desert strip, there are few unique species of land animals. One is the near-threatened Sechuran fox, the smallest of the South American foxes (found in northern Peru), which has a black-tipped tail, pale, sand-colored fur, and an omnivorous appetite for small rodents and seed pods.

Reptiles, Amphibians, Insects & Marine Life

The greatest variety of reptiles, amphibians, insects and marine life can be found in the Amazon Basin. Here, you'll find hundreds of species, including toads, tree frogs and thumbnail-sized poison dart frogs (indigenous peoples once used the frogs' deadly poison on the points of their blow-pipe darts). Rivers teem with schools of piranhas, *paiche* and *doncella* (both are types of freshwater fish), while the air buzzes with the activity of thousands of insects: armies of ants, squadrons of beetles, as well as katydids, stick insects, caterpillars, spiders, praying mantises, transparent moths, and butterflies of all shapes and sizes. A blue morpho butterfly in flight is a remarkable sight: with wingspans of up to 10cm, their iridescent-blue coloring can seem downright hallucinogenic.

Naturally, there are all kinds of reptiles, too, including tortoises, river turtles, lizards, caimans and, of course, that jungle-movie favorite: the anaconda. An aquatic boa snake that can measure more than 10m in length, it will often ambush its prey by the water's edge, constrict its body around it and then drown it in the river. Caimans, tapirs, deer, turtles and peccaries are all tasty meals for this killer snake; human victims are almost unheard of (unless you're Jennifer Lopez and Ice Cube in a low-rent Hollywood production). Far more worrisome to the average human is the bushmaster, a deadly, reddish-brown viper that likes to hang out inside rotting logs and among the buttress roots of trees. Thankfully, it's a retiring creature, and is rarely found on popular trails.

Plants

At high elevations in the Andes, especially in the Cordilleras Blanca and Huayhuash, outside Huaraz, there is a cornucopia of distinctive alpine flora and fauna. Plants encountered in this region include native lupins, spiky tussocks of ichu grass, striking queñua (Polylepis) trees with their distinctive curly, red paper-like bark, in addition to unusual bromeliads. Many alpine wildflowers bloom during the trekking season, between May and September.

In the south, you'll find the distinctive *puna* ecosystem. These areas have a fairly limited flora of hard grasses, cushion plants, small herbaceous plants, shrubs and dwarf trees. Many plants in this environment have developed small, thick leaves that are less susceptible to frost and radiation. In the north, you can find some *páramo* (high-altitude Andean grasslands), which have a harsher climate, are less grassy and have an odd mixture of landscapes, including peat bogs, glacier-formed valleys, alpine lakes, wet grasslands, and patches of scrubland and forest.

National Parks

Peru's vast wealth of wildlife is protected by a system of national parks and reserves with 60 areas covering almost 15% of the country. The newest is the Sierra del Divisor Reserve Zone, created in 2006 to protect 1.5 million hectares of rainforest on the Brazilian border. All of these protected areas are administered by the Instituto Nacional de Recursos Nacionales (Inrena; www.inrena.gob.pe), a division of the Ministry of Agriculture.

Unfortunately, resources are lacking to conserve protected areas, which are subject to illegal hunting, fishing, logging and mining. The government simply doesn't have the funds to hire enough rangers and provide them with the equipment necessary to patrol the parks. That said, a number of international agencies and not-for-profit organizations contribute money, staff and resources to help with conservation and education projects.

Environmental Issues

Peru faces major challenges in the stewardship of its natural resources, with problems compounded by a lack of law enforcement and its impenetrable geography. Deforestation and erosion are major issues, as is industrial pollution, urban sprawl and the continuing attempted eradication of coca plantations on some Andean slopes. In addition, the Carr Interoceánica through the heart of the Amazon may imperil thousands of square kilometers of rainforest.

Reduced growth in mining earnings in the 21st century has led the government to install protectionist measures, much to the detriment of the environment. A law enacted in July 2014 weakened environmental protections by removing Peru's environmental ministry's jurisdiction over air, soil, and water quality standards.

JEREMY PAWLOWSKI/SHUTTERSTOCK ©

Food & Drink

In Peru, fusion was always a natural part of everyday cooking. Over the last 400 years, Andean stews mingled with Asian stir-fries, and Spanish rice dishes absorbed Amazonian flavors, producing the country's famed criollo (creole) cooking. More recently, a generation of experimental young innovators has pushed local fare to gastronomic heights.

Staples & Specialties

Given the country's craggy topography, there's an infinite variety in regional cuisines. But at a national level much of the country's cooking begins and ends with the humble potato – which originally hails from the Andes. (All potatoes can be traced back to a single progenitor from Peru.)

Standout dishes include *ocopa* (potatoes with a spicy peanut sauce), *papa a la huan-caína* (potato topped with a creamy cheese sauce) and *causa* (mashed potato terrines stuffed with seafood, vegetables or chicken). Also popular is *papa rellena,* a mashed potato filled with ground beef and then deep-fried. Potatoes are also found in the chowder-like soups known as *chupe* and in *lomo saltado,* the simple beef stir-fries that headline every Peruvian menu.

Chef Mitsuharu Tsumura at Maido

CRIS BOUNCLE/AFP /GETTY IMAGES ©

★ Most Influential Chefs

Gastón Acurio at Astrid y Gastón (p43)

Virgilio Martínez at Central (p42)

Mitsuharu Tsumura at Maido (p43)

Francesca Ferreyros at IK (p60)

Pedro Miguel Schiaffino at Malabar (p58) and ámaZ(p42)

Other popular items include tamales (corn cakes), which are made in various regional variations – such as *humitas* (created with fresh corn) and *juanes* (made with rice or cassava).

Amazon

Though not as popular throughout the entire country, Amazon ingredients have begun to make headway in recent years. Several high-end restaurants in Lima have started giving gourmet treatment to jungle mainstays, to wide acclaim. This includes the increased use of river snails and fish (including *paiche* and *doncella*), as well as produce such as *aguaje* (the fruit of the moriche palm), yucca (cassava) and *chonta* (hearts of palm). *Juanes* (a bijao leaf stuffed with rice, yucca, chicken and/or pork) is a savory area staple.

Coast

The coast is all about seafood – and ceviche, naturally, plays a starring role. A chilled concoction of fish, shrimp or other seafood marinated in lime juice, onions, cilantro and chili peppers, ceviche is typically served with a wedge of boiled corn and sweet potato. The fish is cooked in the citrus juices through a process of oxidation. (Some chefs, however, have begun to cut back on their marinating time, which means that some ceviches are served at a sashimi-like consistency.) Another popular seafood cocktail is *tiradito,* a Japanese-inspired ceviche consisting of thin slices of fish served without onions, sometimes bathed in a creamy hot-pepper sauce.

Cooked fish can be prepared dozens of ways: *al ajo* (in garlic), *frito* (fried) or *a la chorrillana* (cooked in white wine, tomatoes and onions), the latter of which hails from the city of Chorrillos, south of Lima. Soups and stews are also a popular staple, including *aguadito* (a soupy risotto), *picante* (a spicy stew) and *chupe* (seafood chowder) – all of which can feature fish, seafood and other ingredients.

Other items that make a regular appearance on seafood menus are *conchitas a la parmesana* (scallops baked with cheese), *pulpo al olivo* (octopus in a smashed olive sauce) and *choros a la chalaca* (chilled mussels with fresh corn salsa). On the north coast, around Chiclayo, omelets made with manta ray *(tortilla de manta raya)* are a typical dish.

None of this means that pork, chicken or beef aren't popular. *Ají de gallina* (spicy chicken and walnut stew) is a Peruvian classic. In the north, a couple of local dishes bear repeat sampling: *arroz con pato a la chiclayana* (duck and rice simmered in cilantro, typical of Chiclayo) and *seco de cabrito* (goat stewed in cilantro, chilis and beer).

Highlands

In the chilly highlands, it's all about soups – which tend to be a generous, gut-warming experience, filled with vegetables, squash, potatoes, locally grown herbs and a variety of meats. *Sopa a la criolla* (a mild, creamy noodle soup with beef and peppers) is a regular item on menus, as is *caldo de gallina* (a nourishing chicken soup with potatoes and herbs). In the area around Arequipa, *chupe de camarones* (chowder made from river shrimp) is also a mainstay.

The highlands are also known as the source of all things *cuy* (guinea pig). It is often served roasted or *chactado* (pressed under hot rocks). It tastes very similar to rabbit and is often served whole. River trout – prepared myriad ways – is also popular.

Arequipa has a particularly dynamic regional cuisine. The area is renowned for its *picantes* (spicy stews served with chunks of white cheese), *rocoto relleno* (red chilis stuffed with meat) and *solterito* (bean salad).

For special occasions and weddings, families will gather to make *pachamanca:* a mix of marinated meats, vegetables, cheese, chilis and fragrant herbs baked on hot rocks in the ground.

Top Eats

Arequipa At Zig Zag (p103), the succulent combination meat plate of alpaca, beef and lamb is a carnivore's delight.

Cuzco Elegant Uchu Peruvian Steakhouse (p172) serves stone-grilled alpaca with piquant sauces and twice-baked Andean potatoes.

Iquitos Set at the mouth of the Río Itaya, Al Frio y al Fuego (p266) has scrumptious dishes crafted from Amazon river fish.

Lima The Peruvian capital is something of a 'fish capital' and the chilled ceviche matches the chilled atmosphere at Pescados Capitales (p60).

Trujillo The bamboo-lined Mar Picante (p231) is known for serving up behemoth orders of divine *ceviche mixto.*

Desserts

Desserts tend to be hypersweet concoctions. *Suspiro limeño* is the most famous, consisting of *manjar blanco* (caramel) topped with sweet meringue. Also popular are *alfajores* (cookie sandwiches with caramel) and *crema volteada* (flan). Lighter and fruitier is *mazamorra morada,* a purple-corn pudding of Afro-Peruvian origin that comes with chunks of fruit.

During October, bakeries sell *turrón de Doña Pepa,* a sticky, molasses-drenched cake eaten in honor of the Lord of Miracles.

Drinks

The main soft-drink brands are available, but locals have a passion for Inca Kola – which tastes like bubble gum and comes in a spectacular shade of nuclear yellow. Fresh fruit juices are also popular, as are traditional drinks such as *chicha morada,* a refreshing, non-alcoholic beverage made from purple corn and spices.

Though the country exports coffee to the world, many Peruvians drink it instant: some restaurants dish up packets of Nescafé or an inky coffee reduction that is blended with hot water. In cosmopolitan and touristy areas, cafes serving espresso and cappuccino have proliferated. Tea and *mates* (herbal teas), such as *manzanilla* (chamomile), *menta* (mint) and *mate de coca* (coca-leaf tea), are also available. Coca-leaf tea will not get you high, but it can soothe stomach ailments and it's believed to help in adjusting to high altitude.

Pisco

It is the national beverage – the omnipresent grape brandy served at events from the insignificant to the momentous.

Production dates back to the early days of the Spanish colony in Ica, where it was distilled on private haciendas and then sold to sailors making their way through the port of Pisco. In its early years, pisco was the local firewater: a great way to get ripped – and wake up the following morning feeling as if you had been hammered over the head. By the early 20th century, the pisco sour (pisco with lime juice and sugar) arrived on the scene, and quickly became the national drink. In recent decades, as production has become more sophisticated, piscos have become more nuanced and flavorful (without the morning-after effects).

The three principal types of Peruvian pisco are Quebranta, Italia and Acholado. Quebranta (a pure-smelling pisco) and Italia (slightly aromatic) are each named for the varieties of grape from which they are crafted, while Acholado is a blend of varietals that has more of an alcohol top note (best for mixed drinks). There are many small-batch specialty piscos made from grape must (pressed juice with skins), known as *mosto verde*. These have a fragrant smell and are best sipped straight.

The most common brands include Tres Generaciones, Ocucaje, Ferreyros and La Botija, while Viñas de Oro, Viejo Tonel, Estirpe Peruano, LaBlanco and Gran Cruz are among the finest. Any pisco purchased in a bottle that resembles the head of an Inca will make for an unusual piece of home decor – and not much else.

Where to Eat & Drink

For the most part, restaurants in Peru are a community affair, and local places will cater to a combination of families, tourists, teenagers and packs of chatty businesspeople. At lunchtime, many eateries offer a *menú* – a set meal consisting of two or three courses. This is generally good value. (Note: if you request the *menú,* you'll get the special. If you want the menu, ask for *la carta.*)

Cevicherías – places where ceviche is sold – are popular along the coast, and commonly open for lunchtime service, as most places proudly serve fish that is at its freshest. In the countryside, informal local restaurants known as *picanterías* are a staple. In some cases these operate right out of someone's home.

Embracing Local Cuisine

Peru, once a country where important guests were treated to French meals and Scotch whiskey, is now a place where high-end restaurants spotlight deft interpretations of Andean favorites, including quinoa and *cuy* (guinea pig). The dining scene has blossomed. And tourism outfits have swept in to incorporate a culinary something as part of every tour. In 2000 the country became the site of the first Cordon Bleu academy in Latin America, and in 2009 *Bon Appétit* magazine named Lima the 'next great food city.' In 2017 three Lima restaurants made the list of the World's Best Restaurants, with Virgilio Martínez earning the Chefs Choice Award. And the honors roll on. Of Peru's 3.1 million annual visitors, 40% do gastronomic tourism. And maybe you should too.

Foodie fever has infected Peruvians at every level, with even the most humble *chicharrón* (fried pork) vendor hyperattentive to the vagaries of preparation and presentation. No small part of this is due to mediagenic celebrity chef Gastón Acurio, whose culinary skill and business acumen (he owns dozens of restaurants around the globe) have given him rock-star status.

ALLEN.G/SHUTTERSTOCK ©

Music & the Arts

The country that has been home to both indigenous and European empires has a wealth of cultural and artistic tradition. Perhaps the most outstanding achievements are in the areas of music (both indigenous and otherwise), painting and literature – the last of which received plenty of attention in 2010, when Peruvian novelist Mario Vargas Llosa won the Nobel Prize.

Music

Like its people, Peru's music is an intercontinental fusion of elements. Pre-Columbian cultures contributed bamboo flutes, the Spaniards brought stringed instruments and the Africans gave it a backbone of fluid, percussive rhythm. By and large, music tends to be a regional affair: African-influenced *landó* with its thumping bass beats is predominant on the coast, high-pitched indigenous *huayno,* heavy on bamboo wind instruments, is heard in the Andes and *criollo* waltzes are a must at any dance party on the coast.

Over the last several decades, the *huayno* has blended with surf guitars and Colombian *cumbia* (a type of Afro-Caribbean dance music) to produce *chicha* – a danceable sound closely identified with the Amazon region, growing in popularity even with cool urban

Writer Mario Vargas Llosa

JÖRG CARSTENSEN/PICTURE ALLIANCE VIA GETTY IMAGES ©

★ Must-Read Fiction

The War of the End of the World (Mario Vargas Llosa; 1981)

War by Candlelight (Daniel Alarcón; 2006)

Chronicle of San Gabriel (Julio Ramón Ribeyro; 2004)

Roebuck: Tales of an Admirable Adventurer (Luke Waterson; 2015)

youth. (Well-known *chicha* bands include Los Shapis and Los Mirlos.) *Cumbia* is also popular. Grupo 5, which hails from Chiclayo, is a favorite in the genre.

On the coast, guitar-inflected *música criolla* (*criollo* music) has its roots in both Spain and Africa. The most famous *criollo* style is the *vals peruano* (Peruvian waltz), a three-quarter-time waltz that is fast moving and full of complex guitar melodies. The most legendary singers in this genre include singer and composer Chabuca Granda (1920–83), Lucha Reyes (1936–73) and Arturo 'Zambo' Cavero (1940–2009). Cavero, in particular, was revered for his gravelly vocals and soulful interpretations. *Landó* is closely connected to this style of music, but features the added elements of call-and-response. Standout performers in this vein include singers Susana Baca (b 1944) and Eva Ayllón (b 1956).

Peru is making significant contributions to today's alt-rock scene, with fusion bands such as Uchpa, NovaLima, Bareto, the award-winning Lucho Quequezana, and La Sarita integrating Quechua, Afro-Peruvian and other influences. Band La Mente sets a party tone and Bareto remakes Peruvian *cumbia* classics with great appeal. The contemporary band Barrio Calavera meshes ska, *cumbia, chicha,* reggae, punk and boleros with Latin-American folklore for raucous dance music.

Visual Arts

The country's most famous art movement dates to the 17th and 18th centuries, when the artists of the Cuzco School produced thousands of religious paintings, the vast majority of which remain unattributed. Created by indigenous and *mestizo* (person of mixed indigenous and Spanish descent) artists, the pieces frequently feature holy figures laced in gold paint and rendered in a style inspired by mannerist and late Gothic art – but bearing traces of an indigenous color palette and iconography. Today, these hang in museums and churches throughout Peru and reproductions are sold in many crafts markets.

One of the most well-known artistic figures of the 19th century is Pancho Fierro (1807–79), the illegitimate son of a priest and a slave, who painted highly evocative watercolors of the everyday figures that occupied Lima's streets: fishmongers, teachers and Catholic religious figures clothed in lush robes.

In the early 20th century, an indigenist movement led by painter José Sabogal (1888–1956) achieved national prominence. Sabogal often painted indigenous figures and incorporated pre-Columbian design in his work. As director of the National School of Arts in Lima, he influenced a whole generation of painters who looked to Andean tradition for inspiration, including Julia Codesido (1883–1979), Mario Urteaga (1875–1957) and Enrique Camino Brent (1909–60).

Literature

Mario Vargas Llosa (b 1936) is Peru's most famous writer, hailed alongside 20th-century Latin American luminaries such as Gabriel García Márquez, Julio Cortázar and Carlos Fuentes. His novels evoke James Joyce in their complexity, meandering through time and shifting perspectives. Vargas Llosa is also a keen social observer, casting a spotlight on the naked corruption of the ruling class and the peculiarities of Peruvian society. More than two dozen of his novels are available in translation. The best place to start is *La ciudad y los perros* (The Time of the Hero; 1962), based on his experience at a Peruvian military academy. (The soldiers at his old academy responded to the novel by burning it.)

Another keen observer is Alfredo Bryce Echenique (b 1939), who chronicles the ways of the upper class in novels such as *El huerto de mi amada* (My Beloved's Garden; 2004), which recounts an affair between a 33-year-old woman and a teenage boy in 1950s Lima. Demonstrating a distinctly Peruvian penchant for dark humor is Julio Ramón Ribeyro (1929–94). Though never a bestselling author, he is critically acclaimed for his insightful works, which focus on the vagaries of lower-middle-class life. His work is available in English in *Marginal Voices: Selected Stories* (1993). If you are just learning to read Spanish, his clearly and concisely written pieces are an ideal place to start exploring Peruvian literature.

Also significant is Daniel Alarcón (b 1977), a rising Peruvian-American writer whose award-winning short stories have appeared in the *New Yorker* magazine. His debut novel, *Lost City Radio* (2007), about a country recovering from civil war, won a PEN award in 2008.

If Vargas Llosa is the country's greatest novelist, then César Vallejo (1892–1938) is its greatest poet. In his lifetime, he published only three slim books – *Los heraldos negros* (The Black Heralds; 1919), *Trilce* (1922) and *Poemas humanos* (Human Poems; 1939) – but he has long been regarded as one of the most innovative Latin American poets of the 20th century. Vallejo frequently touched on existential themes and was known for pushing language to its limits, inventing words when real ones no longer suited him.

Traditional Crafts

Peru has a long tradition of producing extraordinarily rendered crafts and folk art. Here's what to look for:

Textiles You'll see intricate weavings with elaborate anthropomorphic and geometric designs all over Peru. Some of the finest can be found around Cuzco.

Pottery The most stunning pieces of pottery are those made in the tradition of the pre-Columbian Moche people of the north coast. But also worthwhile is Chancay-style pottery: rotund figures made from sand-colored clay. Find these at craft markets in Lima.

Religious Crafts These abound in all regions, but the *retablos* (3D ornamental dioramas) from Ayacucho are the most spectacular.

Hiking on the Inca Trail (p210)

SHARPTOYOU/SHUTTERSTOCK ©

Survival Guide

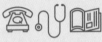

Directory A–Z

Accessible Travel

Peru offers few conveniences for travelers with disabilities. Features such as signs in Braille or phones for the hearing-impaired are virtually nonexistent, while wheelchair ramps and lifts are few and far between, and the pavement is often badly potholed and cracked. Most hotels do not have wheelchair accessible rooms, at least not rooms specially designated as such. Bathrooms are often barely large enough for an able-bodied person to walk into, so few are accessible to wheelchairs.

Nevertheless there are Peruvians with disabilities who get around, mainly through the help of others.

Apumayo Expediciones (☑914-169-665; www.apumayo. com; Jr Ricardo Palma Ñ-11, Urb Santa Monica Wanchaq, Cuzco; ☺9am-6pm Mon-Fri) An adventure-tour company that takes disabled travelers to Machu Picchu and other historic sites in the Sacred Valley.

Conadis (☑01-332-0808; www.conadisperu.gob.pe; Av Arequipa 375, Santa Beatriz, Lima; ☺8am-5pm Mon-Fri) Governmental agency for Spanish-language information

and advocacy for people with disabilities.

Emerging Horizons (www. emerginghorizons.com) Travel magazine for the mobility impaired, with handy advice columns and news articles.

Mobility International (☑USA 541-343-1284; www.miusa.org; 132 E Broadway, Suite 343, USA; ☺9am-4pm Mon-Fri) Advises disabled travelers on mobility issues and runs an educational exchange program.

Accommodations

Peru has accommodations to suit every budget, especially in tourist hubs and cities. Lodgings in Peru are considerably more expensive in tourist areas, such as Lima, Cuzco and the Sacred Valley.

Rates

Note that prices may fluctuate with exchange rates.

Extra charges Foreigners do not have to pay the 18% hotel tax (sometimes included in rates quoted in soles), but may have to present their passport and tourist card to photocopy. A credit card transaction surcharge of 7% or more does not include the home bank's foreign-currency exchange fee. US dollars may be accepted, but the exchange rate may be poor.

Packages In the remote jungle lodges of the Amazon and in popular beach destinations such as Máncora, all-inclusive resort-style pricing is more the norm.

Book Your Stay Online

For more accommodation reviews by Lonely Planet authors, check out http://hotels.lonelyplanet.com. You'll find independent reviews, as well as recommendations on the best places to stay. Best of all, you can book online.

High season In Cuzco, demand is very high during the high season (June to August). Other busy times include Inti Raymi, Semana Santa and Fiestas Patrias, when advance reservations are a must. In Lima, prices remain steady throughout the year; look for last-minute specials online. Paying cash always helps; ask for discounts for long-term stays.

Reservations

Street noise can be an issue in any lodging, so select your room accordingly. It's always OK to ask to see a room before committing. Other things to consider:

Airport arrival Since many flights into Lima arrive late at night, it's inadvisable to begin searching for a place to sleep upon arrival. Reserve your first night ahead; most hotels also can arrange airport pickup.

Late arrival Cheap budget places may not honor a reservation if you arrive late. Even if you've made a reservation, it is best to confirm your arrival time. Late check-in is not a problem at many midrange and top-end hotels, in which case a deposit may be required.

When to Book Around the country, reservations are a necessity for stays during a major festival (such as Inti Raymi in Cuzco) or a holiday such as Semana Santa (Easter Week), when all of Peru is on vacation. In the Amazon, reservations are needed at remote lodges. In smaller villages and areas off the beaten path, service tends to be on a first-come, first-served basis.

Advance payment Some lodges, especially in the Amazon, may require all or part of the payment up front. Make sure your travel plans are firm if you are paying in advance, as securing refunds can be a challenge.

Discounts Reserving online is convenient, but off-season walk-in rates may be lower. At top-end hotels, however, last-minute online deals are the norm, so always check a hotel's website for discounts and special promotional packages.

Room types *Habitación simple* refers to a single room. A *habitación doble* features twin beds while a *habitación matrimonial* has a double or queen-sized bed.

Customs Regulations

○ Peru allows duty-free importation of 3L of alcohol and 20 packs of cigarettes, 50 cigars or 250g of tobacco. You can import US$300 of gifts. Legally, you are allowed to bring in such items as a laptop, camera, portable music player, kayak, climbing gear, mountain bike or similar items for personal use.

○ It is illegal to take pre-Columbian or colonial artifacts out of Peru, and it is illegal to bring them into most countries. If purchasing reproductions, buy only from a reputable dealer and ask for a detailed receipt. Purchasing animal products made from endangered species or even just transporting them around Peru is also illegal.

○ Coca leaves are legal in Peru, but not in most other countries, even in the form of tea bags. People subject to random drug testing should be aware that coca, even in the form of tea, may leave trace amounts in urine.

○ Check with your own home government about customs restrictions and duties on any expensive or rare items you intend to bring back. Most countries allow their citizens to import a limited number of items duty-free, though these regulations are subject to change.

Climate

Cuzco

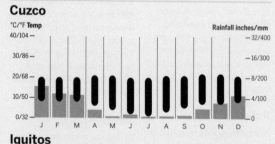

Iquitos

Lima

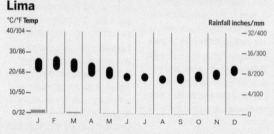

Electricity

Electrical current is 220V, 60Hz AC. Standard outlets accept round prongs, some have dual-voltage outlets which take flat prongs. Even so, your adapter may need a built-in surge protector.

Type A
220V/60Hz

Type A
220V/60Hz

Type C
220V/60Hz

Food

Mid- to high-end restaurants charge a 10% service fee and 19% tax. The following price ranges refer to a main dish.

$ less than S20

$$ S20–S60

$$$ more than S60

Health

It's not unusual to suffer from altitude sickness in the Andes or have tummy problems, despite Peru's wonderful culinary reputation. Peru's many climates mean that travelers will face different risks in different areas. While food-borne as well as mosquito-borne infections happen, many of these illnesses are not life-threatening – but they can certainly ruin your trip. Besides getting the proper vaccinations, it's important that you take insect repellent and exercise care in what you eat and drink.

Before You Go

Since most vaccines don't produce immunity until at least two weeks after they're given, visit a physician four to eight weeks before departure. Ask your doctor for an International Certificate of Vaccination (otherwise known as the 'yellow booklet'), which will list all the vaccinations you've received. This is mandatory for countries that require proof of yellow-fever vaccination upon entry, but it's a good idea to carry it wherever you travel.

Bring medications in their original containers, clearly labeled. A signed, dated letter from your physician describing all medical conditions and medications, including generic names, is also a good idea. If carrying syringes or needles, be sure to have a physician's letter documenting their medical necessity.

Most doctors and hospitals expect payment in cash, regardless of whether you have travel health insurance.

The World Health Organization (www.who.int/ith) offers a free download of its International Travel and Health booklet.

Availability of Health Care

Lima has high-quality 24-hour medical clinics, and English-speaking doctors and dentists. See the guide at the website for the US embassy (http://lima.usembassy.gov). Rural areas may have only the most basic medical services.

Life-threatening medical problems may require evacuation. For a list of medical evacuation and travel insurance companies, see the website of the US State Department (http://travel.state.gov).

Pharmacies are known as *farmacias* or *boticas*, identified by a green or red cross. They offer most of the medications available in other countries, though tampons, birth-control pills and other contraceptives (even condoms) are scarce outside metropolitan areas and not always reliable, so stock up in cities or from home.

Altitude Sickness

Altitude sickness may result from rapid ascents to altitudes greater than 2500m (8100ft). In Peru, this includes Cuzco, Machu Picchu and Lake Titicaca. Being physically fit offers no protection. Symptoms may include headaches, nausea, vomiting, dizziness, malaise, insomnia and loss of appetite. Severe cases may be complicated by fluid in the lungs (high-altitude pulmonary edema) or swelling of the brain (high-altitude cerebral edema). If symptoms persist for more than 24 hours, descend immediately by at least 500m and see a doctor.

The best prevention is to spend two nights or more at each rise of 1000m. Diamox may be taken starting 24 hours before ascent. A natural alternative is ginkgo.

It's also important to avoid overexertion, eat light meals and abstain from alcohol. Altitude sickness should be taken seriously; it can be life threatening when severe.

Insurance

Having a travel-insurance policy to cover theft, loss, accidents and illness is highly recommended. Always carry your insurance card with you. Not all policies compensate travelers for misrouted or lost luggage. Check the fine print to see if it excludes 'dangerous activities,' which can include scuba diving, motorcycling and even trekking. Also check if the policy coverage includes worst-case scenarios, such as evacuations and flights home.

You must usually report any loss or theft to local police (or airport authorities) within 24 hours. Make sure you keep all documentation to make any claim.

Worldwide travel insurance is available at www.lonelyplanet.com/travel-insurance. You can buy, extend and claim online anytime – even if you're already on the road.

Internet Access

○ Most regions have excellent internet connections and reasonable prices; it is typical for hotels and hostels to have wi-fi or computer terminals.

○ Family guesthouses, particularly outside urban areas, lag behind in this area.

○ Internet cafes are widespread.

Legal Matters

Legal assistance Your own embassy is of limited help if you get into trouble with the law in Peru, where you are presumed guilty until proven innocent. If you are the victim, the *policía de turismo* (tourist police; Poltur) can help, with limited English. Poltur stations are found in major cities.

Bribery Though some police officers (even tourist police) have a reputation for corruption, bribery is illegal. Beyond traffic police, the most likely place officials might request a little extra is at land borders. Since this too is illegal, those with time and fortitude can and should stick to their guns.

Drugs Avoid having any conversation with someone who offers you drugs. Peru has draconian penalties for possessing even a small amount of drugs; minimum sentences are several years in jail.

Police Should you be stopped by a plainclothes officer, don't hand over any documents or money. Never get into a vehicle with someone claiming to be a police officer, but insist on going to a real police station on foot.

Protests It's not recommended to attend political protests or to get too close to blockades – these are places to avoid.

Detention If you are imprisoned for any reason, make sure that someone else knows about it as soon as possible. Extended pretrial detentions are not uncommon. Peruvians bring food and clothing to family members who are in prison, where conditions are extremely harsh.

Complaints For issues with a hotel or a tour operator, register your complaint with the **National Institute for the Defense of Competition and the Protection of Intellectual Property** (Indecopi; 📞01-224-7800; www.indecopi.gob.pe) in Lima.

LGBT+ Travelers

Peru is a strongly conservative, Catholic country. While most believe that legalizing same-sex civil unions will happen soon, the initiative has met resistance from the Peruvian Congress in the past, despite the adoption of similar measures in neighboring countries in the Southern Cone. While many Peruvians will tolerate homosexuality on a 'don't ask; don't tell' level when dealing with foreign travelers, LGBT+ rights remain a struggle. As a result, many Peruvians don't publicly identify.

Public displays of affection among homosexual couples is rarely seen. Outside gay clubs, it is advisable to keep a low profile. Lima is the most accepting of gay people, but this is on a relative scale. Beyond that, the tourist towns of Cuzco, Arequipa and Trujillo tend to be more

tolerant than the norm. Social media platforms Tinder and Grindr can connect travelers to the gay scene.

FYI: the rainbow flag seen around Cuzco and in the Andes is *not* a gay pride flag – it's the flag of the Inca empire.

Maps

The best road map of Peru is the 1:2,000,000 *Mapa Vial* published by Lima 2000 and available in better bookstores. The 1:1,500,000 *Peru South and Lima* country map, published by International Travel Maps, covers the country in good detail south of a line drawn east to west through Tingo María, and has a good street map of Lima, San Isidro,

Miraflores and Barranco on the reverse side.

For topographical maps, go to the **Instituto Geográfico Nacional** (IGN; 📞01-475-3030, ext 119; www.ign.gob.pe; Aramburu 1190-98, Surquillo; 🕐8:30am-5pm Mon-Fri), with reference maps and others for sale. In January the IGN closes early, so call ahead. High-scale topographic maps for trekking are available, though sheets of border areas might be hard to get. Geological and demographic maps and CD-ROMs are also sold.

Up-to-date topo maps are often available from outdoor outfitters in major trekking centers such as Cuzco, Huaraz and Arequipa. If you are bringing along a GPS unit, ensure that your power source adheres to Peru's 220V, 60Hz AC standard and always carry a compass.

A Note about Prices

Prices are generally listed in Peruvian nuevos soles. However, many package lodgings and higher-end hotels will only quote prices in US dollars, as will many travel agencies and tour operators. In these cases, we list prices in US dollars.

Both currencies have experienced fluctuations in recent years, so expect many figures to be different from what you have read.

Money

The nuevo sol ('new sun') comes in bills of S10, S20, S50, S100 and (rarely) S200. It is divided into 100 céntimos, with copper-colored coins of S0.05, S0.10 and S0.20, and silver-colored S0.50 and S1 coins. In addition, there are bimetallic S2 and S5 coins with a copper-colored center inside a silver-colored ring.

US dollars are accepted by many tourist-oriented businesses, though you'll need nuevos soles to pay for local transportation, meals and other incidentals.

Counterfeit bills (in both US dollars and nuevo soles) often circulate in Peru. Merchants question both beat-up and large-denomination bills. Consumers should refuse them too.

To detect fakes check for a sheer watermark and examine a metal strip crossing the note that repeats Peru in neat, not misshapen, letters. Colored thread, holographs and writing along the top of the bill should be embossed, not glued on.

ATMs

- *Cajeros automáticos* (ATMs) proliferate in nearly every city and town in Peru, as well as at major airports, bus terminals and shopping areas.

- ATMs are linked to the international Plus (Visa) and Cirrus (Maestro/Master-Card) systems, as well as American Express and other networks.

- Users should have a four-digit PIN. To avoid problems, notify your bank that you'll be using your ATM card abroad.

- If your card works with Banco de la Nación, it may be the best option as it doesn't charge fees (at least at the time of writing).

- Both US dollars and nuevos soles are readily available from Peruvian ATMs.

- ATMs are normally open 24 hours.

- Your home bank may charge an additional fee for each foreign ATM transaction.

- For safety reasons use ATMs inside banks with security guards, preferably during daylight hours. Cover the keyboard for PIN entry.

Changing Money

The best currency for exchange is the US dollar, although the euro is accepted in major tourist centers. Other hard currencies can be exchanged, but usually with difficulty and only in major cities. All foreign currencies must be in flawless condition.

Cambistas (money changers) hang out on street corners near banks and *casas de cambio* (foreign exchange bureaus) and give competitive rates (there's only a little flexibility for bargaining), but are not always honest. Officially, they should wear a vest and badge identifying themselves as legal. They're useful after regular business hours or at borders where there aren't any other options.

Credit Cards

Midrange and top-end hotels and shops accept *tarjetas de crédito* (credit cards) with a 7% (or greater) fee. Your bank may also tack on a surcharge and additional fees for each foreign-currency transaction. The most widely accepted cards in Peru are Visa and MasterCard.

Taxes & Refunds

o Expensive hotels add a 18% sales tax (though foreigners do not have to pay this) and 10% service charge; the latter is generally not included in quoted rates.

o A few restaurants charge combined taxes of more than 19%, plus a service charge (*servicio* or *propina*) of 10%.

o There is no system of sales-tax refunds for shoppers.

Tipping

Restaurants Tip 10% for good service.

Porters and tour guides Tip each separately at the end of the trip.

Taxis Tip not required (unless drivers have assisted with heavy luggage).

Opening Hours

Hours are variable and liable to change, especially in small towns, where hours are irregular. Posted hours are a guideline. Lima has the most continuity of services. In other major cities, taxi drivers often know where the late-night stores and pharmacies are located.

Banks 9am to 6pm Monday to Friday, some 9am to 6pm Saturday

Restaurants 10am to 10pm, many close 3pm to 6pm

Museums Often close on Monday

Government offices and businesses 9am to 5pm Monday to Friday

Shops 9am to 6pm, some open Saturday

Public Holidays

Major holidays may be celebrated for days around the official date.

Fiestas Patrias (National Independence Days) is the biggest national holiday, when the entire nation seems to be on the move.

New Year's Day January 1

Good Friday March/April

Labor Day May 1

Inti Raymi June 24

Feast of Sts Peter & Paul June 29

National Independence Days July 28–29

Feast of Santa Rosa de Lima August 30

Battle of Angamos Day October 8

All Saints Day November 1

Feast of the Immaculate Conception December 8

Christmas December 25

Safe Travel

Use basic precautions and a reasonable amount of awareness to avoid a robbery. Some tips:

o Crowded places such as bus terminals, train stations, markets and fiestas are the haunts of pickpockets; wear your day pack in front of you or carry a bag that fits snugly under your arm.

o Thieves look for easy targets, such as a bulging wallet in a back pocket or a camera held out in the open; keep spending money in your front pocket and your camera stowed when it's not in use.

o Passports and larger sums of cash are best carried in a money belt or an inside pocket that can be zipped or closed – or better yet, stowed in a safe at your hotel.

o Snatch theft can occur if you place a bag on the ground (even for a few seconds), or while you're

Government Travel Advice

The following government websites offer travel advisories and information on current hot spots.

Australian Department of Foreign Affairs (www. smarttraveller.gov.au)

British Foreign Office (www.gov.uk/foreign-travel-advice/peru)

Canadian Department of Foreign Affairs (www. dfait-maeci.gc.ca)

US State Department (www.travel.state.gov)

asleep on an overnight bus; never leave a bag with your wallet and passport in the overhead rack of a bus.

○ Don't keep valuables in bags that will be unattended.

○ Blending in helps: walking around town in brand-new hiking gear or a shiny leather jacket will draw attention; stick to simple clothing.

○ Leave jewelry and fancy watches at home.

○ Hotels – especially cheap ones – aren't always trustworthy; lock valuables inside your luggage or use safety deposit services.

○ Walk purposefully wherever you are going, even if you are lost; if you need to examine your map, duck into a shop or restaurant.

○ Always take an official taxi at night and from the airport or bus terminals. If threatened, it's better just to give up your goods than face harm.

Telephone

A few public pay phones operated by Movistar and Claro are still around, especially in small towns. They work with coins or phone cards, which can be purchased at supermarkets and groceries. Often internet cafes have 'net-to-net' capabilities (such as Skype), to talk for free.

Cell Phones

In Lima and other larger cities you can buy SIM cards for unlocked phones for about S15. Credit can be purchased in pharmacies and supermarkets. Cell-phone reception may be poor in the mountains or jungle.

Emergency & Important Numbers

Directory assistance	☎103
National tourist information (24hr)	☎511-574-800
Police	☎105

Phone Codes

When calling Peru from abroad, dial the international access code for the country you're in, then Peru's country code (51), then the area code without the 0 and finally, the local number. When making international calls from Peru, dial the international access code (00), then the country code of where you're calling to, then the area code and finally, the local phone number.

In Peru, any telephone number beginning with a 9 is a cell-phone number. Numbers beginning with 0800 are often toll-free only when dialed from private phones. To make a credit- card or collect call using AT&T, dial 0800-50288. For an online telephone directory, see www.paginasamarillas .com.pe.

Time

○ Peru is five hours behind Greenwich Mean Time (GMT). It's the same as Eastern Standard Time (EST) in North America. At noon in Lima, it's 9am in Los Angeles, 11am in Mexico City, noon in New York, 5pm in London and 4am (following day) in Sydney.

○ Daylight Saving Time (DST) isn't used in Peru.

○ Punctuality is not one of the things that Latin America is famous for, so be prepared to wait around. Buses rarely depart or arrive on time. Savvy travelers should allow some flexibility in their itineraries.

Toilets

Peruvian plumbing leaves something to be desired. There's always a chance that flushing a toilet will cause it to overflow, so you should avoid putting anything other than human waste into the toilet. Even a small amount of toilet paper can muck up the entire system – that's why a small, plastic bin is routinely provided for disposing of the paper. This may not seem sanitary, but it is definitely better than the alternative of clogged toilets and flooded floors. A well-run hotel or restaurant, even a cheap one, will empty the bin and clean the toilet daily. In rural areas, there may be just a rickety wooden outhouse built around a hole in the ground.

Public toilets are rare outside of transportation terminals, restaurants and museums, but restaurants will generally let travelers use a restroom (sometimes for a charge). Those in terminals usually have an attendant who will charge you about S0.75 to enter and then give you a few sheets of toilet paper. Public restrooms frequently run out of toilet paper, so always carry extra.

Visas

Tourists are permitted a 183-day, non-extendable stay, stamped into passports and onto a tourist card called a Tarjeta Andina de Migración (Andean Immigration Card). Keep it – it must be returned upon exiting the country. If you will need it, request the full amount of time to the immigration officer at the point of entry, since they have a tendency to issue 30- or 90-day stays.

Those who enter Peru via the Lima airport or cruise ship do not receive a tourist card; their visits are processed online.

If you lose your tourist card, visit the **Oficina de Migraciónes** (Immigration Office; ☎01-200-1000; www.

migraciones.gob.pe; Prolongación España 734, Breña; ☺8am-1pm Mon-Fri) or obtain a replacement copy via the website. Information in English can be found online. Extensions are no longer officially available.

Anyone who plans to work, attend school or reside in Peru for any length of time must obtain a visa in advance. Do this through the Peruvian embassy or consulate in your home country.

Carry your passport and tourist card on your person at all times, especially in remote areas (it's required by law on the Inca Trail). For security, make a photocopy of both documents and keep them in a separate place from the originals.

Women Travelers

Machismo is alive and well in Latin America. Most female travelers to Peru will experience little more than shouts of *mi amor* (my love) or an appreciative hiss. If you are fair-skinned with blond hair, however, be prepared to be the center of attention. Peruvian men consider foreign women to have looser morals and be easier sexual conquests than Peruvian women and will often make flirtatious comments to single women.

Unwanted attention Staring, whistling, hissing and catcalls in the streets is common and

best ignored. Most men rarely, if ever, follow up on the idle chatter (unless they feel you've insulted their manhood). Ignoring all provocation and staring ahead is generally the best response. If someone is particularly persistent, try a potentially ardor-smothering phrase such as *soy casada* (I'm married). If you appeal directly to locals, you'll find most Peruvians to be protective of lone women, expressing surprise and concern if you tell them you're traveling without your family or husband.

Bricheros It's not uncommon for fast-talking charmers, especially in tourist towns such as Cuzco, to attach themselves to gringas. Known in Peru as *bricheros,* many of these young Casanovas are looking for a meal ticket, so approach any professions of undying love with extreme skepticism. This happens to men too.

First impressions Use common sense when meeting men in public places. In Peru, outside of a few big cities, it is rare for a woman to belly up to a bar for a beer, and the ones that do tend to be prostitutes. If you feel the need for an evening cocktail, opt for a restaurant. Likewise, heavy drinking by women might be misinterpreted by some men as a sign of promiscuity. When meeting someone, make it very clear if only friendship is intended. This goes double for tour and activity guides. When meeting someone for the first time, it is also wise not to divulge where you are staying until you feel sure that you are with someone you can trust.

Climate Change & Travel

Every form of transport that relies on carbon-based fuel generates CO2, the main cause of human-induced climate change. Modern travel is dependent on airplanes, which might use less fuel per kilometer per person than most cars but travel much greater distances. The altitude at which aircraft emit gases (including CO2) and particles also contributes to their climate change impact. Many websites offer 'carbon calculators' that allow people to estimate the carbon emissions generated by their journey and, for those who wish to do so, to offset the impact of the greenhouse gases emitted with contributions to portfolios of climate-friendly initiatives throughout the world. Lonely Planet offsets the carbon footprint of all staff and author travel.

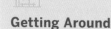

Transportation

Getting There & Away

Air

Peru (mainly Lima) has direct flights to and from cities all over the Americas, as well as to continental Europe. Other locations require a connection. The international departure tax is included in ticket costs.

Land & River

Because no roads bridge the Darien Gap, it is not possible to travel to South America by land from the north. Driving overland from neighboring Bolivia, Brazil, Chile, Colombia and Ecuador requires careful logistical planning.

Bus and train International bus companies go to Chile, Ecuador, Colombia, Bolivia, Brazil and Argentina. Smaller regional companies do cross-border travel, but on a more-limited basis. The only rail service that crosses the Peru border is the train between Arica (Chile) and Tacna on Peru's south coast.

Boat Getting to Peru by boat is possible from points on the Amazon River in Brazil and from Leticia (Colombia). There are also port cities on Peru's Pacific coast.

Tickets With any form of transport, it may be a bit cheaper to buy tickets to the border, cross over and then buy onward tickets on the other side, but it's usually much easier, faster and safer to buy a cross-border through ticket. When traveling by bus, check carefully with the company about what is included in the price of the ticket, and whether the service is direct or involves a transfer, and possibly a long wait, at the border.

Getting Around

Peru has a constant procession of flights and buses connecting the country. In particular, driving routes to the jungle have improved drastically. Keep in mind, poor weather conditions can cancel flights and buses. Strikes can be another obstacle in regional travel – consult travel experts on the routes you will be taking.

Air

Most domestic airlines have offices in Lima. Smaller carriers and charters are also an option. The most remote towns may require connecting flights, and smaller towns are not served every day. Many airports for these places are no more than a dirt strip.

Be at the airport two hours before your flight departs. Flights may be overbooked, baggage handling and check-in procedures tend to be chaotic, and flights may even leave *before* their official departure time because bad weather is predicted.

Most airlines fly from Lima to regional capitals, but service between provincial cities is limited.

LATAM (☑01-213-8200; www. latam.com; Av José Pardo 513, Miraflores) Reliable service to Arequipa, Chiclayo, Cuzco, Iquitos, Juliaca, Piura, Puerto Maldonado, Tacna, Tarapoto and Trujillo. Additionally it offers link services between Arequipa and Cuzco, Arequipa and Juliaca, Arequipa and Tacna, Cuzco and Juliaca, and Cuzco and Puerto Maldonado. With international services as well.

LC Perú (☎01-204-1300; www. lcperu.pe; Av Pablo Carriquirry 857, San Isidro; ☺9am-7pm Mon-Fri, to 5pm Sat) Flies from Lima to Andahuaylas, Arequipa, Ayacucho, Chachapoyas, Chiclayo, Cajamarca, Huánuco, Huaraz, Iquitos, Trujillo and Huancayo (Jauja) on smaller turbo-prop aircraft. Gets low marks for frequent cancellations and the difficulty in obtaining a refund.

Peruvian Airlines (☎01-715-6122; www.peruvianairlines.pe; Av José Pardo 495, Miraflores; ☺9am-7pm Mon-Fri, to 5pm Sat) Flies to Arequipa, Cuzco, Piura, Iquitos, Jauja, Pucallpa, Tarapoto, Tacna and internationally to La Paz, Bolivia.

Star Perú (☎01-213-8813; www.starperu.com; Av Espinar 331, Miraflores; ☺9am-6:45pm Mon-Fri, to 1pm Sat) Domestic carrier, flying to Ayacucho, Cuzco, Huanuco, Iquitos, Pucallpa, Puerto Maldonado and Tarapoto.

Viva Air (☎01-705-0107; www.vivaair.com; Aeropuerto Internacional Jorge Chávez; ☺hours vary) Budget flights to Arequipa, Piura, Cuzco, Iquitos and Tarapato.

Tickets

Most travelers travel in one direction overland and save time returning by air. You can sometimes buy tickets at the airport on a space-available basis, but don't count on it.

Peak season The peak season for air travel within Peru is late May to early September, as well as around major holidays. Buy tickets for less popular destinations as far in advance as possible, as these infrequent flights book up quickly. It's almost impossible to buy tickets just before major holidays, notably Semana Santa (the week leading up to Easter) and Fiestas Patrias (the last week in July). Overbooking is the norm.

Discounts Domestic flights are usually cheaper when advertised on the Peruvian website (versus its international version), so if you can wait until you arrive to Peru to buy regional tickets, you may save money.

Reconfirming flights In remote areas, buying tickets and reconfirming flights is best done at airline offices; otherwise, you can do so online or via a recommended travel agent. Ensure all flight reservations are *confirmed and reconfirmed* 72 and 24 hours in advance; airlines are notorious for overbooking and flights are changed or canceled with surprising frequency, so it's even worth calling the airport or the airline just before leaving for the airport. Confirmation is especially essential during the peak travel season.

Bicycle

Safety The major drawback to cycling in Peru is the country's bounty of kamikaze motorists. On narrow, two-lane highways, drivers can be a serious hazard to cyclists. Cycling is more enjoyable and safer, though very challenging, off paved

roads. Mountain bikes are recommended, as road bikes won't stand up to the rough conditions.

Rentals Reasonably priced rentals (mostly mountain bikes) are available in popular tourist destinations, including Cuzco, Arequipa, Huaraz and Huancayo. These bikes are rented to travelers for local excursions, not to make trips all over the country. For long-distance touring, bring your own bike from home.

Transporting bicycles Airline policies on carrying bicycles vary, so shop around.

Boat

There are no passenger services along the Peruvian coast. In the Andean highlands, there are boat services on Lake Titicaca. Small motorized vessels take passengers from the port in Puno to visit various islands on the lake, while catamarans zip over to Bolivia.

In Peru's Amazon Basin, boat travel is of major importance. Larger vessels ply the wider rivers. Dugout canoes powered by outboard engines act as water taxis on smaller rivers. Those called *peki-pekis* are slow and rather noisy. In some places, modern aluminum launches are used.

Bus

Buses are the usual form of transportation for most Peruvians and many travelers. Fares are cheap and services are frequent on the major long-distance routes, but buses are of varying quality. Don't always go with the cheapest option – check their safety records first. Remote rural routes are often served by older, worn-out vehicles. Seats at the back of the bus yield a bumpier ride.

Many cities do not have a main bus terminal. Buses rarely arrive or depart on time, so consider most average trip times as best-case scenarios. Buses can be significantly delayed during the rainy season, particularly in the highlands and the jungle. From January to April, journey times may double or face indefinite delays because of landslides and bad road conditions.

Fatal accidents are not unusual in Peru.

Avoid overnight buses, on which muggings and assaults are more likely to occur.

Classes

Luxury buses Invariably called Imperial, Royal, Business or Executive, these higher-priced express services feature toilets, movies and air-conditioning. Luxury buses serve paltry snacks and don't stop.

Bus-camas Feature seats which recline halfway or almost fully. Better long-distance buses stop for bathroom breaks and meals in special rest areas with inexpensive but sometimes unappetizing fare. Almost every bus terminal has a few kiosks with basic provisions.

Económico For trips under six hours, you may have no choice but to take an *económico* bus,

and these are usually pretty beaten up. While *económico* services don't stop for meals, vendors will board and sell snacks.

Costs & Reservations

Schedules and fares change frequently and vary from company to company; therefore, quoted prices are only approximations.

Fares fluctuate during peak and off-peak travel times. For long-distance or overnight journeys, or travel to remote areas with only limited services, buy your ticket at least the day before. Most travel agencies offer reservations but overcharge shockingly for the ticket. Except in Lima, it's cheaper to take a taxi to the bus terminal and buy the tickets yourself.

You can check schedules online (but not make reservations, at least not yet) for the major players, including the following:

Cruz del Sur (www.cruzdelsur.com.pe)

Oltursa (www.oltursa.com.pe)

Ormeño (📞01-472-1710; www.grupo-ormeno.com.pe; Av Javier Prado Este 1057)

Transportes Línea (www.linea.pe)

Car & Motorcycle

● Distances in Peru are long so it's best to bus or fly to a region and rent a car from there. Hiring a taxi is often cheaper and easier.

● At roadside checkpoints, police or military conduct

meticulous document checks. Drivers who offer an officer some money to smooth things along consider it a 'gift' or 'on-the-spot fine' to get on their way. Readers should know that these transactions are an unsavory reality in Peru and Lonely Planet does not condone them.

● When filling up, make sure the meter starts at zero.

Car Rental

Major rental companies have offices in Lima and a few other large cities. Renting a motorcycle is an option mainly in jungle towns, where you can go for short runs around town on dirt bikes, but not much further.

Economy car rental starts at US$25 a day without the 19% sales tax, 'super' collision-damage waiver, personal accident insurance and so on, which together can climb to more than US$100 per day, not including excess mileage. Vehicles with 4WD are more expensive.

Make sure you completely understand the rental agreement before you sign. A credit card is required, and renters normally need to be over 25 years of age.

Driver's License

A driver's license from your own home country is sufficient for renting a car. An International Driving Permit (IDP) is only required if you'll be driving in Peru for more than 30 days.

Road Rules & Hazards

Bear in mind that the condition of rental cars is often poor, roads are potholed (even the paved Pan-American Hwy), gas is expensive, and drivers are aggressive, regarding speed limits, road signs and traffic signals as mere guides, not the law. Moreover, road signs are often small and unclear.

- Driving is on the right-hand side of the road.
- Driving at night is not recommended because of poor conditions, speeding buses and slow-moving, poorly lit trucks.
- Theft is all too common, so you should not leave your vehicle parked on the street. When stopping overnight, park the car in a guarded lot (common in better hotels).
- Gas or petrol stations (called *grifos*) are few and far between.

Local Transportation

In most towns and cities, it's easy to walk everywhere or take a taxi. Using local buses, *micros* and *combis* can be tricky, but is very inexpensive.

Tours

Travelers who prefer not to travel on their own, or have a limited amount of time, have ample tours to choose from. Travel with knowledgeable guides comes at a premium. It's worth it for highly specialized outdoor activities like rafting, mountaineering, bird-watching or mountain biking.

If you want to book a tour locally, Lima, Cuzco, Arequipa, Puno, Trujillo, Huaraz, Puerto Maldonado and Iquitos have the most travel agencies offering organized tours. For more specialized, individual or small-group tours, you can generally hire a bilingual guide starting at US$20/80 per hour/day plus expenses (keep in mind exchange rates may affect this); tours in other languages may be more expensive. Some students or unregistered guides are cheaper, but the usual caveat applies – some are good, others aren't.

For more guide listings, check out www.leaplocal.org, a resource promoting socially responsible tourism.

Train

The privatized rail system, PeruRail (www.perurail.com), has daily services between Cuzco and Aguas Calientes, aka Machu Picchu Pueblo, and thrice-weekly services between Cuzco and Puno on the shores of Lake Titicaca. There are also luxury passenger services between Cuzco, Puno and Arequipa twice weekly. **Inca Rail** (☎084-25-2974; www.incarail.com; Portal de Panes 105, Plaza de Armas; 1 way S231-330; ⊙8am-9pm Mon-Fri, 9am-7pm Sat, to 2pm Sun) also offers a service between Ollantaytambo and Aguas Calientes.

Train buffs won't want to miss the lovely **Ferrocarril Central Andino** (☎01-226-6363; www.ferrocarrilcentral.com.pe; Estación Desamparados; round-trip adult/child 12 & under tourist class S600/300, standard class S450/225), which reaches a head-spinning altitude of 4829m. It usually runs between Lima and Huancayo from mid-April to mid-November. In Huancayo, cheaper trains to Huancavelica leave daily from a different station. Another charmingly historic railway makes inexpensive daily runs between Tacna on Peru's south coast and Arica, Chile.

Language

Spanish pronunciation is not difficult as most of its sounds are also found in English. You can read our pronunciation guides below as if they were English and you'll be understood just fine.

Peruvian Spanish is considered one of the easiest varieties of Spanish, with less slang in use than in many other Latin American countries, and relatively clear enunciation.

To enhance your trip with a phrasebook, visit **lonelyplanet.com**. Lonely Planet iPhone phrasebooks are available through the Apple App store.

Basics

Hello.
Hola.   *o*·la

How are you?
¿Qué tal?   ke tal

I'm fine, thanks.
Bien, gracias.   byen *gra*·syas

Excuse me. (to get attention)
Disculpe.   dees·*kool*·pe

Yes./No.
Sí./No.   see/no

Thank you.
Gracias.   *gra*·syas

You're welcome./That's fine.
De nada.   de *na*·da

Goodbye./See you later.
Adiós./Hasta luego.   a·*dyos*/as·ta *lwe*·go

Do you speak English?
¿Habla inglés?   *a*·bla een·*gles*

I don't understand.
No entiendo.   no en·*tyen*·do

How much is this?
¿Cuánto cuesta?   *kwan*·to *kwes*·ta

Can you reduce the price a little?
¿Podría bajar un   po·*dree*·a ba·*khar* oon
poco el precio?   *po*·ko el *pre*·syo

Accommodations

I'd like to make a booking.
Quisiera reservar   kee·*sye*·ra re·ser·*var*
una habitación.   *oo*·na a·bee·ta·*syon*

How much is it per night?
¿Cuánto cuesta   *kwan*·to *kwes*·ta
por noche?   por *no*·che

Eating & Drinking

I'd like ..., please.
Quisiera ..., por favor.   kee·*sye*·ra ... por fa·*vor*

That was delicious!
¡Estaba buenísimo!   es·*ta*·ba bwe·*nee*·see·mo

Bring the bill/check, please.
La cuenta, por favor.   la *kwen*·ta por fa·*vor*

I'm allergic to ...
Soy alérgico/a al ... (m/f)   soy a·*ler*·khee·ko/a al ...

I don't eat ...
No como ...   no *ko*·mo ...

chicken	*pollo*	*po*·yo
fish	*pescado*	pes·*ka*·do
meat	*carne*	*kar*·ne

Emergencies

I'm ill.
Estoy enfermo/a. (m/f)   es·*toy* en·*fer*·mo/a

Help!
¡Socorro!   so·*ko*·ro

Call a doctor!
¡Llame a un médico!   *ya*·me a oon *me*·dee·ko

Call the police!
¡Llame a la policía!   *ya*·me a la po·lee·*see*·a

Directions

I'm looking for (a/an/the) ...
Estoy buscando ...   es·*toy* boos·kan·do ...

ATM
un cajero   oon ka·*khe*·ro
automático   ow·to·*ma*·tee·ko

bank
el banco   el *ban*·ko

... embassy
la embajada de ...   la em·ba·*kha*·da de ...

market
el mercado   el mer·*ka*·do

museum
el museo   el moo·*se*·o

toilet
los servicios   los ser·*vee*·syos

tourist office
la oficina de   la o·fee·*see*·na de
turismo   too·*rees*·mo

Behind the Scenes

Acknowledgements

Climate map data adapted from Peel MC, Finlayson BL & McMahon TA (2007) 'Updated World Map of the Köppen-Geiger Climate Classification', *Hydrology and Earth System Sciences*, 11, 1633–44.

Illustrations pp208-9 by Michael Weldon

This Book

This 2nd edition of Lonely Planet's *Best of Peru* guidebook was curated by Brendan Sainsbury and researched and written by Brendan, Alex Egerton, Carolyn McCarthy, Phillip Tang and Luke Waterson. The previous edition was curated by Phillip and written by Phillip, Greg Benchwick, Alex, Carolyn and Luke. This guidebook was produced by the following:

Destination Editor Bailey Freeman

Senior Product Editor Saralinda Turner

Regional Senior Cartographer Corey Hutchison

Product Editor Ronan Abayawickrema

Book Designer Ania Bartoszek

Assisting Book Designer Gwen Cotter

Assisting Editors Andrew Bain, Katie Connolly, Andrea Dobbin, Emma Gibbs, Jennifer Hattam, Lou McGregor, Alison Morris, Kristin Odijk, Claire Rourke, Fionnuala Twomey

Cover Researcher Wibowo Rusli

Thanks to Hannah Cartmel, Shona Gray, Sandie Kestell, Amy Lynch, Genna Patterson, Kathryn Rowan

Send Us Your Feedback

We love to hear from travelers – your comments keep us on our toes and help make our books better. Our well-traveled team reads every word on what you loved or loathed about this book. Although we cannot reply individually to postal submissions, we always guarantee that your feedback goes straight to the appropriate authors, in time for the next edition. Each person who sends us information is thanked in the next edition, the most useful submissions are rewarded with a selection of digital PDF chapters.

Visit lonelyplanet.com/contact to submit your updates and suggestions or to ask for help. Our award-winning website also features inspirational travel stories, news and discussions.

Note: We may edit, reproduce and incorporate your comments in Lonely Planet products such as guidebooks, websites and digital products, so let us know if you don't want your comments reproduced or your name acknowledged. For a copy of our privacy policy visit lonelyplanet.com/privacy.

Index

ANNA HARRIS

LONELY PLANET IN THE WILD

Send your 'Lonely Planet in the Wild' photos to social@lonelyplanet.com
We share the best on our Facebook page every week!

Symbols & Map Key

Look for these symbols to quickly identify listings:

◉	Sights	✕	Eating
✦	Activities	☻	Drinking
➌	Courses	✪	Entertainment
➐	Tours	🛍	Shopping
✸	Festivals & Events	❶	Information & Transport

These symbols and abbreviations give vital information for each listing:

🌿 Sustainable or green recommendation

FREE No payment required

☏	Telephone number	🚌	Bus
⏱	Opening hours	⛴	Ferry
P	Parking	🚊	Tram
⊘	Nonsmoking	🚆	Train
❄	Air-conditioning	📖	English-language menu
@	Internet access	🥕	Vegetarian selection
🛜	Wi-fi access		
🏊	Swimming pool	👶	Family-friendly

Find your best experiences with these Great For... icons.

	Art & Culture		History
	Beaches		Local Life
	Budget		Nature & Wildlife
	Cafe/Coffee		Photo Op
	Cycling		Scenery
	Detour		Shopping
	Drinking		Short Trip
	Entertainment		Sport
	Events		Walking
	Family Travel		Winter Travel
	Food & Drink		

Sights

- 🏖 Beach
- 🐦 Bird Sanctuary
- Buddhist
- 🏰 Castle/Palace
- ✝ Christian
- Confucian
- 🕉 Hindu
- ☪ Islamic
- Jain
- ✡ Jewish
- Monument
- 🏛 Museum/Gallery/Historic Building
- Ruin
- Shinto
- Sikh
- Taoist
- Winery/Vineyard
- Zoo/Wildlife Sanctuary
- ◉ Other Sight

Points of Interest

- Bodysurfing
- ⛺ Camping
- Cafe
- Canoeing/Kayaking
- Course/Tour
- Diving
- Drinking & Nightlife
- ✕ Eating
- ✪ Entertainment
- Sento Hot Baths/Onsen
- 🛍 Shopping
- Skiing
- Sleeping
- Snorkelling
- Surfing
- Swimming/Pool
- Walking
- Windsurfing
- Other Activity

Information

- Bank
- Embassy/Consulate
- Hospital/Medical
- @ Internet
- Police
- Post Office
- Telephone
- Toilet
- Tourist Information
- ● Other Information

Geographic

- 🏖 Beach
- ⊢◄ Gate
- Hut/Shelter
- Lighthouse
- Lookout
- ▲ Mountain/Volcano
- Oasis
- Park
-)(Pass
- Picnic Area
- Waterfall

Transport

- Airport
- BART station
- ✕ Border crossing
- Boston T station
- 🚌 Bus
- Cable car/Funicular
- Cycling
- Ferry
- Metro/MRT station
- Monorail
- P Parking
- Petrol station
- Subway/S-Bahn/Skytrain station
- Taxi
- Train station/Railway
- Tram
- Tube Station
- Underground/U-Bahn station
- ● Other Transport

Phillip Tang

Phillip grew up on a typically Australian diet of *pho* and fish'n'chips before moving to Mexico City. A degree in Chinese and Latin-American cultures launched him into travel and then writing about it for Lonely Planet's *Canada*, *China*, *Japan*, *Korea*, *Mexico* and *Vietnam* guides. See his writing at hellophillip.com; photos @mrtangtangtang; and tweets @ philliptang.

Luke Waterson

Raised in southwest England, Luke quickly became addicted to exploring out-of-the-way places. Completing a Creative Writing degree at the University of East Anglia, he shouldered his backpack and vowed to see as much of the world as possible. Luke specialises in writing on South America – he contributes to the LP *Peru* and *Ecuador* guides, and his debut novel *Roebuck*, set in the 16th-century Amazon jungle, was published in December 2015. For updates about his writing, fact and fiction, visit lukeandhiswords.com.

Our Story

A beat-up old car, a few dollars in the pocket and a sense of adventure. In 1972 that's all Tony and Maureen Wheeler needed for the trip of a lifetime – across Europe and Asia overland to Australia. It took several months, and at the end – broke but inspired – they sat at their kitchen table writing and stapling together their first travel guide, *Across Asia on the Cheap*. Within a week they'd sold 1500 copies. Lonely Planet was born.

Today, Lonely Planet has offices in Franklin, London, Melbourne, Oakland, Dublin, Beijing, and Delhi, with more than 600 staff and writers. We share Tony's belief that 'a great guidebook should do three things: inform, educate and amuse'.

Our Writers

Brendan Sainsbury

Born and raised in the UK in a town that never merits a mention in any guidebook (Andover, Hampshire), Brendan didn't leave Blighty until he was 19. Making up for lost time, he's since squeezed 70 countries into a sometimes precarious existence as a writer and professional vagabond. His rocking-chair memories will probably include staging a performance of *A Comedy of Errors* at a school in war-torn Angola and running 150 miles across the Sahara Desert in the Marathon des Sable. In the last 11 years, he has written over 40 books for Lonely Planet, covering everything from Castro's Cuba to the canyons of Peru.

Alex Egerton

A news journalist by trade, Alex has worked for magazines, newspapers and media outlets on five continents. He spends most of his time on the road checking under mattresses, sampling suspicious street food and chatting with locals as part of the research process for travel articles and guidebooks. When he is not traveling, you'll find him at home in Popayán, southern Colombia.

Carolyn McCarthy

Carolyn specializes in travel, culture and adventure in the Americas. She has written for *National Geographic*, *Outside*, *BBC Magazine*, *Sierra Magazine*, *Boston Globe* and other publications. Carolyn has contributed to 40 guidebooks and anthologies for Lonely Planet. For more information, visit www.carolynmccarthy.org or follow her Instagram travels @mccarthyoff map.

◄————————— More Writers ————————◄

STAY IN TOUCH LONELYPLANET.COM/CONTACT

AUSTRALIA The Malt Store, Level 3, 551 Swanston St, Carlton, Victoria 3053 03 8379 8000, fax 03 8379 8111

IRELAND Digital Depot, Roe Lane (off Thomas St), Digital Hub, Dublin 8, D08 TCV4, Ireland

USA 124 Linden Street, Oakland, CA 94607 510 250 6400, toll free 800 275 8555, fax 510 893 8572

UK 240 Blackfriars Road, London SE1 8NW 020 3771 5100, fax 020 3771 5101

 twitter.com/ lonelyplanet
 facebook.com/ lonelyplanet
 instagram.com/ lonelyplanet
 youtube.com/ lonelyplanet
 lonelyplanet.com/ newsletter